WHAT'S ON HER MIND

WHAT'S ON HER MIND

The Mental Workload of Family Life

ALLISON DAMINGER

PRINCETON UNIVERSITY PRESS

PRINCETON & OXFORD

MIX
Paper | Supporting
responsible forestry
FSC® C008955

Published by Princeton University Press
41 William Street, Princeton, New Jersey 08540
99 Banbury Road, Oxford OX2 6JX

press.princeton.edu

GPSR Authorized Representative: Easy Access System Europe - Mustamäe tee 50, 10621 Tallinn, Estonia, gpsr.requests@easproject.com

All Rights Reserved

Library of Congress Cataloging-in-Publication Data

Names: Daminger, Allison, 1990– author.
Title: What's on her mind : the mental workload of family life / Allison Daminger.
Other titles: What is on her mind
Description: Princeton : Princeton University Press, [2025] | Includes bibliographical references and index.
Identifiers: LCCN 2024044811 (print) | LCCN 2024044812 (ebook) | ISBN 9780691245386 (hardback) | ISBN 9780691245393 (ebook)
Subjects: LCSH: Families—United States—Psychological aspects. | Families—United States. | Households—United States. | Patriarchy—United States. | BISAC: SOCIAL SCIENCE / Gender Studies
Classification: LCC HQ 536 .D3225 2025 (print) | LCC HQ 536 (ebook) | DDC 155.9/240973—dc23/eng/20250127
LC record available at https://lccn.loc.gov/2024044811
LC ebook record available at https://lccn.loc.gov/2024044812

British Library Cataloging-in-Publication Data is available

Editorial: Rachael Levay and Erik Beranek
Production Editorial: Ali Parrington
Text and Jacket Design: Katie Osborne
Production: Erin Suydam
Publicity: Maria Whelan

Illustrations by Connie Meyer

This book has been composed in Arno with TT Commons Pro and Recent Grotesk

Printed in the United States of America

10 9 8 7 6 5 4 3 2 1

For E. L., with gratitude

CONTENTS

WHAT'S ON HER MIND

INTRODUCTION

The hospital cafeteria was hushed in the lull between breakfast and lunch. Jackie, a White dietitian employed on one of the hospital's upper floors, sat across from me radiating nervous energy.[1] "It's me and my husband, Matthew," she began when I asked about her family. "I'm thirty-two. Oh my god, how old am I? I'm thirty-two. I'm going to be thirty-three in a week. Actually, next week. . . . Matthew and I have been together for seventeen years and married for eight soon—eight next week. And then we also have our two-point-two-five-year-old,[2] who is a boy and very cute."

Jackie and I met because she and Matthew had each agreed to participate in separate interviews about their household labor patterns. But I wasn't interested in the activities we typically think of as "housework." If I were, I would have tallied the minutes Jackie and Matthew each spend on action-oriented chores like cooking, cleaning, shopping, and home maintenance.[3] And by that temporal measure, I would have identified *Matthew* as the primary household laborer. Jackie herself estimates he does 80 percent of such labor, though Matthew diplomatically describes his share as "a bit more" than half. He has likely accumulated more childcare hours, too: for the first eighteen months of their son's life, Matthew acted as his primary caregiver while working part-time from home.

It's worth underscoring the fact that Matthew's domestic contributions are far greater than those of most men, both past and present.[4] And yet the metric of time spent on chores and childcare gives us an incomplete understanding of how he and Jackie work together, because it leaves out most of their *cognitive* labor. Simply put, cognitive household labor is a set of mental processes aimed at figuring out what the family requires, what it owes to others, and how best to ensure that both requirements and obligations are fulfilled. Most often, this takes the form of anticipating household members' needs, identifying options

1

for meeting them, deciding how to proceed, and following up after the fact. While Matthew stir-fried and vacuumed, Jackie's mind whirred: "It sounds kind of unfair to him," she apologized, before suggesting she does 90 percent of the family's cognitive labor. Matthew declined to offer a specific breakdown and instead described Jackie's cognitive load as "astronomically more" than his.

To uncover this overlooked form of work, I focused my conversations with Jackie and Matthew on their *mind-use* rather than their time-use.[5] Before the interviews, I asked each of them to keep a diary of all the family-related decisions they made, contemplated, or debated over the course of a recent day. The log Jackie handed me that morning was among the most extensive I'd collected thus far. It contained 26 entries, ranging from how many crackers she could give her toddler without ruining his dinner to whether she should take up a second, part-time job to help make ends meet.[6] Yet Jackie apologized for her log's brevity. Usually, she explained, her days felt like a never-ending stream of family-related decision making. "But, because I've been so crazy busy—this happens sometimes, that I actually *work* at work—you'll see chunks of time [in the log] where I'm not doing something, whereas I feel it's often every hour. I'll be like, 'Oh, I need to do this for our family.' And I don't feel like it was as often as usual."

I asked Jackie to tell me more about one of the decisions she'd listed: whether the family needed anything besides black beans from the grocery store. Jackie recalled that they'd planned to make bean burritos the previous night for dinner but realized, too late, that all the family had on hand were dry beans. "We were supposed to make beans"—that is, cook the dry beans, a lengthy process—"either on the weekend or last night, but we hadn't because we didn't have it on the [meal planning] board, and so nobody remembered." Jackie, who stopped at the store on her way home from work to pick up canned beans, approximated her train of thought while wandering the grocery aisles: "What do we need? Do we need a snack? Do we have enough snacks for the week? Do I need to buy mangos? Should I buy some bananas? I don't think my husband thinks any of that, which is funny. . . . It's the [grocery] list. The list is the list, and that is it. No more, no less. The list. The end."

Jackie's tendency to think two steps ahead was a recurrent theme as we continued discussing her decision log. Tracking household supplies? "It's always me," she noted, "unless Matthew needs his own deodorant, and then he'll buy it at a grocery store. . . . Whereas, for my deodorant, I'm like, 'Maybe we should go to Target because we also need da-da-da.'" Coming up with backup plans? When the family's washer broke, Jackie posted a query on a neighborhood forum while Matthew was troubleshooting in the basement. By the time he emerged, defeated, she had identified three local repair companies and a neighbor willing to lend a *Consumer Reports* guide in the event they needed a new machine.

Matthew, who is also White, joined us in the cafeteria just as Jackie and I were finishing our interview. He looked the part of the graduate student he is: college T-shirt and baggy shorts, wire-rimmed glasses perched on his nose. Jackie headed upstairs for a meeting, leaving Matthew and me to talk while he ate leftovers from the notorious bean burritos, supplemented with fries from the cafeteria. Matthew, too, had completed a decision log for the previous day, though his contained one-third as many entries as his wife's. And as I soon discovered, Jackie had been the one to instigate several of the decisions he did record. At 3:10 p.m., for example, Matthew wrote that he was researching new lunchboxes for their toddler. How, I asked, had that come up? "There was this smell emanating [from his old lunchbox]," Matthew explained. "We tried all sorts of wipes and cleaning and maintenance and stuff, but it's just not going away. We think there's thread inside that got gunky somehow." Asked whether he and Jackie had discussed a plan for replacing the lunchbox, he recalled, "We did. And then she started doing a bunch of research on it. So, I told her to stop." He worried Jackie had too much on her mental to-do list and "wanted to take something off her plate."

When I asked Matthew to approximate his own mental list of things to do, errands to run, and issues to address, he started with professional responsibilities ("Snippets of code that I have to [write]. Readings I have to do. Labs to grade.") before naming several home improvement projects: "We'd like to buy a new couch at some point. We have some serious work to do in the backyard that just takes forever. . . . The basement is a mess." But Matthew guessed Jackie's list would be "whatever I just said, times fifty. She knows the exact steps in every single one of those things [I listed]. . . . So, like, 'Get a new bedframe.' Her list would be, 'Go here, look at their bedframes, go here, look at their bedframes, think about styles. Think about what would look good in our room.' . . . She would take it as a starting point for a web of concerns."

Matthew exaggerated, but only somewhat. Jackie's mental list went on approximately four times as long as his, including the following excerpt:

> The kitchen needs to be cleaned. It's disgusting. We need a better system for cleaning the kitchen. We should make a list for how we're going to do our chores. The laundry isn't getting done quick enough. We need a better system for doing the laundry. . . . We need to clean out our son's toys

because he's been sitting with the same toys. There's literally infant toys in there. He doesn't use those anymore. . . . We should get some more age-appropriate toys for him. . . . I've been wanting to start a scrapbook thing for him forever, for the first year of his life. . . . I have three books to read about parenting, but I also want to read the three books I took [from the library] that are pleasure reading. . . . I was thinking about switching his pediatrician, having to gather all that stuff together, and interview the new pediatrician that my friend had recommended.

After hearing her list, I understood why Jackie described herself as "exhausted mentally" while Matthew fretted that she "carries a lot of load that I don't."

I've now interviewed the members of 76 different-gender and 18 LGBTQ+[7] couples—172 individuals total—about their cognitive labor practices.[8] In this book, I draw on their stories to argue that our current, time-centered metrics lead us to *underestimate* gender gaps in household contributions. New insights emerge when we supplement familiar questions about how people use their time with careful attention to how they use their mind. Cognitive labor operates as a near-constant "background job"—to quote one of my interviewees—for the spouse who acts as cognitive laborer-in-chief. And among the majority of different-gender couples, including Jackie and Matthew, that chief cognitive laborer is a woman. In most of these "Woman-led" couples, the female partner *also* completes the bulk of the physical work for her family. Matthew is unusual among men in my study, because he completes a larger share of the family's physical household labor.[9]

After explaining *how* Woman-led couples divide up cognitive labor, I turn to the question of *why* their allocation is so lopsided. Most couples draw on a narrative I call "personal essentialism": they argue that it is an individual's nature, independent of their gender, that either facilitates or inhibits their cognitive labor activities. Women, in their telling, just happen to be more organized and future-oriented; men are only coincidentally more scattered and present-focused. But this explanation does not stand up to scrutiny. Cognitive labor prowess is as much a function of learned skill as innate capacity, and I show how structural and cultural forces nudge women toward investing more in building and subsequently deploying those skills in the domestic context.

But while Woman-led couples comprise the majority of my sample, their experiences are not universal. In Balanced and Man-led couples, respectively, different-gender partners either share equally in cognitive labor or the male partner completes the majority. Meanwhile, most queer couples are Imbalanced in their approach to cognitive labor (i.e., they divide it unequally between partners), though a handful of Balanced couples manage to split it equally. Despite these variations, what many of these couples share is a strong sense of their own agency, which they leverage to shape and reshape their cognitive labor allocation in ways that work for them. Their experiences, both positive and negative, simultaneously illustrate the challenges associated with operating against dominant social structures and the opportunities available to those willing to try.

Stalled and Uneven

Your interpretation of Jackie and Matthew's story depends on whether you focus more on the full or empty half of the proverbial glass: Do you celebrate Matthew's active fathering as a sign of progress toward gender equality? Lament Jackie's larger cognitive burden as a marker of persistent inequality? Parallel questions plague anyone who contemplates the broader state of gender relations in twenty-first-century America. For the optimists among us, encouraging statistics abound. Compared to their foremothers, today's women have considerably more education.[10] They make more money.[11] They are better represented in the halls of power.[12] These were the trends I knew best before beginning this research. After a childhood dominated by "girl power" messaging,[13] I came of age believing gender inequality to be more historical curiosity than persistent feature of twenty-first-century life. In fairness to my younger self, I was not wholly naive. Cultural touchstones such as Anne-Marie Slaughter's viral *Atlantic* article "Why Women Still Can't Have It All"[14] and Sheryl Sandberg's bestseller *Lean In*[15] came out shortly after my college graduation, drawing renewed attention to contemporary gender inequalities. Still, it wasn't until graduate school that I fully appreciated the enigma that is our current gender moment.

In historical terms, it is true American women have never had it better. But if the comparison point is contemporary men rather than prior generations of women, a different conclusion emerges. American women earn roughly 82 cents for every dollar men earn, and even less if they are Black, Native, or Hispanic.[16] Women are woefully underrepresented in the upper echelons of business and politics.[17] Women are more likely to be living below the poverty line.[18] And women do more of the physical housework and childcare for their families, Jackie and Matthew's counterexample notwithstanding.[19]

This more dismal set of statistics is at odds with what many Americans say they want. Many—though certainly not all—Americans endorse gender equality or something close to it.[20] And yet our practices, particularly when it comes to how we arrange our homes and families, routinely conflict with those ideals.[21] In the early 1960s, when my mother was born, the average married woman spent nearly 34 hours per week on housework, roughly seven times as many hours as the average married man.[22] By the time I was a young child three decades later, that ratio had shrunk to about 1.9, in part because men increased their hours, but mostly because women decreased theirs.[23] Thirty years after that, when my niece was born in 2022, the female-to-male housework ratio had barely budged.[24]

Sociologist Paula England sees patterns like this one as evidence of a "stalled and uneven" gender revolution.[25] Stalled, because decades past the feminist victories of the 1960s and 1970s, women haven't yet reached full equality with men; more troublingly, the rate of change has slowed, stopped, and in some cases even reversed. Uneven, because some gender gaps have closed further than others.

One interpretation of these facts is that not enough time has passed.[26] In the aftermath of any revolution, old behaviors are often slow to align with new ideals. Institutions like businesses, schools, and government agencies often resist change, particularly when it requires investments of time, money, and other resources.[27] Eventually, though, behaviors catch up with beliefs. If women haven't yet reached parity with men, perhaps we just need to be patient.

The problem is that this story of a slow but gradual convergence of men's and women's fortunes doesn't fit the data. Instead, on several key metrics we see a period of rapid change coinciding with women's mass entry into the paid labor force, followed by a long plateau in which gender convergence trickles off or stops altogether.[28] This is the pattern for physical household labor: massive change in the 1960s through 1980s followed by more than three decades of relative stasis. Why did the physical housework revolution stall out? And why has the cognitive housework revolution barely started?

Doing Gender on the Second Shift

I first encountered Arlie Hochschild's seminal book The Second Shift as a graduate student. Though the text was nearly thirty years old, I found myself underlining and dog-earing every other page, stunned by the way Hochschild seemed to capture both my peers' and my parents' household labor dynamics. Hochschild was writing in 1989, at the tail end of a major overhaul in women's lives. In the preceding decades, women had entered the workforce in huge numbers.[29] But this seismic shift in women's paid work contributions did not presage an equivalent revolution in men's housework contributions.[30] Instead, many women were now working the equivalent of two jobs, including the housework Hochschild famously described as their "second shift." Though I hadn't planned to study gender in graduate school, this encounter with Hochschild's work steered me onto a new path. I wanted to understand why many women were *still* working that double shift—and how the story might change if we considered forms of household labor Hochschild largely overlooked.[31]

On the former point, I was in good company: though Hochschild's study is perhaps the best-known, the question of why women do so much household labor has preoccupied hundreds of social scientists over multiple decades.[32] Many have looked to economics, reasoning that a couple's domestic labor allocation is largely a function of their paid labor allocation.[33] That is, the spouse who earns more money or works longer hours for pay will do a smaller share of the chores at home. Why? Higher earnings create dependency on the part of the lower earner, which gives the primary breadwinner more power to bargain their way out of distasteful tasks. The laws of comparative advantage push spouses to specialize, which often means the higher earner's career takes priority. Finally, time spent at work is typically incompatible with time spent on physical housework or childcare: if your spouse is at the office until 8:00 p.m. most nights, they cannot help with dinner and bedtime for your toddler.[34]

These economic theories are nominally gender-neutral. If couples are merely responding to economic incentives or logistical constraints, the identity of the breadwinner shouldn't matter. But something curious happens among the minority of different-gender couples with a woman in the chief earner role. Sociologist Veronica Tichenor put it bluntly in the subtitle of her 2005 book: "Successful wives can't buy equality." Rather, such women often do double duty as chief earner *and* chief housekeeper.[35] This asymmetry hints that a couple's labor allocation is not just about earnings or hours. It's also about gender. More specifically, it's about cultural beliefs regarding gender— what do we believe women and men should do for their families?—and, on a deeper level, about how those beliefs are reflected and refracted in the way individuals "do" their gender.[36]

The idea of "doing" one's gender sounds odd to those of us accustomed to thinking of gender as a personal quality—something we *are*. But many sociologists understand gender as more akin to an activity. In this view, "woman" is not an inherent feature of who I am but rather a role I continually enact.[37] We each do our gender in myriad ways, ranging from how we clothe and groom ourselves to the hobbies we pursue and the ways we communicate. Women can wrestle and men can pirouette, but doing so is socially risky. In the words of the original "doing gender" theorists, Candace West and Don Zimmerman, to do gender is to "engage in behavior *at the risk of gender assessment*."[38] Behaving in ways that run counter to others' understanding of our gender makes us particularly vulnerable to their judgment.

Housework—the tasks we complete, those we skip, and the ways we do so—is yet another arena for doing gender.[39] For women, doing gender has historically meant completing most of the physical housework and childcare tasks. For men, it has long entailed ignoring or underperforming such tasks, with the notable exception of certain "male-typed" chores like taking out the trash and tending to the lawn.[40] But missing from most studies of how we do gender via housework is a consideration of what it means to do gender in the context of *cognitive* household labor.[41] And as it turns out, deeply ingrained notions of what gender means and how it should manifest shape the way we use our minds as well as our minutes.

Our Gendered Selves

Americans are famous—some might say infamous—for their individualist streak. Where other cultures emphasize family and group membership, Americans celebrate "self-made" and "self-reliant" individuals.[42] We encourage young people to find and follow their passion or calling.[43] We implore one another to remain true to who we are and to surround ourselves with those who appreciate our unique quirks.[44] Though these messages seem largely positive, even banal, they have an underexplored shadow side. Popular discourse tells us our personalities and preferences are innate elements of our innermost selves. But this individualistic message obscures the role of context. In a narrow sense, we underestimate how our circumstances bring out different sides of us: delivering a lecture, I am authoritative; at dinner with friends, I'm laid-back.[45] More broadly, we overlook the ways our social location—that is, our unique combination of characteristics like gender and race and class—shapes our sense of self.

Many sociologists of gender argue that each of us has a "gendered self," but they aren't referring to fundamental differences in men's and women's psyches.[46] Rather, they're pointing out that our understanding of who we are is shaped (largely outside our awareness) by cultural ideas about what gender means. Consider the act of choosing a career, one of many decisions where we're encouraged to let personal passion be our guide. As sociologist Erin Cech compellingly documents in a recent book, when men and women follow this advice they tend to self-select into different jobs.[47] Women are overrepresented in the so-called "helping" fields, like nursing, teaching, and social work. Men are overrepresented in technical and mechanical fields like engineering, computer science, and the trades.[48]

My best friend and her husband are a case in point. She teaches at an elementary school. He owns a car-detailing business. One could interpret their career choices as evidence of innate gender difference: women gravitate toward people (in this case, young children); men gravitate toward things (in this case, cars).[49] Indeed, 89 percent of elementary school teachers are women, and 82 percent of auto dealers are male.[50] When men and women have the freedom to choose their occupational paths, they often choose differently.

Another way to explain it, however, is that as a child my friend was celebrated for behaving in a nurturing way toward her friends and her dolls, given copious opportunities to babysit, and instructed by female elementary school teachers she saw as role models. Along the way, she developed a sense of herself as patient and caring, and she eventually identified teaching as an ideal way to make use of these gifts. Meanwhile, her husband was given toy cars to play with, encouraged when he displayed mechanical aptitude, and invited to help his father in the garage. He developed a keen sense of spatial awareness and channeled his energies into learning the ins and outs of various car models. Both my friend and her husband chose their profession, and neither, I suspect, would be happy in the other's occupational shoes. And yet their career choices were likely shaped by their gender as much as their innate personal qualities.

In other words, when we act in ways that feel instinctive, natural, or in line with who we are, we are often *also* doing gender. To be clear, I'm not arguing that personality is a myth or that there's no such thing as an authentic preference. Rather, I'm arguing that we tend to *overestimate* the effects of individual difference and *underestimate* the effects of social forces, including gender, on who we are and what we want. Nature and nurture work in concert, but our tendency is to focus too heavily on the former when it comes to explaining our personality and preferences.[51]

When I asked different-gender couples why they divide cognitive housework unequally, I heard the same focus on individual nature. They told me things like, "She's just way more organized," and "He's more of a go-with-the-flow guy." In other words, they argued that personality and temperament dictate one's cognitive labor role in a household. The problem is that when we understand cognitive labor as deeply personal, an extension of *who we are* rather than merely *what we do,* its gendered nature gets obscured. Overwhelmingly, female interviewees were the ones identified as "type-A" and "the planner"—characteristics central to what I term the "Superhuman" archetype. Meanwhile, their male partners—including high-powered surgeons and meticulous project managers—were described as laid-back "Bumblers" who lacked sufficient planning skills.

In effect, my interviewees' deft use of the Bumbler and Superhuman archetypes replaced gender essentialism with *personal* essentialism: they reframed long-standing gender stereotypes as individual differences. This meant that couples who endorsed egalitarianism ended up perpetuating inequality, all the while believing—or, at least, telling themselves—gender had little to do with their cognitive labor arrangement. Focusing on personality meant they could avoid confronting the social and cultural forces that make gender traditionalism the path of least resistance for so many. Meanwhile, couples who desired change were thwarted by their belief that it would be impossible. After all, our cultural obsession with finding and enacting one's authentic self tells us it's unreasonable to ask a Superhuman woman to suddenly embrace spontaneity or a Bumbler man to begin planning two steps ahead. Framing cognitive labor allocations as a function of innate qualities rather than learned skills helped trap couples in patterns misaligned with their ideals.

"Just on My List for Now"

Among most couples I spoke with, cognitive labor inequality was narrated as an inevitable consequence of personality difference. But a notable minority broke from this mold. Roughly one-fifth of the different-gender couples I interviewed were Balanced (i.e., each partner carried a roughly equal cognitive load) or Man-led (i.e., the male partner took on more of the cognitive labor). Among the LGBTQ+ interviewees, whom I shorthand as "queer couples" throughout the book, cognitive labor inequality was the norm; I refer to these couples as "Imbalanced." However, that inequality was quantitatively and qualitatively different than the inequality I observed among Woman-led couples like Jackie and Matthew. Together, the queer and nontraditional different-gender couples highlight alternate ways of understanding the relationships among gender, self, and cognitive labor.

Whitney, a Latina woman who works in sales, chuckled while recalling her father singling out his daughters for domestic chores. "'Go help your mom with the dishes,'" he would say. "You know, like, 'Girls, go do that.'" In response, Whitney remembered telling him, "'My husband will wash the dishes for me. I'm not washing the dishes.' I guess I've always been a bit rebellious against that perception [that housework was women's work]." The dishwashing husband never materialized; instead, Whitney married Vanessa, a cheerful woman who gestures emphatically as she speaks. "It's a big benefit to be a queer couple," Vanessa, who is White, asserted. "There just isn't an established role, at least for us. . . . So any chore, or any household thing, it's a conversation." Whitney offered a similar sentiment:

> We're very equal partners, I would say. We don't have that sort of expectation where there's, this, like, "Well, you're just automatically going to do this. And I'm automatically gonna do that." I think part of that . . . [is] the fact that we're both women, though. So it has to be a little bit more deliberate for us. But I would say it's easy for one of us to feel lazy and let the other one do it, no matter what gender we are. And we purposefully try not to do it that way.

Whitney and Vanessa's strong mutual commitment to equality did not translate into a 50/50 labor allocation. Both spouses agreed that Vanessa completes more of the cognitive labor for their family, which at the time of our interviews included one toddler and a baby on the way.[52] "I'm the planner of the two of us," Vanessa, a communications manager, explained. "I'm the one who schedules appointments, calls doctors, does all our insurance stuff, is always thinking about that kind of stuff. Whitney wouldn't go to the dentist if I didn't schedule her." Whitney concurred: "[Vanessa] is the admin of our home for sure."

Vanessa may be the household's primary cognitive laborer, but Whitney and Vanessa are not simply a same-gender version of Jackie and Matthew. Both women referenced traditional gender archetypes, even as their labor patterns simultaneously scrambled them. Vanessa described Whitney as "such a mom, in that she thinks about every little thing [with our son], and she's anxious about it all the time." Whitney complained that in the early days of parenthood, Vanessa acted "like a scared new dad" awaiting Whitney's parenting instructions. Why, then, was "scared new dad" Vanessa the one managing their toddler's diet, scheduling his pediatrician appointments, and coordinating the childcare schedule? When I posed a version of this question to Vanessa, she paused for a minute before venturing a guess: "[Whitney is] the moment-to-moment stuff, and she's the very long-term. Whitney's not, like, 'I'm thinking ahead to next week,' or even three months out. She's either, like, '[Our son's] future' and 'His career path' and 'His education,' or 'What coat is he wearing right now?'"

Like Whitney and Vanessa, most of the queer couples I interviewed were Imbalanced—that is, they divide cognitive labor unequally, defying the simplistic stereotype of queer couples as egalitarian.[53] But Imbalanced queer couples' version of cognitive inequality differed markedly from that of their different-gender peers. Queer respondents cited individual personality to explain their division, yet they rarely described personas that mapped neatly onto the Superhuman and Bumbler archetypes I observed among different-gender couples. Vanessa's suggestion that Whitney attended to the immediate present and the far future, while Vanessa handled most of the in-between, was unique to this pair, but my conversations with queer couples revealed a wide range of similarly idiosyncratic explanations.

Queer and nontraditional different-gender couples alike also evinced a more flexible understanding of the relationship between their cognitive labor allocation and their innate selves. "We're not super stuck in our ways, in that we have to be rigid," explained Whitney. "We're quick to pivot if we need to." Asked to explain why she is the one responsible for certain household tasks, Vanessa concluded, "It's a combination of things I'm just stronger at, [things] I actually like doing, and things that are just on my list for now." The belief that a cognitive labor arrangement could be informed, but not dictated, by perceived personality differences did not ensure perfect equality. This belief did, however, seem to help partners like Vanessa and Whitney find a mutually satisfying equilibrium.

Collecting the Data

In the pages to come, I draw from the stories of 172 parents representing 94 distinct couples. Across countless kitchen, café, and office tables, they opened up about the big and the small stuff of their lives. The earliest interviews took place in the summer of 2017, after I put out a call for college-educated, different-gender couples parenting young children. The transition to parenthood is often accompanied by an increased household labor load and a more gender-traditional division of that labor.[54] I was curious to see how these changes would play out in the cognitive labor sphere, among a demographic group (i.e., the highly educated) known for their strong endorsement of gender-egalitarian ideals.[55] But I later wondered whether the cognitive labor patterns I'd observed so far were an "upper-middle-class thing": to what extent did they generalize beyond a very narrow, privileged slice of the population? Thus, in late 2019 I returned to the field for a second round of interviews, this time with different-gender couples from a wider range of educational and occupational backgrounds. Finally, in 2022 I conducted a third round of interviews with LGBTQ+ parents. I wanted to understand how cognitive labor operated outside the context of a different-gender relationship: Was there greater equality? Did couples use different logic to explain their arrangements?

The individuals who ultimately shared their stories with me were, by many measures, a diverse bunch. Some were in their twenties, others in their fifties. Some lived in the center of a major city, others on the periphery of a sleepy suburban town. They labored as construction workers, carpenters, doctors, and dietitians (to name but a few occupations), or they served as full-time caregivers for their children.

Still, they are by no means a representative sample of the U.S. population, and my results thus cannot showcase the full range of behaviors, beliefs, and circumstances that shape American families' cognitive labor dynamics. By design, all of my interviewees are parents; the majority are also legally married and reside in one of two East Coast states (New Jersey and Massachusetts).[56] As a group, they trend affluent (with a median household income of $155,000), though I spoke with couples occupying many distinct rungs on the class ladder.[57] At one end, Valerie and her partner Joe, neither of whom finished college, were barely scraping by on an annual income of $21,000; at the other, Kara and Joel, who both held graduate degrees, lived very comfortably on more than $300,000. I expected to find significant differences in the cognitive labor patterns of couples like these, given prior research on class differences in household labor allocation and gender ideology.[58] Indeed, my analysis turned up some variations, particularly in the way interviewees of different social classes talked about gender. However, these cross-class differences were minor compared to the overwhelming similarities I observed among couples across the socioeconomic spectrum. Thus, I have opted to describe class differences where relevant but have not made it a primary focus of my analysis.

My sample is also overwhelmingly White (84 percent) and U.S.-born (88 percent), an important limitation given the growing body of research showing how gender operates differently across races, ethnicities, and immigrant statuses.[59] Because I spoke with so few members of specific groups other than White, U.S.-born individuals, I cannot confidently speak to the question of how cognitive labor patterns vary across these dimensions, and my results should not be interpreted as a universal norm.[60] I describe any differences

I did observe as hypotheses to be explored in future research rather than definitive conclusions.

Once I figured out *whom* to interview, my next challenge was figuring out *how* to interview them. My working assumption was that cognitive labor would be an unfamiliar concept, one that many respondents had not named for themselves, let alone found a way to communicate to a stranger. So, I developed a tool I hoped would help make the invisible visible to both interviewer and interviewee. I emailed each participant a "decision diary" a few days before we were scheduled to meet and asked them to complete it ahead of their interview. This diary was modeled after the time diaries popular in traditional studies of housework, in which participants keep a minute-by-minute log of their activities.[61] But rather than their actions, I asked my respondents to keep track of all the family-related *decisions* they made or contemplated over a twenty-four-hour period.

When we sat down together—most often in their home, sometimes in a library or coffee shop, and occasionally in an office cafeteria or break room—the diaries my interviewees kept provided ample fodder for the first half of our conversation. Some of the decisions participants recorded were mundane ("decided to order takeout for dinner") and others monumental ("decided to place an offer on a house"). I peppered them with questions about both. Later, we transitioned into a discussion of more abstract topics, such as how they make joint decisions with their spouse and what portion of the physical and cognitive household labor they each complete.

Because I required both partners to participate in separate interviews, I was able to directly compare the way they talked about similar events. Though many participants half-jokingly asked if I could tell them what their partner said, I always demurred. Even if I had shared, they might have been disappointed. Few partners directly contradicted one another, perhaps because they knew I would also be speaking with their spouse. Still, the details they shared or omitted offered important clues as to what role the interviewee had played in any given interaction.

My second and third rounds of interviews resembled the first, albeit with tweaks to the protocol that reflected my evolving understanding of the issues. For example, I added detailed questions about participants' backstory (i.e., their upbringing, career trajectory, and relationship history) in hopes of understanding the pathways that led them to their present (in)equality. I also replaced the decision diaries with a deck of cards printed with cognitive and physical household tasks.[62] Participants sorted the cards into piles based on who typically handles each task in their household and explained their reasoning aloud during and after the exercise. Finally, I relaxed the requirement that both partners participate in the study, lest I inadvertently screen out unhappy couples. I strongly encouraged dual participation, however, and in most cases (roughly 80 percent) was still able to interview both members of each couple. Readers interested in the finer points of my study design will find considerably more detail in the appendix.

Organization of the Book

Our story begins in chapter 1 with an abridged history of activists' and scholars' attempts to define and study household labor. For good reason, researchers in this field have primarily looked to the clock to assess and compare household contributions. But this focus on time has an unfortunate side effect: it shrinks the experience of household labor down to its most visible components and leaves out large swaths of the work that goes into maintaining a household and raising children. I suggest we supplement familiar time-use metrics with attention to "mind-use" and introduce cognitive labor as the key component of this dimension of household life.

Chapters 2–4 center the Woman-led couples who comprise the majority of my interviewees. In chapter 2, I show why current, time-based estimates likely understate gender gaps in household labor. The fathers I interviewed are a far cry from the distant dads lampooned in popular media and lamented in earlier eras of social science research.[63] Most are heavily involved in family decision making, and many devote considerable time to chores and childcare. But it is primarily women whose minds are disproportionately dedicated to household affairs. Women in different-gender couples do more cognitive work overall and are particularly likely to take on the most burdensome aspects of this labor.

Puzzlingly, this inequality persists even though most respondents in Woman-led couples expressed a desire for an equal (or equal-ish) cognitive labor allocation. Yet as I document in chapter 3, this apparent contradiction between ideal and reality rarely translated into sustained efforts to change. This disconnect was possible because most couples recast gendered inequalities as personal quirks. As one respondent explained, "It's not a gender thing, it's a *me* thing." This "personal essentialist" narrative alleviated the pressure couples might otherwise feel to live up to their egalitarian ideals. It also discouraged reallocation—it is difficult, and perhaps unkind, to ask one's partner to become someone they are not—even as it helped minimize spousal conflict.

Contrary to the personality-based explanations favored by my interviewees, I argue in chapter 4 that successful completion of cognitive labor depends as much on one's skills and capacities as on innate traits. The catch is that men and women in Woman-led couples *invest* differently in building relevant skills and, even in areas where they have similar abilities, they *deploy* them differently between their paid work and home. The skills men bring to their employment, for instance, are frequently overlooked in the domestic context. I show how these twin processes of gendered investment and deployment are driven as much by social forces, such as norms that hold women more accountable for domestic outcomes, as by individual choices. But regardless of their origins, these skill-related patterns end up creating and sustaining the perceived personality differences they are said to merely reflect.

Is this gendered division of cognitive labor inevitable? In the final two chapters, I turn away from Woman-led couples like Jackie and Matthew to explore alternative ways of understanding and allocating cognitive labor. In chapter 5, I describe the small subset of different-gender couples who have a Balanced or Man-led division. Their diverse experiences, not all of them positive, reveal both the promise and the peril of operating outside the status quo. The most satisfied of these nontraditional couples perceive a match between who they are and what their circumstances demand of them, and they view themselves as active agents in the design of their cognitive labor arrangements.

Meanwhile, the labels "Man-led" and "Woman-led" make little sense when applied to queer couples like Vanessa and Whitney, whose experiences I document in chapter 6. Instead, I describe these couples as Balanced or Imbalanced depending on their cognitive labor allocation. The majority fell into the latter camp. Yet both the magnitude of their cognitive inequality and the ways they made sense of it set them apart from most Woman-led couples. For one, queer couples tended to be more cognizant of their labor patterns and to grapple with them jointly rather than individually. For another, though queer respondents frequently cited personality to explain their cognitive labor allocation, they rarely described "selves" that mapped onto existing gender stereotypes. These couples were not, however, uniformly untroubled by cognitive labor–related conflict or dissatisfaction, and the sources of their struggles help bring the obstacles to greater equality into stark relief.

Building on these insights, I conclude with a vision for an expanded sociology of household labor that places as much emphasis on mind-use as time-use. Though the associated measurement challenges are formidable, the payoff will be worthwhile. Understanding gender inequality in the twenty-first century depends on our ability to track subtle distinctions in men's and women's experiences of household life, as well as the evolving narratives that sustain those distinctions. To move beyond the status quo, we will need to do more than exhort women to lean in at work and men to step up at home. I close the book with a series of recommendations for actors ranging from policymakers to institutions to couples. Change is possible. But achieving it will require us to rethink deeply entrenched assumptions about who we are and who we might yet become.

CHAPTER 1

DOING, FEELING—AND THINKING

At 6:40 a.m. on a June Wednesday, Kristen, a White woman in her early thirties, confronted a hungry two-year-old. Her son Ethan, the toddler in question, "is what we like to call a handful," Kristen told me affectionately a few days later. Right now, though, he was mostly hungry. Kristen mentally ticked through breakfast options: "I'm thinking about, what has Ethan eaten this week? What's stuck and what hasn't? Is he eating enough protein? Which he tends to not. . . . And I'm also thinking about the timing of it all, and the things that have to come after it. To clean up, to get him dressed on time for school." She eventually settled on scrambled eggs and orange juice.

Just as she was pulling the eggs off the stove, Kristen's husband, Alan, also White, joined them in the kitchen and asked Ethan whether he wanted anything else to eat. "Yogurt!" Ethan proclaimed. Kristen was annoyed by the disruption but took it in stride. "I asked [Alan], 'Can you wait until we get him to eat some protein?' From the egg. The yogurt's protein, too, but it was like, I've already made this. So I convinced Ethan to eat a couple bites, and then he could eat the yogurt Alan brought."

According to the log Kristen kept that day and shared with me later, the egg versus yogurt debate was over by 6:50 a.m. But even as it was unfolding, Kristen's attention was fragmented. When she grabbed an egg from the fridge, she noted a dwindling supply of both milk and yogurt and made a mental note to stop by the grocery store later. While cajoling Ethan to eat, she saw that angry red blotches had reemerged on his cheeks and decided to pull out the bottle of allergy medicine. At 7:00 a.m., Kristen ventured upstairs with Ethan to his bedroom. As she rummaged through his dresser drawers, a recent email from Ethan's day-care center came to mind. "'This is the start of summer,'" Kristen paraphrased, "'so make sure you clean out cubbies and you take away any [clothes] left over from winter.'" She'd already picked up Ethan's snow pants and boots, but she knew he still had fleece pants she should bring home. Back downstairs, Kristen's brain pinged again: she should probably pull Ethan's teacher aside to talk about potty-training plans. He'd been having some success at home, and it seemed like a good time to start weaning him off diapers at day care, too.

Kristen's log was quiet from day-care drop-off through midafternoon as she pushed through meetings and deadlines related to her work as a public policy analyst. Around 3:30 p.m., though, she began making plans. Dinner with the cousins would be nice, wouldn't it? Kristen texted her sister-in-law about coming over the next evening and then her husband to let him know about the plan. She also mentally filed away several issues to discuss with Alan after he returned home from his project management job, including news she'd received via email about a lice outbreak at Ethan's day care.

When later rolled around, Kristen steered the conversation with Alan toward another contentious question: was it time to push Ethan's bedtime back? She explained her concerns:

> We've had a couple nights over the last week or so that have been way too early. Like 4 a.m., [Ethan is] trying to get up and out. Alan and I keep circling back to—this is my question, I keep asking the question. . . . Because in the back of my head I keep hoping that as Ethan gets older, he'll be able to go to bed later, we'll be able to eat together [as a family], and [he'll] go to bed later and presumably sleep later.

Alan, however, preferred having child-free time in the evening so he and Kristen could eat and talk together in peace. Recalling the same conversation, he explained:

> This has happened before, where we'll have a couple of nights where, for whatever reason, he gets up early . . . Kristen got up with Ethan earlier because I got up with him, tried to soothe him and get him back to bed, and he's just like, "No, Daddy!" and ran by me to our bedroom and climbed into bed with Kristen. I wasn't going to be able to do anything. I basically said [to Kristen], "Let's give it one more night. I don't think two nights is enough of a sample size."

After some back-and-forth, the spouses agreed to continue the status quo, as Alan had requested. Reflecting back on the conversation a few days later, Kristen's frustration was apparent: "As someone who got up twice last night, I think [the bedtime question] is pretty big. But I'm also someone of the mind that . . . I just want an answer. I want someone to tell me, 'This is how you fix the problem.' I don't have that."

In this chapter, we begin to make sense of Kristen's experiences on that June Wednesday. Alongside the familiar chores—like cooking and driving Ethan to and from day care—that occupied her time, Kristen's mind was constantly scanning for potential problems, sorting through her options for solving them, making countless decisions, and monitoring the effects of decisions she'd already made. "Housework," at least as it's commonly understood, doesn't adequately capture these aspects of her day. Kristen's experiences are forms of *cognitive labor*, akin to the work of project-managing the home. Alan, too, engaged in such labor, though his contributions were less extensive and took different forms. In the pages that follow, I map the contours of this understudied dimension of household life and explain what we lose when we leave mind-use out of the housework story.

But first: what, exactly, *is* that housework story, and why is it oriented around physical labor and time-use in the first place? Despite its associations with drudgery, unpaid domestic labor has been a lightning rod for countless Americans wrestling with lofty questions about morality, economics, and modernity. Generations of feminist activists and social scientists have campaigned—and continue campaigning—to gain societal recognition for housework as both a valuable social contribution *and* a burden that falls too heavily on the shoulders of women.[1] One unfortunate side effect of that historic fight was the reduction of household labor to a single, physical component governed by the metric of time.

Putting Housework on a Pedestal

Because every story must begin somewhere, we pick up the housework narrative at the turn of the nineteenth century. Prior to the Industrial Revolution in the United States, both men's and women's labor was largely aimed at producing what Marx called "use-value."[2] Families grew crops to feed themselves, spun wool to clothe themselves, and built houses to shelter themselves. Work and home were largely one and the same. The 1800 U.S. Census reflected this conception: "housewives" (i.e., women whose primary job was caring for their families) were classified as productive workers. By the 1900 census, however, these same housewives had been recast as "dependents" alongside children and the elderly.[3] Why?

In short, because they were not paid for their efforts. Cooking could be productive labor, but only if you were employed as a cook for another household.

The same activity, when uncompensated and performed for family members, no longer counted. With the rise of a capitalist market economy, "exchange-value" had come to dominate use-value: individuals grew crops, sewed garments, and assembled homes and furniture in hopes of earning money, which they could then exchange for the goods they needed.[4] In the process, the world of paid work (aka "the market") and the world of unpaid household labor (aka "the domestic") split in two.[5]

This separation of spheres was more than a spatial distinction: domestic life was increasingly positioned as everything the market was not. Where the latter was competitive, individualistic, and governed by economic logic, the former was collaborative, communal, and governed by moral virtues.[6] The stark distinction between cold, unfeeling market and warm, comfortable home dovetailed nicely with existing ideas about the gender binary: "home" was coded as feminine, "market" as masculine. But if home was to be a true haven where men could take refuge from the vagaries of the market, women's daily activities needed to be more clearly demarcated from men's. Hence the reclassification of women from workers to dependents: women were not "laboring," they were cultivating a wholesome family atmosphere and passing on Christian values to the next generation.[7] Nineteenth-century feminists took issue with this classification of unpaid domestic tasks. The notion of home as haven *seemed* to put women on a pedestal. But in the process, they argued, it also downplayed their contributions and kept them financially dependent on the men in their lives.[8]

It's important to note that this simplified narrative overlooks important class and racial differences.[9] For centuries, poor women and women of color had been exchanging their labor for wages—or, in the case of enslaved persons, for nothing at all—while White and wealthy families profited from their efforts.[10] Still, prior to the Industrial Revolution, poor women often earned income from work they did from their homes—gardening, taking in boarders, selling milk and cheese from their cows—rather than out in the wider world.[11] Wage labor conducted outside the home became much more common for poor and working-class women only in the wake of the Industrial Revolution.

But these were not the women who had been placed on a pedestal of purity. Nor were they the women for whom White, middle-class feminists were fighting.[12] Instead, those feminists aimed to improve the lot of the White, middle-class housewife. One of their key goals was to recast unpaid housework as *economically productive*. To do this, they sought a common scale for measuring women's non-market work and men's market work. Eventually, they settled on time, which could be translated into dollars.

Hildegarde Kneeland, a pioneering home economist, summarized the resulting "wages for wives" campaign as a push to calculate "an estimated wage, based on the cost of replacing the housewife by a paid worker in the home. Since her husband would have to meet this cost if the housewife withdrew her services, [the campaigners] propose that [the estimated wage] be taken as the amount which she earns and therefore as the amount which her husband should pay her."[13] To reach this estimated wage figure, Kneeland explained, one multiplied the number of hours a housewife spent on various tasks by "the wage rates customarily paid" to workers who sold equivalent services on the market.[14] If the average maid earned 50 cents per hour, then a housewife was effectively saving her husband 50 cents for each hour she spent on laundry and cleaning.

The "wages for wives" campaigners hoped that quantifying unpaid household activities and translating them into economic terms would in turn raise their status in a society dominated by the profit imperative. They largely accepted the idea that housework was women's purview, but they wanted the economic value of that work celebrated alongside its moral value.[15] Time—and its direct connection, via hourly wages, to money—seemed like the key to accomplishing their goal.

The "wages for wives" campaigners did not make significant headway before feminist advocacy around housework faded, largely replaced by attention to female suffrage.[16] They did, however, set the stage for our modern understanding of housework as physical labor that is best measured in units of time. The housework question would reemerge several decades later in the context of second-wave feminism. This time, social scientists would be paying more attention, and they, too, would look to the clock.

Quantifying and Commodifying

The academic study of housework was largely the providence of home economists from the late nineteenth century through the mid-twentieth.[17] In the field's heyday, home economists argued that the principles used by management theorists to improve paid work in factories—tactics like economizing movements and designing ergonomically optimized workspaces—would apply equally well to home-based labor.[18] Like the activists before them, few questioned the idea that domestic chores were a woman's responsibility, but most firmly believed those chores need not be quite so taxing.

Sociologists, meanwhile, were relatively late to the idea that housework might fall under their purview. Prior to the 1960s, many mainstream sociologists believed men and women were fundamentally different creatures with distinct social roles that mapped onto the separate spheres: women belonged to the private, domestic realm and men to the public, market realm.[19] In consequence, write Myra Marx Ferree and colleagues in their history of women in the discipline, women were "rarely of interest to sociologists, unless as deviants ('nuts and sluts') or as wives and mothers (family sociology being understood largely by studying women, and only women)."[20] But as educational and employment opportunities for women expanded in the mid-1900s, female sociologists arrived in greater numbers, bringing fresh perspectives that challenged once-dominant views of gender, work, and family. Gradually, sociologists moved away from the idea that men and women "naturally" belonged in different places. They increasingly interpreted the segregation of men and women into public and private roles as evidence of gender inequality rather than of a well-functioning social order.[21]

Sociological research on household labor exploded in the latter half of the twentieth century, with hundreds of articles on related topics published between 1989 and 1999 alone.[22] In the pages of those articles, scholars worked to generate the sort of precise definition and reliable metrics that could lend credibility to the study of household labor as a social problem rather than a niche "women's issue." These scholars converged on a set of concrete, observable activities few critics would dispute as housework: cooking, cleaning, laundry, and home maintenance. Several additional categories, including bill-paying, shopping, and childcare, regularly made the list, too.[23] And like the activists who came before them, these scholars primarily measured housework in minutes and hours.

Their focus on time-use had several advantages. For one, it was associated with "serious" disciplines like scientific management, in which engineers sought to shave seconds off factory workers' routine movements to boost their efficiency and productivity.[24] For another, the conversion of housework efforts to minutes made it easier to compare individuals' workloads and, thus, document inequality. If we know that an at-home mother averages sixty hours weekly on housework and childcare, we have a concrete way to compare her contributions to her breadwinner husband's, though he is paid and she is not: time serves as the common scale, just as the "wages for wives" campaigners recognized.[25] Knowing that the average married mother spends nearly twice as much time on housework as her male counterpart gives us an intuitive sense of their relative burdens and allows us to track fluctuations in the size of those burdens over time. Time can also be plausibly (if imperfectly) converted to monetary value, usually via hourly wage rates. This conversion allows scholars to estimate women's contributions to the national economy or simply the household balance sheet.[26] In short, the specificity and concreteness of time helped legitimize both scholars' *and* activists' arguments about housework's importance and drew public attention to its unequal distribution by gender.

The major problem with the time perspective, however, is that many household activities evade temporal measurement. This is not a contemporary discovery. As far back as 1929, home economist Kneeland warned that accurately measuring women's time in childcare would be a nightmare. "It is no easy task to decide when the time should be counted as work and when as leisure," she warned. "With the actual physical care of children, the dressing and bathing and feeding, there is little uncertainty. But with training and 'oversight' the figure will tend to be either too low or too high."[27] "Planning and other management" tasks would similarly elude capture, Kneeland predicted: "The time which appears in the record will invariably be too low, since much of this 'head work' is done while the hands of the housewife are engaged in one of her manual tasks."[28]

Picking up this thread decades later, several feminist sociologists pointed out further limitations of the now customary definition and measurement of housework. Writing about women's "invisible labor" in 1987, Arlene Kaplan Daniels noted that while specific tasks can be delegated to others, "it is usually the wife and mother who notices what needs to be done and when."[29] Hanna Papanek identified "family status production" as a specific category of under-appreciated work that involved sending thoughtful holiday cards, making an elaborate spread for dinner with your spouse's boss, and otherwise ensuring the family's positive reputation in the community.[30] Sara Ruddick and Susan Walzer independently argued that the practice of mothering involved a distinct form of thought as well as action,[31] while Carolyn Rosenthal identified "kinkeeping" as the work women performed to hold extended families together,[32] and Helen Mederer argued for distinguishing between accomplishing and managing household tasks.[33]

Unfortunately, the advice of such pioneering thinkers has not been sufficiently heeded. Contemporary housework studies still overwhelmingly focus on concrete tasks like cooking and cleaning and still overwhelmingly measure housework burdens in hours and minutes.[34] Researchers distribute surveys that ask participants to estimate how much time they spend on various chores in an average week, or time diaries in which they record their activities minute by minute.[35] The cost, it seems, of garnering recognition for housework as a legitimate object of social scientific study was a reduction in its complexity and nuance.

While many thinkers from Kneeland forward have recognized the limitations of predominant definitions and measurements of housework, scholars have not yet coalesced around a viable alternative. We lack a clear definition of what Kneeland called "head work," a definition that recognizes it as a unique dimension of household life with qualities that require innovative measurement strategies. Concepts like "kinkeeping" and "family status production" are too specific, while constructs like "invisible labor" are too vague, defined in negative terms that don't give us a clear sense of what to look for.[36]

One promising model is "emotional labor," an idea that emerged from sociologist Arlie Hochschild's research on service workers such as flight attendants.[37] Hochschild noticed that part of the attendants' job was to maintain a cheerful, upbeat demeanor regardless of how customers treated them. An attendant who completed all the requisite job tasks—making announcements, pushing the beverage cart, instructing passengers to buckle up—but failed to smile while doing so would face her employer's disapproval. In other words, a core part of her job was emotional labor: intentionally managing and displaying her feelings in context-appropriate ways.

In its original incarnation, emotional labor was a concept reserved for the paid work sphere. Hochschild coined the related term "emotion work" to describe similar processes in the domestic sphere: a man trying not to lose his temper with his children at bedtime, a woman comforting her spouse after a fight with his boss.[38]

Emotion work is an ideal model for those of us seeking to move beyond a unidimensional understanding of housework as a physical endeavor. It is both specific enough to be precisely identified and broad enough to apply to a wide range of circumstances. Professionally and personally, most of us must routinely struggle to bring our feelings in line with the norms dictated by our environment. These "emotional" efforts constitute a second dimension of domestic work alongside the more familiar, action-based kind I refer to as "physical" household labor.

In the decades since it entered the popular lexicon, however, "emotional labor"—much like "invisible labor"—has become a catchall term for a wide range of misfit activities not captured by the dominant housework paradigm, from deciding when the bathroom needs cleaning to remembering a family member's birthday.[39] Hochschild herself has lamented the "blurriness of the thinking" around this topic. "We're trying to have an important conversation but having it in a very hazy way, working with a blunt concept," she told a journalist in 2018.[40] To be sure, language evolves over time, and a core part of the intellectual enterprise is elaborating and refining earlier thinking. But the tendency to describe everything that does not fit the familiar housework model as "emotional labor" may conceal more than it reveals. When a concept comes to mean everything, it loses its potency. We're overdue for a new, three-dimensional understanding of housework as a combination of doing, feeling, and *thinking*.

Defining the Cognitive Dimension

With this backstory in mind, let's return to Kristen, whom we followed earlier through a busy but typical day-in-the-life. Kristen's *physical labor*, like cooking breakfast, dressing Ethan, and driving him to day care, is most readily apparent. If we dig a little deeper, we can also make out her *emotional labor*. When Alan offered Ethan a more appealing breakfast option than the egg Kristen was already scrambling, she did her best to remain upbeat despite her irritation. When Ethan awoke—again!—at 4 a.m., Kristen kept her frustration in check. But these activities, which I shorthand as *doing* and *feeling*, respectively, leave out broad swaths of Kristen's experience: *thinking*. This *cognitive labor* constitutes a third, relatively underexamined dimension of household work.[41]

In broad terms, cognitive household labor is a set of mental processes aimed at ensuring all family members' needs are met and that the family fulfills its obligations to others. It has four chief components: anticipating issues, identifying options, making decisions, and monitoring the results.[42] In a prototypical case, these four components unfold sequentially, beginning with anticipation, to form a cognitive "episode." Of course, reality is messier than this theoretical model, which presumes each stage will be clearly delineated and proceed in sequence. In practice, straight lines often look more like recursive loops; episodes are initiated but never completed; steps are combined or skipped altogether. Before diving into that complexity, however, let's first consider the ideal-typical case, as depicted in figure 1.1.

Every cognitive labor episode begins with a catalyst that sets off the whole operation. Often this catalyst is the sudden recognition of a problem, unfulfilled need, or new opportunity. *Didn't I see something on social media about spring soccer registration? We should start shopping for the holidays soon. Our health insurance coverage is about to expire.* This *anticipation* work is like a series of metaphorical pings, the psychic equivalent of a smartphone abuzz with

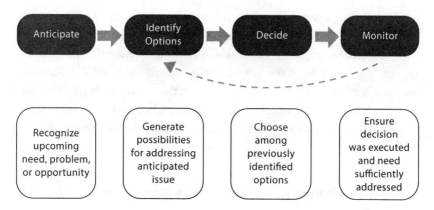

FIGURE 1.1. Four components of a cognitive labor episode.

notifications. Like their digital cousins, mental pings often emerge unbidden: in the shower, on the commute home, halfway through an important meeting. Human brains find open loops unsettling, so these pings often recur until some resolution is reached: a task is executed, responsibility is delegated to a spouse, or the issue is determined unworthy of further attention.[43] Kristen's anticipation included noticing her family was nearly out of milk and that Ethan was suffering from seasonal allergies.

Step two in the cognitive labor sequence is *identifying options*, or coming up with possibilities for addressing the anticipated issue. For complex matters, identification may unfold over days, weeks, or even months. Before selecting a day care for the first time, many of my interviewees polled friends, combed online forums and review sites, and assembled a spreadsheet comparing the features of local childcare facilities. Before choosing a vacation destination, they read up on the merits and drawbacks of various seaside towns. Before finalizing a Thanksgiving menu, they bookmarked numerous recipes for cranberry sauce and stuffing. More often, however, identification was far less formal, resembling a simple brainstorm rather than a fact-finding mission. At 5:30 p.m., they stood in front of the pantry, scanning the shelves and imagining what might become dinner. When rain scuttled Saturday afternoon plans, spouses took turns throwing out alternatives: The roller rink? Extra screen time? A visit to Grandma's? In Kristen's case, identification meant sorting through possible breakfast foods for Ethan, figuring out which clothes would be most appropriate for the weather and his daily activities, and preemptively googling "how to treat lice."

From this set of methodically or haphazardly assembled options, individuals or couples next *decide*. Decision making can range from snap judgment to lengthy deliberation. It can be a solo process or a tense negotiation between spouses, grounded in instinct or in careful consideration of pros and cons. *We'll book this hotel. Let's enroll our son in the local Head Start preschool. I'll skip the pancakes and just serve cereal for breakfast.* Often, though not always, a decision triggers the kind of physical action that might show up in a time log: making a phone call, assembling a meal, packing a bag. Kristen made many decisions during the day she tracked for me, some of them in conjunction with her husband. She picked out eggs for her son's breakfast, invited her sister-in-law over for dinner, and decided it was best to adopt a "wait-and-see" approach to the possibility of lice.

While a decision may seem like the endpoint of the process, there is one more cognitive labor component to account for: *monitoring the results*. Decisions are not always executed immediately, nor are their effects entirely predictable. Monitoring is required to ensure the decision was actually carried out as planned and to determine whether it accomplished its purpose. If not, it's back to the drawing board to identify and select a new option. The monitoring step is especially critical when the outcome of a decision hinges on another person's action. *Did my wife ever call the plumber? Did my daughter's teacher answer my email?*

If the decision was meant to solve a problem, monitoring can also mean assessing the solution's efficacy. *Did changing my daughter's diet resolve her symptoms, or do we need to make another appointment with the pediatrician? Did the baking soda remove the stain, or do I need to research alternative remedies?* Monitoring is anticipation's cousin, in the sense that both involve scouting out needs and problems. They differ in that anticipation is about putting something new *on* the radar, whereas monitoring is about determining when it can come *off*. For Kristen, monitoring meant checking to make sure Ethan's rash went away, staying in touch with his teacher to hear how potty training was going at day care, and waiting to see whether he returned to a more reasonable wake-up time.

Burdens and Benefits

The four components of cognitive labor are ever-present for many of us, to the point where we might reasonably wonder: is this really "work"? Despite their centrality to our lives, "work" and "labor" are slippery concepts to define. Academics and pundits alike have arguably gone a bit labor-crazy, inventing (or, more charitably, identifying) ever-multiplying forms: reproductive labor, emotional labor, office housework, and so on.[44] So I'd forgive you for bringing some skepticism to this text. Surely, there are corners of our lives that cannot or should not be labor-ized!

Part of the problem is that many of us associate "work" with burden, drudgery, or even exploitation. Understandably, we may hesitate to apply such a label to tasks like planning our child's birthday party. Thinking instead about work as *effortful, goal-directed activity* helps us separate it from its more negative connotations.[45] As most employees can attest, the category of "work" encompasses a range of more and less onerous activities. Some are intrinsically rewarding, while others are merely a means to the end of a paycheck. Many of us can name the enjoyable components of our jobs (for me, that's writing) and contrast them with boring or painful components (applying for grants). Both writing and grant applications are critical to my success as an academic. Yet I experience writing as a creative act, whereas grant applications are primarily appealing insofar as they enable me to do the writing and research I love. Put another way, writing is both intrinsically rewarding *and* an important means to the end of career success. It is work, but work that I enjoy, at least on good days.

Similar principles apply to unpaid work, where a combination of task characteristics and idiosyncratic preferences determines just how laborious our labor feels. Time-use researchers have established that (shockingly) cleaning-related tasks feel especially burdensome to the average person, whereas cooking is more middling.[46] For some, preparing a meal is an enjoyable hobby that also happens to be a good way to keep the family healthy and food costs in check; for others it's primarily a tedious chore. Broadly speaking, physical housework is consistently rated as less enjoyable than leisure activities and even paid work.[47] The popularity of services and devices promising to reduce housework time—cleaning services, meal delivery kits, Instant Pots, robot vacuums—confirms our intuitive sense that housework is, for many, something to be avoided or minimized. Echoing several other interviewees, Brandi joked that in her ideal world, "I would do 0 percent" of the household labor.

Childcare, though often included under the "household labor" umbrella, is a bit more complicated. Both childcare and housework are effortful and goal-directed—in the case of the former, the goal is to raise happy, healthy offspring, and in the latter, to maintain a functioning home. But while more time doing chores is usually seen as undesirable, more time spent caring for children is not as clearly negative.[48] Few parents pine for more cleaning time; many wish they could devote more hours to their children.[49] That care may be effortful (i.e., might involve labor), but such effort is often seen as intrinsically rewarding in a way housework is not.[50]

Cognitive labor occupies a similar gray area. Most of my interviewees could name at least one cognitive task they couldn't stand: meal planning, finding home repair people, filing a tax return. But there were others, like planning a child's birthday party or finding the ideal place to vacation, that at least some interviewees quite enjoyed. Sometimes, the very tasks they found most draining were the same ones they could not imagine handing over to anyone else. Some portion of this variation can be chalked up to personal preference, social norms, and individual circumstances. But my data also point to several characteristics of cognitive labor that shape individuals' experiences of it in predictable ways. On one side is the *burden* this work imposes; on the other are its offsetting *benefits*.[51]

The *burden* of a cognitive activity is largely a function of its *complexity* and *abstractness*. The most complex tasks are a metaphorical juggling act in which the cognitive laborer must track multiple inputs, coordinate with various players, and allocate finite resources. Simpler tasks are more like tossing a ball into the air and catching it: there are only a few variables to consider. Orchestrating a cross-country move is complex; planning a playdate is (hopefully) comparatively simple.

The abstractness of a cognitive task also impacts its burden. A highly abstract task is pervasive and unbounded: it has neither a defined start nor end and cannot be deferred to a more convenient time or place. Carla aptly described the problem with such tasks: "Sometimes, it pops into my head, like, god, I should really get extra stuff [e.g., new clothes] for our daughter. I kind of wish that didn't pop into my head during the day . . . that I could actually just be working when I'm working." Instead, anticipatory thoughts like these followed Carla wherever she went, interrupting her concentration at inopportune moments. The task of making sure a child had the right clothing, and enough of it, was practically endless. Less abstract tasks, meanwhile, have a more defined beginning and end and can often be scheduled. Identifying someone to repair the roof, for instance, might involve setting aside an hour on Saturday to make some calls—and come with the added satisfaction of crossing the item off a to-do list once the roofer is confirmed.[52]

On the other side of the equation, a cognitive task's *benefits* are a function of its *visibility* and *stakes*. High-visibility tasks are those others can easily recognize—and thus appreciate. Cognitive work surrounding unusual or one-off events, such as planning a vacation, tends to be more visible than the work that goes into maintaining the status quo, like keeping the pantry stocked with staple foods. Decision-making work, the outcome of which is often communicated to others and translated into concrete action, is typically the most visible of the four cognitive labor components. Anticipation and monitoring work are comparatively invisible, sometimes even to the laborer herself. Holly, like many respondents, was baffled by my questions about how she tracked household inventory: "Umm, it's usually in my head. I generally have a good idea of how much we have of stuff." The idea that constantly monitoring the supply of toothpaste was work for which Holly was responsible had not occurred to her. Though critical to her household's functioning, Holly's hidden work was unlikely to be counted when she or her husband reflected on their contributions to the family. In contrast, more visible tasks like finding an apartment to rent were easier to receive "credit" for, either from oneself or one's spouse.

The benefits of a cognitive task also depend on the stakes involved: to what extent does the task represent an opportunity to exercise influence over some valued outcome or to prevent problems ranging from annoyance to catastrophe? Some cognitive tasks, such as figuring out where to relocate or which apartment to rent, have high stakes: they carry lasting consequences or come with large financial implications. The more cognitive work one puts into such a task, the better their ability to sway the outcome—and, thus, the family's trajectory—in their preferred direction.[53] By contrast, much of the day-to-day cognitive work of running a home and raising a family is relatively low-stakes, at least in any one instance.[54] Choosing a new home is distinct from choosing a takeout restaurant; selecting a new car is distinct from selecting a new bedspread (although, again, individual preferences are idiosyncratic; if I looked hard enough, I'm sure I could find someone who cares more about the bedspread than the car).

The stakes of any given issue sometimes depend on a household's level of financial precarity. For an upper-middle-class family, a decision about whether to take a child to the pediatrician would likely hinge on whether their symptoms were severe enough to warrant the inconvenience. For a low-income family, the question of cost—specifically, what paying for the appointment would require them to sacrifice elsewhere in the budget—ups the ante and, in turn, the cognitive labor required to make the best decision. Stacey, an administrative assistant for whom money was tight, recalled a recent trip to a big-box store: "I had to decide whether to buy three months' worth of contacts or six months', because you can save $40 if you buy the six, but we just had some pretty big expenses. So I was reluctant to put the money into it, but I decided to just make the long-term investment and get six months of lenses even though it was a higher upfront cost than I anticipated." For someone in a less precarious financial position, a decision like this would likely be less fraught, and thus less cognitive labor–intensive.

Burden and benefit are often, but not always, correlated: more effort frequently means more reward. Managing a home renovation, for example, falls into the high-benefit, high-burden category. Even if you never lift a hammer, this can be grueling work. It requires you to coordinate multiple schedules (the contractor wants to come next week; your spouse requests that work not begin until after the holidays) and balance aesthetic and financial priorities (is it worth springing for the more expensive option, or is our second choice good enough?). While there will be an endpoint—the construction is finished!—that conclusion may be months in the future. In the meantime, the cognitive laborer may be frequently and unpredictably asked for a response to some urgent question (there's a six-week backorder on those tiles; do you still want them?) even as she tries to concentrate on the paid work that's funding this renovation in the first place.

But despite the complexity, this is not a thankless task. Progress on the renovation is quite salient: yesterday the wall was empty; today there's a bathtub. Even if you did not lift a finger to install that tub, it is still a visible "product" of your oversight. As the renovator-in-chief, you are also ideally positioned to ensure that your design sensibilities and financial priorities are reflected in the finished product. You consult your spouse, of course, but perhaps you don't bug them with *every* decision; nor do you show them every possible paint color or backsplash option. Troy, who managed a major renovation of his family's home, explained: "There were a lot of difficult decisions with the house, and a lot of times where I would have to meet kind of daily with the contractors . . . and make decisions on the fly." Any issue he thought "mattered" he would raise with his wife, but he admitted that he "might not be right" all the time about where to draw the line between "matters and doesn't matter."

On the opposite end of the spectrum (low-burden, low-benefit) are tasks like managing the disposal of household trash. Unless you live in a town with stringent recycling rules, this work is relatively simple: no need to coordinate with family members; just keep an eye on the trash can. It's also concrete and regular. Trash pickup happens on a weekly basis, making it easy to set a calendar reminder or incorporate into a weekly routine. Thoughts about the trash are unlikely to interfere with the rest of your week. In the scheme of things, however, trash management is not a high-stakes activity. Remembering it's garbage day doesn't give you much sway over the family's trajectory. Because it's so routine, it's also unlikely to be visible to your family members, who may only notice when you slip up and forget to drag the cans to the curb on time.

Many tasks feature a more complex mixture of burdens and benefits that fall somewhere between these two extremes. Managing the family calendar, for instance, can be highly burdensome but is usually only moderately beneficial. Successful calendar management requires tracking inputs in many forms: an email from the school, a post on a community group forum, a text from a friend, a paper invitation, a conversation over dinner. The calendar-keeper must keep track of the preferences and constraints of their spouse, children, childcare providers, and other players. *Luis has that Thursday afternoon meeting that always runs over, so we should plan dinner for 7 p.m. to be safe. The babysitter mentioned she'd be out of town that night, so we should check to see if Grandpa's available instead.* Further complicating matters, those preferences and constraints may shift unpredictably, threatening to topple the carefully constructed house of cards and saddle the calendar manager with the even harder task of sifting through the rubble.

In addition to its complexity, calendar management is extremely abstract. There is no real beginning or end, no taking a break or resolving to deal with the schedule over the weekend. The family calendar marches on regardless, and falling behind can have disastrous—or at least annoying—consequences. *We missed the sign-up deadline for our son's favorite camp, and now we have to break the news that he won't be joining his friends in the cabins. The pediatrician charges a fee for no-shows and doesn't have checkup appointments open for another month.* The significance of such consequences—and thus the stakes of any given calendar decision—depends partly on a family's financial situation: for some, a no-show fee is merely unfortunate; for others, it throws the entire budget out of whack.

Unlike physical tasks such as cooking and cleaning, which can only be done at home, the calendar follows respondents everywhere. Adding insult to injury, there is no product or endpoint for the calendar manager to point to as proof of their contribution. A spouse might see an event written on a calendar square but have no way of knowing how much thought and energy went into getting it there. "Saturday, 3 p.m., soccer game at Clement Field" does not reflect the back-and-forth with the coach about the rescheduled match or the effort to move another child's playdate, which conflicted with the new game time. As sociologist Arlie Hochschild points out, appreciation can go a long way toward softening the burden of household labor.[55] Low-visibility tasks like calendar management rarely garner a spouse's praise; like taking out the trash, the work is primarily noticed when something goes awry. *I told you I had a meeting and couldn't make that parent-teacher conference! That's not going to work; my mother told me she and my stepdad are out of town that weekend and can't babysit.*

Finally, though keeping track of the schedule is undoubtedly crucial to a family's continued functioning, it is not typically influential in itself. The calendar manager might keep track of scheduled soccer matches, sure, but she doesn't decide whether soccer is worth doing in the first place. On the margins, control over the schedule can prove useful: if you prefer to sleep in on weekends, you might preemptively schedule appointments for later in the day. If you'd rather not be out late two nights in a row, you might not share your full availability with the friend planning a dinner party. But in the overall scheme of things, calendar management is relatively low-influence work.

Low-burden but high-benefit cognitive tasks are considerably less common in my data. Under certain circumstances, however, decision making can fall into this category. Some couples separate the work of identifying options from the work of deciding among them.[56] One partner does extensive research to narrow the universe of possibilities down to just a few hotels, takeout restaurants, or rental apartments. Then, the other partner selects their top choice from this shortlist. She does not have to deal with the complexity of the research task, but she does have the opportunity to exert her influence, either by selecting one of the choices presented or by vetoing the options and asking her partner to go back to the drawing board and identify alternatives. In business terms, these are the cognitive tasks with the highest return on investment. And as we'll see in the next chapter, not only is cognitive labor unequally distributed by gender; women in different-gender couples are also disproportionately saddled with its more burdensome components.

The Trouble with Time

While properties like abstractness and (in)visibility impact the cognitive laborer's experience, some of these same qualities have important implications for how we *study* cognitive labor—and help explain why doing so has proven so difficult. Kneeland's 1929 warning that "planning and management" work would be difficult to capture in minutes and hours turned out to be incredibly prescient.[57]

Despite the obstacles Kneeland anticipated, there have been several notable attempts to measure non-physical household labor in a rigorous way. One of the best examples comes from a 2014 study by sociologist Shira Offer, who sought to quantify and compare mothers' and fathers' time spent on mental labor, which she defined as "the planning, organization, coordination, and management of everyday tasks and duties," both paid and unpaid.[58] Respondents in Offer's study were paged at random intervals over the course of a week and asked what they were doing, how they were feeling, and what was on their mind. The results showed only minimal gender differences in the time men and women spent on family-related mental labor: such labor made up nearly identical proportions of men's and women's total mental labor time (roughly 30 percent).[59] In an earlier study, economists Anne Winkler and Thomas Ireland calculated the amount of time American adults reported spending on "household management"—such as dealing with finances or organizing schedules—in an average week. They found that this work had a negligible footprint in respondents' lives, comprising little more than an hour of the week (1.2 hours for women, 0.9 hours for men).[60]

These results were surprising to Offer, who expected to find larger gender differences, and to Winkler and Ireland, who suspected the estimates they report represent "a substantially understated lower bound."[61] Such findings also stand in stark contrast to popular depictions of women as chief mental laborers who find their efforts taxing. A string of articles about cognitive labor–related phenomena went viral around the time I began this research. In a comic titled "You Should've Asked,"[62] the French artist Emma depicts a frazzled woman whose male partner waits for her instructions rather than taking initiative on housework and childcare tasks. "The mental load," Emma writes, "is almost completely borne by women. It's permanent and exhausting work. And it's invisible." In Harper's Bazaar, journalist Gemma Hartley wrote a searing personal essay about being "fed up" with her husband's failure to recognize the mental and emotional work she was doing and worried that the mental load carried "almost exclusively by women translates into a deep gender inequality that is hard to shake."[63]

Though these viral articles are not in themselves a reliable metric, their resonance suggests they tapped into a widely shared experience. What explains the disconnect between the work of scholars like Offer, Winkler, and Ireland, which suggests cognitive labor is negligible and gender differences in its performance minor, and the testimony of Emma or Hartley? Are women exaggerating the role of cognitive labor in their lives?

I don't think so. Rather, I suspect the disconnect stems from incompatibility between the tools and typologies that have worked so well in the study of physical labor and those we'll need to study its cognitive counterpart. It's difficult, perhaps impossible, to accurately measure time spent on cognitive labor. Because most of this work takes place internally, it would be of little use for a researcher to follow couples around their home with a stopwatch as Frederick Winslow Taylor once did for workers on the factory floor. I can record the time it takes for someone to clean their home by observing their movements; I cannot intuit what's going through their mind as they vacuum.

Then again, most of the research on physical housework also relies on some degree of self-report rather than direct observation. But if we simply ask people to estimate how much time they spend on cognitive labor, they will almost certainly struggle to name an accurate figure. As I noted earlier, cognitive tasks like anticipation and monitoring tend to be invisible—or at least obscured—even to the person doing the work. When I posed specific questions about those tasks, respondents had a lot to say. But without that prompting, they tended to overlook anticipation and monitoring (and, somewhat less often, identification and decision making). Part of the problem is that until very recently, words and concepts related to cognitive labor haven't been part of mainstream discourse. And when we don't have a name for what we're experiencing, it's hard to talk about it with any specificity.[64] Kristen, the woman we met at the beginning of this chapter, suspected that the decision log she'd kept was incomplete: "I started [logging] and was like, 'Is this a decision or a daily task?' . . . There are things I know I've thought about that I didn't log, and things that I logged that I don't know qualify."

Let's say, for argument's sake, Kristen did have the language she needed to recognize her own and her husband's cognitive labor. The next challenge would be converting that understanding into minutes and hours. According to her decision log, which included columns for "start" and "end" times, the incidents I described earlier occupied only twenty-eight minutes of Kristen's day.[65] Further, nearly all twenty-eight of those minutes overlapped with other activities, such as working for her employer, cooking, driving, and interacting with her son. If, as many time-use studies do, I had asked Kristen to record her "primary activity" during those minutes, her time would be recorded as "cooking," "driving," and "childcare."[66]

Because I asked specifically about a mental process, decision making, Kristen was on the lookout for tasks that might not otherwise have been top of mind. Yet the time stamps she recorded seemed somewhat arbitrary: two minutes to notice they were running low on milk, which overlapped with ten minutes figuring out what Ethan should have for breakfast; five minutes making plans for the weekend, which overlapped with time spent working for pay. I asked for time stamps, and Kristen gave them to me. Yet the diffuse and overlapping nature of her cognitive activities made them hard to translate into minutes. Faced with this same challenge, other interviewees recorded start times but no end times, noted the same start and end time, recorded multi-hour blocks for issues like what to do for dinner,[67] or simply left off time stamps altogether.

But once again for argument's sake, imagine we *were* able to come up with an accurate tool for measuring time spent in cognitive labor. Even still, we would remain far from the underlying goal of understanding the *impact* cognitive work has on the laborer. It's not that cognitive labor doesn't take time, as anyone who's spent hours researching a new car or planning a holiday meal or gathering documentation for a tax return can attest. The problem is that the number on the stopwatch bears only limited relation to the costs borne—or, for that matter, the benefits accrued.

Research in psychology and behavioral science tells us that decision making is mentally taxing.[68] Holding too many things in our minds at once can inhibit our performance. In computing terms, our mental "bandwidth" is frustratingly finite. This means there are opportunity costs associated with our mental experience, as well as with our time and money. If I spend $12 on my favorite sandwich (roasted veggies and goat cheese on focaccia from a local deli), that's $12 I can no longer invest, put toward a new pair of jeans, or save for a rainy day. Similarly, if I'm preoccupied by concerns about the childcare schedule for the upcoming week, I am probably not concentrating fully on the quarterly report I'm writing.

The abstract nature of many cognitive tasks meant this work seeped into all corners of respondents' days. Both leisure time and paid work time were subject to interruption by an errant thought: *I should get milk on my way home. Did the babysitter confirm she could stay late on Thursday?* The mental "pings" that interrupted at all hours bear only partial resemblance to their digital counterparts, however. Many knowledge workers, myself included, opt to put their cell phones on silent or in another room when they need to concentrate fully on a task, because even the possibility of being interrupted can be a deterrent to focus. It is common wisdom in productivity circles that it's a bad idea to keep an email client open throughout the day, because the arrival of a message—whether or not one chooses to answer it right away—disrupts concentration.[69] I might spend only sixty cumulative minutes reading and answering email throughout my workday, but if that hour is scattered in small chunks across the day, this time estimate will vastly undercount the productivity costs of my fragmented attention.[70]

Unfortunately, the mind is not a device that can be switched into silent mode or deposited in the next room. And while any one instance of cognitive labor might seem a minor annoyance, the cumulative effects of many "small" or split-second acts can be substantial. If I asked you to remember one upcoming event, you could probably commit it to memory in a few seconds. But if I fed you an intermittent stream of events to remember over the course of a day, those thirty-second increments would add up to something far greater than the sum of their parts.[71] Mindy offered a memorable analogy to illustrate this concept:

> [Planning and organizing] wouldn't really bother me. It's just that I have so many other things that it makes it—it's like brushing your teeth when you're really tired. Normally you don't mind, you know. But when you're exhausted, it somehow seems like . . . you can't possibly brush your teeth before you go to bed.

Mindy believed many of the issues she was managing were small in themselves. She attributed her exhaustion to their accumulated weight.

Unfortunately, this is not the part where I reveal a simple mind-use metric that can replace time-use in the study of cognitive labor. But that's actually my point: when housework of any kind is reduced to a single number, such as hours per week, we lose as much as we gain. Scholars of physical labor know this trade-off well. Some tasks, like cooking and transporting children to school, must be done frequently, and there is little leeway to delay or reschedule such work.[72] Regardless of what's happening at the office, the children will need an evening meal. But there are other household tasks that happen irregularly and can be pushed off if needed. The lawn must be mowed, but it need not happen on a weekday, and there is usually little harm in skipping a week if other concerns are more pressing. Mowing the lawn and feeding the kids dinner might take similar amounts of time in an average week, but to treat these as equivalent would be misleading.

I don't mean to suggest that time is irrelevant, nor that we should cease studying household labor in quantitative terms. Rather, I'm calling for a more holistic understanding of what that work entails and how it impacts us, one that considers time-use and mind-use side by side. The cost of getting household activities recognized as a form of labor—and housework inequalities recognized as a legitimate object of sociological study—was a reduction in complexity and nuance. Our collective focus on what people *do* with their minutes and hours has crowded out a consideration of how they *think*. And, as the next chapter shows, the absence of cognitive labor from our models distorts our understanding of how gender continues to shape household life.

CHAPTER 2

THE GENDERED DIVISION OF COGNITIVE LABOR

When I arrived at her home, Kathleen was gruff: "Are you Allison?" To be fair, she had only just pulled into the driveway herself and was struggling to wrangle an uncooperative preschooler from her car seat. Kathleen beckoned me to follow her through the front door, preemptively apologizing for the mess. "I do clean," she promised, "but everyone else just messes it up." The entryway was indeed cluttered with coats, shoes, boxes, and other items we maneuvered around on our way to the dining room. Kathleen and I sat adjacent to one another and across from her daughter Laurel, who occupied herself cutting construction paper into unrecognizable shapes and occasionally interrupting with loud pronouncements ("I want a popsicle!").

Consistent with her initial greeting, Kathleen, a White woman, was blunt throughout our interview. She summarized her relationship with her husband, Chris, this way: "So he sort of pursued me and we went out. We started dating. Now we have two kids and they live in this house. With a hairy dog." Still, it seemed clear her unsentimental demeanor masked deep affection. Her older daughter Chloe is "nice, she's kind, she's flexible. She's awesome. She's got a lot of friends. They just like her because she likes everybody." Similarly, "everybody likes Chris," Kathleen explained. "He's, like, the nicest guy on the planet."

When I interviewed Chris, an Asian American man, he described himself as the family "softie": "I'm like, if we think we can afford something for the kids, I say yes." Chris prided himself on being different from his own father, whom he saw as a breadwinner but not much more: "My dad was kinda—and he still is—just the money: 'Here's money.'" Like his father, Chris works full-time (as a police officer; Kathleen is also employed full-time, as a guidance counselor), but he was determined to be more present for his daughters.

From what I could tell, he'd succeeded. "He's just very into the kids," said Kathleen. "He plays with them. He's Fun Dad. . . . He's taking Chloe to Chuck E. Cheese on the last day of school. That's what they do, that's their thing." His parenting wasn't all play, however.[1] While Chris and I spoke, we sat at a picnic table in the backyard watching Laurel on the swing set. Multiple times during the interview—when Laurel got stuck on a swing, wanted a snack, was afraid of a bug—Chris paused our conversation to attend to her. "If you need it, here's insect repellant. The bugs will stay away from you," Chris counseled, handing Laurel the bottle. A moment later: "You don't spray the bugs, you spray yourself!"

But Kathleen had one major complaint about Chris. "He doesn't antici-pate!" she exclaimed:

> I get so frustrated. Like if I don't tell him what to do with the kids, he doesn't do it. They'll just sit around the house inside on a beautiful day and not do anything because he's, like, playing his guitar. . . . I'm like, really? "I have things to do. You need to do something with these children. This is what you need to do." I wish he would just do that, take the initiative. Drives me crazy.

Chris confirmed his wife's story from his own perspective. When it came to managing their daughters' lives, "I'm just the passenger," Chris mused. He ran errands, dropped his eldest at camp, and took time off work to attend impor-tant school events, but Kathleen steered the ship. She oversaw the family budget and implored Chris to reduce his spending; monitored their daughters' diet to ensure sufficient vegetable content; researched extracurricular activities that would lure them away from screens. Though their calendar was nominally shared, Chris admitted neglecting it: "Kathleen's a little better about checking the calendar than I am. She'll be like, 'I put it on the calendar!' and it's like, 'Oh, yeah, I didn't really look.'" Occasionally, Chris said, "I might come up with something [to do], and Kathleen will be like, 'Yeah, that's a good idea,' and I'll see it through. But a lot of times, the daily activities, Kathleen's the one that's organizing that, like, 'We're gonna go here, we're gonna do this.' And I'm just kind of like, 'Okay, I'm along for the ride.'"

In other words, Kathleen acted as primary cognitive laborer for their household, the metaphorical air traffic controller directing the planes in the family fleet. She is in good company. Roughly four-fifths of the different-gender couples I interviewed were Woman-led, in that the female partner car-ried a heavier cognitive load. Given what we know about gender imbalances in other kinds of household work, this is hardly surprising.[2] Nevertheless, the finding that women carry a heavier cognitive load is significant, because it means that we—scholars, policymakers, and everyday people alike—have been undercounting their contributions to household life. When we add mind-use to the more prevalent time-use metrics, gender gaps start to look more like chasms, and cracks appear in apparently equitable foundations. These chasms and cracks are difficult to see, in part because they are hard to measure using time-based tools and in part because they are often obscured by greater balance in more salient components of household life: physical household labor and, within the cognitive sphere, decision making.

In Kathleen and Chris's case, the cognitive labor was heavily weighted toward Kathleen, but the physical labor was less clearly skewed. Both Chris and Kathleen described Chris as an involved father and husband. "I don't think it's about the typical, like, the woman stays home and does the housework and the cooking and the cleaning," Kathleen insisted. "It's not like that. 'Cause he'll do the dishes. He prepares [the children's] lunch in the morning." Chris testified that he does "DIY stuff," as well as making breakfast for the kids, coaching his older daughter's sports team, and folding about half the laundry. He was also heavily involved in family decision making. Though Kathleen identified after-school activities for their daughters, she conferred with Chris before enrolling them. Kathleen kept a closer eye on the ebbs and flows of their bank account, but she and Chris decided together whether they could afford a big purchase. It was the relatively low-benefit, high-burden work of anticipating and monitoring where the largest gaps emerged between the two spouses.

In the coming pages, I'll describe the cognitive labor patterns I observed among Woman-led couples like Kathleen and Chris in more detail: how do spouses share—or not—in this work? Despite the name I've given this group, women in Woman-led couples did not practice across-the-board cognitive leadership; men, too, played important cognitive roles in their families. I'll also explain how cognitive and physical labor allocations interact and examine the relationship between spouses' career characteristics and their cognitive labor patterns. Physical and cognitive labor patterns are neither independent of nor perfectly correlated with each other, and cognitive inequalities are not fully explained by men's greater average earnings or work hours. Before all that, though, let's talk about how I reached these conclusions. My skepticism of traditional, time-based methods for studying household labor is by now well established. How, then, did I determine whether a couple was Woman-led, Man-led, or something in between?

Diaries and Domains

One common way to evaluate household labor contributions is top-down: ask people to estimate the amount of time they spend cooking in an average week, say, or what proportion of the laundry they do.[3] The problem is that people are better at recalling specific details than what generally happens.[4] Imagine I'm interested in your eating habits. One way to learn about them would be to ask you how many servings of fruit and vegetables you eat in an average day. Unless you're following a restrictive diet, this is likely a hard question: most of us are accustomed to thinking in terms of meals rather than servings. You could make a reasonable guess—4–6?—but your answer would likely be influenced by your knowledge of what you *should* be eating and, perhaps, what you eat on your best, most veggie-forward days.[5]

Another way to get at the same question is bottom-up, starting with specific recent events and extrapolating broader patterns from there. Instead of asking about your average servings, I could ask what you had for breakfast this morning. "I scarfed down a bowl of cereal before running out the door," you might tell me. "But that's because I was running late. Usually, I have scrambled eggs and a piece of toast. And if it's a Saturday my husband makes blueberry pancakes." Next, I could ask similar questions about lunch and dinner—what did you eat yesterday, and how does that compare to what you normally eat?—and compile your responses to conclude that on most days you get only three servings of produce.

This latter approach resembles my strategy for assessing couples' mind-use patterns. I did ask interviewees to estimate the overall proportion of physical and cognitive labor they completed, but not until the very end of the interview. By then, I'd already collected many data points from sources like the decision diaries they'd completed ahead of time, their description of "the last time [a particular event] happened," and even the way we scheduled our interview.[6] From these data, I extracted all references to cognitive labor (whether completed by the interviewee or their partner) and compiled them into a list that often ran into the dozens. Here are two examples drawn from my notes about Carla, the mother of a kindergartener:

- Trying to figure out which activity daughter should do, given feedback from school that she needs more team-based activity. Carla plans most of child's enrichment activities; husband Robert will agree with general idea, but then she finds a provider and fits it into schedule.

Domain	Cognitive Labor Examples	
Food	Deciding what meals to cook	Ensuring consistent supply of groceries
Basic Childcare	Deciding what to pack in child's lunch	Monitoring child's clothing needs
Children's Engagement	Researching summer camp options	Tracking child's academic progress
Logistics/ Scheduling	Maintaining family calendar	Resolving a schedule conflict
Cleaning/ Laundry	Remembering when sheets need to be changed	Coordinating with paid cleaning service
Finances	Ensuring bills are paid on time	Deciding how to allocate assets
Social Relationships	Selecting gifts for upcoming birthdays	Coordinating a playdate
Shopping	Identifying item needed	Choosing a brand/model
Home/Car Maintenance	Recognizing an item in need of repair	Finding repair professional
Travel/ Leisure	Planning vacation itinerary	Finding activities for a holiday weekend

FIGURE 2.1. Names and examples of each cognitive labor domain.

– Problem with shower: she contacted contractor to get it fixed but hasn't heard back. Says that with those repair issues, no clear role—both partners complain and then eventually one person takes initiative.

Next, I sorted the entries in each list into ten domain categories: logistics and scheduling, social relationships, cleaning and laundry, food, shopping, travel and leisure, finances, maintenance, basic childcare, and managing children's engagement with the wider world.[7] Figuring out which sport Carla's daughter should play fell under "managing children's engagement," whereas the shower issue fell under "maintenance." (Figure 2.1 defines and gives examples of all ten domains.) I also sorted each couple's list based on cognitive labor subtype (i.e., anticipate, identify options, decide, monitor) to look for general patterns that crosscut specific domains. For instance, Carla and her husband, Robert, tended to make decisions together, but, with limited exceptions, Carla was the one to initiate conversations about upcoming issues.

By compiling and carefully analyzing clues like these, I could usually determine who led and who followed, cognitively speaking, in each domain.[8] Carla led five domains: food, logistics, social relationships, shopping, and travel. Robert led finances and laundry, and the spouses shared childcare- and maintenance-related cognitive labor. Because Carla led five domains to Robert's two, I classified this couple as Woman-led.[9] This label fit most different-gender couples, but not all of them. In chapter 5 we'll examine the roughly one-fifth of different-gender couples I classified as Balanced or Man-led.

Gendered Burdens

In Woman-led couples, women like Kathleen and Carla had very different cognitive labor experiences than men like Chris and Robert. Not only did they carry a larger overall share of this work, their cognitive labor was more heavily weighted toward the relatively high-burden but low-benefit work of anticipating and monitoring. Men's cognitive workload, meanwhile, was smaller overall and contained a larger proportion of high-benefit decision-making work. In the following sections, I describe women's and men's cognitive specialties in turn before outlining areas of overlap in which spouses tended to share—at least nominally—in the cognitive labor.

Women's Cognitive Specialties

By definition, women in Woman-led couples acted as cognitive leader in more domains than men. Kathleen led eight of the ten domains (all except the travel/leisure and maintenance domains), whereas Carla led five. Most Woman-led couples fell somewhere in this range.[10] Relationship management, logistics and scheduling, shopping, cleaning and laundry, and both kinds of cognitive childcare were the most feminized cognitive domains, led by women in more than 70 percent of different-gender couples. For Suzanne, the cognitive work of relationship management included keeping track of friends' and family members' birthdays and reminding her husband, Michael, to send a text or sign a card she'd purchased. Logistics and scheduling meant transferring

important dates from their four kids' school and sports schedules onto a calendar on the fridge. Shopping involved keeping track of items they needed to
return or exchange, and cleaning and laundry leadership meant Suzanne was
the one who figured out how to remove troublesome stains from a shirt and
reminded Michael to clean the bathroom. Cognitive childcare entailed remembering when it was time to give their son his medication and helping him
come up with a costume to wear for the 100th day of school.

Across domains, women were overwhelmingly the ones completing the
abstract and low-visibility work of anticipating problems and upcoming needs.
This was true even in areas outside their expertise. While women were less
likely than men to *execute* many physical repair tasks, for instance, they frequently brought such issues to their husband's attention. Lisa explained, "I
kind of keep a running list [for my husband] of, 'Hey, when you've got a few
minutes, X needs doing.' . . . I hate when walls get dinged up, so I'll ask him to
paint a little patch or something." This was largely a mental list, Lisa said, but
when it gets long, "I'll text him and say, 'Here, when you get a chance, do these
things.'" Similarly, Sheila reported that maintenance tasks such as changing
lightbulbs were among the small number of housework tasks in her husband's
purview. However, the anticipation work was Sheila's: "I'll notice that the
lightbulb needs changing, and I'll be like, 'I really need you to change this bulb.
Here are the lightbulbs that I bought.'" Nina keeps a "kick list of things that we
need to fix" written on a whiteboard and alerts her husband to any urgent issues. According to her husband, Julian, "she almost 100 percent of the time
notices things" and either completes the repair herself or brings the issue to
his attention. In each case, these women took on the nebulous—and never-
ending—job of making sure the house was in working order, while their husband's physical repair work was both more time bound and more visible.

Outside the maintenance realm, women were often the ones anticipating
the need for a grocery trip and soliciting input from their partner while preparing a shopping list. "I'll tell him, 'Think of something you want to cook,' and
he'll text me later, after he thinks," said Holly. Women looked ahead to the
weekend. "Lisa does come up with the ideas [for weekend activities] more
often than I do," mused Steve. "She's always thinking about what's going to
happen." Women noted minute changes in their children's well-being. "I can
tell if they're coughing and stuff," said Chris, "but I'd rather let Kathleen deal
with it. Not deal with it, but I think she's just more in tune to it than I am."
Women noticed when the trash bins were overflowing and grime was accumulating. "She asked me to vacuum and take out some garbage," recalled Tyler

of his wife, Holly, "because we had some packing peanuts that really needed to go into the trash. . . . Usually my job is the bathroom, which I refused to do because we didn't have the right cleaning supplies for me, but now we have the right supplies, so I'm back on bathroom duty." In this case, Holly's cognitive work became visible only when it faltered: she'd failed to anticipate that they needed a resupply of the bleach-free cleaners Tyler preferred, and Tyler boycotted bathroom cleaning until she purchased more.

Women also engaged in the mental chess required to anticipate an infant's sleep schedule and time activities around it. Leah explained that she gets frustrated by her husband Mateo's "relaxed" approach to running errands. Whereas Leah was always trying to anticipate possible consequences of a delay—"Okay, if I don't [go to the store] now, the baby will be tired, and then she will fall asleep, maybe when we're still at home, and then it's getting complicated, and then she's in a bad mood, and then I'm stressed"—she saw Mateo as blissfully unaware of the need for urgency and careful time management. While Leah pushed for them to leave promptly, "He's like, 'I need my shoes, I need coffee,' and then checking emails again."

Identifying options was a more varied category overall, but certain subtypes of this work tended to fall to women. Some identification work was informal, a rapid response to a pressing need. The parent home alone with the crying child figured out how to soothe her. The more experienced cook came up with meal ideas on the fly when 6 p.m. rolled around and dinner hadn't yet been started. The partner who learned about a potential scheduling conflict began brainstorming workarounds. But factors like proximity and expertise were not randomly distributed. Women often had more solo time with their children and expertise in a wider range of domestic tasks; thus, they were somewhat more likely to do this informal identification, a point I return to in more detail in chapter 4.[11]

More extensive identification work was less clearly gender-typed; both men and women had distinct specialties. Women overwhelmingly handled research related to children and gift-giving. Women were nearly always the ones to find candidate babysitters, summer camps, and pediatricians. When a couple came across a parenting conundrum, women were usually the ones to do the online research or collect advice from friends and service providers. As Liz explained, "I kind of give [my husband] the expert info, and then we talk it out and [decide], 'What are we comfortable with?'" Women also specialized in picking out gifts, even when their partner made the actual purchase. "[My husband] would buy gifts. I would send him to the store, [but] I would tell him what to get, 100 percent," explained Kim. Likewise, Shaun said that for children's birth-days or baby showers, his wife "would tell me what she wanted and I'd be the one to go get it. . . . [She would say,] 'Hey, go get me a three-pack of onesies.' . . . I would run out, but she would be the one to determine [what to get]."

Just as women were often the ones to notice problems in the first place, they were also frequently the ones to monitor the issue and follow up later to ensure successful resolution. Nina found that the act of delegating a physical task to her husband, Julian, did not preclude her from monitoring the outcome. Sev-eral weeks before our interview, she asked Julian to schedule a flu shot for their toddler. When she checked in a few days later, the task remained undone: "He couldn't, like, he literally, physically couldn't find the fifteen minutes in his workday to fit it in. . . . Maybe if I had left him with that task for a couple weeks he might've found the time. But I want him to get it done and get [our daughter] her flu shot." In the end, Nina scheduled the shot herself. Similarly, Heather often "tasks" her husband, Jeremy, with specific to-dos via email: "I'll say, like, 'I've tasked you,' or 'You've been tasked.'" Once she sent off the email, I asked, was she able to stop thinking about the delegated task? "Not really," Heather admitted, "until he'll email me and say like, 'Okay, this is done.' . . . So I have to follow up with him and say, 'Did that actually get done? If not, can you do it tomorrow?' So it's not really off my plate mentally until I know that it's done."

Women's extensive involvement in anticipation and monitoring work across domains is significant: these are among the most burdensome and least directly beneficial components of cognitive labor. The burden stems largely from their abstract, temporally unbound nature. "Successful" anticipation and monitor-ing means near-constant vigilance. A trip to the kitchen provokes a mental note to buy more eggs. The changing of the seasons inspires an email to the summer camp. Efforts to sleep are interrupted by the sudden realization that the realtor never confirmed tomorrow's appointment.

This work is never quite done, cannot be scheduled, and remains largely invisible—except when something goes awry: there are no eggs on hand for pancakes, there's a last-minute scramble for summer childcare, someone else moves first to make an offer on the house. As a result, many women found themselves frequently on edge, their minds awash with plans and reflections. Bridget, a product manager married to a software engineer, described her an-ticipation and monitoring work as "a background job in my head": "I definitely do more thinking about household stuff during the day while I'm at work. I can multitask some of that stuff. So I will, on my commute, see a Facebook post, or . . . I'm like, 'Oh, I ordered a pair of pants, and I scheduled this, thing, and I drafted this email,' and my husband is, like, reading the *New York Times* [on his commute]." The phrase "background job," a concept Bridget co-opted from software development, helped her husband understand what she meant when she said she was "always thinking" about household issues.

Men's Cognitive Specialties

Although women's cognitive load was large and burdensome, men in Woman-led couples also made important cognitive contributions. Most acted as cognitive leader for at least one domain. Though no domain was led by men in the majority of different-gender couples, finance and maintenance came closest.[12] Men frequently handled long-term or big-picture financial matters, such as managing an investment portfolio or determining how much the family could afford to pay for a home or for childcare.[13] Isaac, who was worried about making ends meet while his wife was unemployed, recalled:

> I did a whole exercise several months ago, where I went back and looked at our expenses and figured out that we were spending too much. [My wife and I] had some general discussion about it, but we still have not sat down and actually looked at all these little numbers, and categories of expenses, and so forth to figure out, where could we possibly cut? I tend to handle [financial matters]. We'll discuss it, then I'll say, "This is what I think we should do. What do you think?"

Isaac's wife, Joanna, admitted that she knew finances were "a topic Isaac would like to discuss much further than we have," but she was avoiding the conversation. She was about to return to paid work after taking time out to care for their young children and hoped the additional income would resolve their financial troubles.

In the maintenance domain, men more often managed home renovations, researched solutions to minor mechanical problems, and kept track of car maintenance schedules. Chris typically finds contractors or repair people because, according to Kathleen, "He's so good at that. He's good at finding people to come and do things." Katie leaves "anything related to cars"—comparing models, looking for deals, remembering when it's time to change the oil—to her husband. Roger and Kelli were redoing their basement when we spoke. Though Kelli was aware of the process, the renovation "has kind of been Roger's project," she explained. Roger described himself as the "point person":

I work with [the contractors] except in cases where they want particularly large decisions made and then both of us talk with them. As things come up or when they're going to be doing things, I just let Kelli know over the course of the days what's going on, and if there are any choices we need to make that are minor, then I'll let [the contractors] know what I think is probably the case. And then I'll double-check with her and then I'll go back and confirm with them.

Though women were usually the main anticipators, there were exceptions in which men played this role, usually in areas related to their domain expertise (primarily home and yard maintenance or financial management) or, in a few notable cases, to children's sports. Alex listened to a podcast about an unusual swimming technique and insisted his daughter be taught by an instructor who specialized in it. Tiffany described her husband as perpetually on the lookout for opportunities for their children to participate in organized sports: "Any [sport] that they've ever been interested in, he will typically see it on, you know, our [local] Facebook page." Notably, these same men were less attuned to more feminized activities within the wider realm of sports. Alex left the extracurriculars he felt less strongly about to his wife: "If it's ballet, you know, it's whatever." When Tiffany's daughter expressed an interest in gymnastics, which her husband does not consider a sport, "he wanted no parts of it. He would go and watch [our daughter], but other than that, he's obviously not looking for gymnastics [opportunities]."

Men also participated meaningfully in some forms of identification work. As the examples above indicate, men often found home repair workers and assessed options for investing their savings. "Gadget" research was also dispro-portionately man-led: men routinely led the search for cars, household appli-ances, and new technologies—and, later, were responsible for monitoring their functioning and troubleshooting problems. When they ran into prob-lems with their tap water, Nathan researched the pros and cons of purchasing a refillable water dispenser. Danielle noted that her partner's growing interest in smoked meats led him to research and buy a smoker—although, as the primary chef, she would be more likely to actually use the new device. Kristen said of her husband that when they needed something new, Alan "takes a lot of pleasure in picking out whatever the new item is. And doing the research on it." I asked whether that was true of all shopping or just certain items, and Kristen clarified: "I would say any kind of household product. Not, like, clean-ing supplies, but any kind of gadget or electronic, anything that's a tool for our family to use. . . . In our last house, he bought the dishwasher. He did the research on it, he looked at the fridges, all that kind of stuff." Though Melanie said that in general, "I do the more 'thinking' things," technology was a notable carve-out for her husband, Stan: "I'm like, 'Electronics? You can deal with [that].' . . . He's more involved, like getting them, and he gets the insurance on them, and it ends up in his name." When their iPads broke, the kids knew to turn to Stan for troubleshooting.

Shared—and "Shared"—Cognitive Work

Neither men nor women had a monopoly on decision making, which was instead a primarily shared activity. Though Chris described Kathleen as "the matriarch," for instance, she valued his input and said she rarely made a unilateral decision on issues of any significance. Partners reported consulting each other "about all sorts of things" (Isaac), "no matter how little" (Douglas), to the point where they were "semi-codependent" (Jackie).[14] Questions that involved a significant outlay of resources, represented a deviation from routine, or impacted both partners were almost always up for discussion. Jackie's husband, Matthew, reported making most work-related decisions on his own, but "almost everything else, I think we at least try to bounce off each other or make each other aware of." Heather explained that "we both bring each other in on most decisions," to the point where it was "maybe too much." Her husband, Jeremy, agreed that "we're constantly consulting."

Kara drew a favorable contrast between her own, collaborative relationship with her husband, Joel, and other, more specialized marriages. Any question about their one-year-old son, she argued, required both her and Joel's perspectives:

> There are some couples where there's, like, wife domains and husband domains, and things that [fall within] the "wife" domain, she'll just do. My sister and her husband, I think, are like this. When it came to planning my nephew's first birthday, she did everything, and I don't even think she told her husband what the plan was; he was happy either way. I think even though I have more time to do that type of thing, Joel likes to be involved and give his opinion.

Joel concurred in his own interview: "We make most decisions together. We've observed [that], compared to other couples, we talk a lot more about relatively minor decisions."

Though the rhetoric of collaboration loomed large in respondents' accounts, it obscured variation in the degree to which decision making was truly shared. In some cases, couples deliberated and debated options together, using information they collected independently or that one partner identified and shared with the other. Jill explained that with big decisions—most recently, whether to build an extension on their house—she and her husband will "leave no stone unturned." They debate the pros and cons of each option and then table the discussion until both partners have mulled over the best path forward. Similarly, Alan and Kristen recently sat down together to make a "want, need, not" list for their housing search. "So, for each element of a house," Alan explained, the spouses decided together, "what do we *need* for our family, what would be cool if it was there, and what can it *not* be."

Just as often, however, "joint" decision making entailed one partner—most often, the woman—making a preliminary decision and offering the other an opportunity to veto it. Said Brooke, "I bring [my husband] in a lot to help with decisions, because even though I kind of make a decision, I need him to agree with it for me to feel like it's a decision." Semi-unilateral decisions like Brooke's were usually spearheaded by the partner cognitively responsible for the domain in question. Because women typically led more domains, they also did more of this kind of decision making; men more often provided a veto or rubber stamp. Although Jenna and Peter mutually agreed to enroll their daughter in a music class, for instance, it was Jenna who found the class and alerted Peter. Similarly, Desiree and Danny decided together to buy a second stroller after some debate. However, it was Desiree who suggested the need for a more compact option, identified a good model, and nudged Danny until he acquiesced to the purchase. Despite her commitment to joint decision making, Kara's description of the planning for their son's birthday suggested she came up with a plan and then shared it with Joel, who signed off: "I wanted to make sure we talked about it, so that it was, 'I think we should get bagels.' [He said,] 'Great! Bagels sound good.'"

This dynamic was particularly apparent in couples' decisions about formal childcare. In sharp contrast to the men depicted in earlier studies of household labor, most of the men I interviewed spoke knowledgeably about the couple's search for the right day care and offered a clear rationale for their choice,[15] and many women described their childcare decisions using pronouns like "we" and "our" that suggested spousal collaboration. Only when I pressed for details did I learn that in nearly all cases, the female partner initiated the childcare search and identified a shortlist of options before inviting her husband to tour the finalist centers, help select one, and assess the financial implications of their top choice.[16] Brooke recalled the process of finding a day care:

> When we found out we were pregnant, we started researching it halfway along and so, we went to two different places, and [the place we chose] was close by and we got references that were very good. We also use cloth diapers, and they allowed that, which a lot of day cares don't, and the hours worked for us and it was also a decent price, so all those things made it worthwhile.

Her husband, Jason, corroborated her memory of a joint search: "We looked at two places, and then there's one nearby that had a good reputation. Just very flexible with scheduling. Their kind of program is something that we liked, and it's very convenient, so we agreed that we'd send [our daughter] there." But when I asked Brooke for more information about the research process, she clarified:

> I was mostly researching it, and I would schedule when we could maybe go, and check in with Jason if he could go too. . . . He was involved in going for the tours and then discussing how we felt after the tours, so I wasn't making the decision on my own. We both shared the pros and cons of the two places and how we felt about them, and then I spoke with the references and shared what the references said with Jason.

It seemed clear that while Brooke and Jason may have mutually *agreed* on their day care, the legwork fell more heavily on Brooke.

Women who steered decision making in this fashion sometimes bore more of the associated "risk": if the decision later turned out to be suboptimal, they shouldered more blame. Carla described a fraught decision a few months earlier over which extracurriculars to enroll their kindergartener in; ultimately, she and her spouse, Robert, chose soccer:

> Deciding on these activities for the Fall, [I] was very much like, "What do you think she should do? . . . Does it matter that she's not participating in a sport and not doing something with a group and not learning how to be a good sport, per se?" And I'm maybe overanalyzing it, but [my husband]'s not analyzing it at all. He's like, "Yeah, sure." And now we're in it, and she doesn't like it. . . . She's not good at soccer, and other kids are outperforming her, but I think that's fine. And he's kind of like, "Why did we sign up for soccer? . . . Why are we doing this if she hates it so much?" And then I feel this burden and responsibility having signed her up, like I'm the one putting her in this situation.

Though Robert had signed off on the decision to enroll their daughter in a soccer league, his secondary role in the choice meant he felt limited responsibility to problem-solve when challenges arose later on.

Men's involvement in decision making, exaggerated or not, is notable. A long scholarly tradition infers a couple's power dynamics from their decision-making dynamics, holding that whichever partner gets the "final say" in more domains has more power.[17] The couples I interviewed preferred to make mutual decisions rather than give either partner the last word.[18] But in practice, couples' commitment to joint decision making meant that men often received "credit" for their involvement in family life without having to put in the same level of preparatory work required to reach the decision stage or without experiencing the same pressure to make the right call. In the terms I laid out in the last chapter, decision making is relatively high-benefit cognitive work: it's more visible than anticipation or monitoring and, often, carries important stakes related to how a couple spends limited resources or parents their children. Joint decision making meant men got to play an important role in shaping their family's trajectory while incurring fewer of the anticipation, monitoring, and, to a lesser extent, identification costs required to ensure the decision was well-informed and timely. *Nominally* joint decision making was valuable, too, because it allowed both partners to see men as cognitively involved in domestic life, even as the decision process often cost them less, a point I'll return to in chapter 3.

The Relationship between Cognitive and Physical Labor

If I had only looked at the "doing" work, I might have reached very different conclusions about the gendered nature of household life among the couples I spoke with. Recall police officer Chris and guidance counselor Kathleen, who were extremely lopsided cognitively (she led eight of ten domains). They weren't quite equal in their division of physical labor—Kathleen did more, and especially more of the repetitive and time-sensitive "core" tasks[19]—but they were a lot less lopsided in their physical than in their cognitive labor allocation. This pattern (significant inequality in the cognitive dimension coupled with more moderate inequality in the physical dimension) was the dynamic I observed most often among Woman-led couples.[20] Many different-gender partners took turns cooking, folding laundry, and driving children to friends' houses, even as the female partner made the meal plan, noticed when they were low on detergent, and scheduled the playdates.

Couples themselves offered two competing arguments about the relationship between cognitive and physical labor. One group implied they were separable, describing *offsetting* patterns in the two dimensions: she completed most of the cognitive labor, they said, but he handled most of the physical labor. Trevor said that cognitive labor was "a 70/30 split toward [my wife], whereas with physical activities, like groceries, taking the bike [for repair], it would be more like 70 percent in my favor." In qualitative terms, Jenny and Shaun described her as the household's "brain" and him as the brawn who carried out the plans she devised. Similarly, Calvin asserted, "[My wife] does more of the mental and I'm the one who carries it out, gets it finished."

A second group of respondents understood cognitive and physical work as *inextricably linked*. Colleen, who subscribed to this theory, recalled her husband asking her to "'make me a list, and I'll do the things on the list.'" She was not amused by his request: "I'm like, if I make the list, then that means I already had to think about it, and I might as well just do it." In Colleen's mind, it was at best inefficient, and at worst impossible, to separate the conception and execution of tasks. The person who thought about an issue and crafted a plan should be the one to carry it out. Nicole recounted a failed experiment in which she had tried to separate out the cognitive and physical work by creating a shopping list but sending her husband to the grocery store: "While he's shopping you get twenty messages, like, 'Is this the right [item]? Is this the right milk?'" Her husband lacked context for the ingredients listed: he couldn't infer whether red onions would be a fine substitute for white, or whether it was worth splurging for the good tomatoes. Nicole no longer bothered asking him to grocery shop, believing that it required less effort to do both the shopping and list-making herself.

There were elements of truth to both perspectives. Some couples did find ways to decouple the cognitive and physical components of a task. Most often, this meant that women retained the cognitive labor and delegated the physical. Carla explained, "If I say [to my husband], 'Buy [our daughter] two pairs of leggings,' he will go out and buy her two pairs of leggings, without resentment." He "doesn't have problems" doing any physical task Carla asks him to, but "it's just—it wouldn't occur to him to do that" on his own. Sonya said she and her husband, Ray, "have come a long way" from the early days of parenting, when she felt like she was doing everything. Now Ray "changes all [our son's] diapers when he's home. I do all the cooking, but he does all—he makes their lunches.

He gets them milk in the morning, and breakfast. . . . We split the kids for bedtime." But although Ray is "very good at doing whatever I delegate to him," Sonya admitted that "he on his own doesn't look around the house and think, 'Oh, we need more soap.' Or, 'oh, we're running low on diapers.' Or, 'hey, gee, [the kids] are growing out of their clothes.'"[21] Ray described the same pattern, explaining that while "I'm very active and I'm involved . . . I'm not, you know, making the list and divvying up the duties."

But while cognitive and physical tasks could usually be decoupled with some effort, couples' assertion that the two dimensions were perfectly offset was more often narrative tool than accurate description.[22] Only a handful of Woman-led couples were true offsetters, in that he did most of the physical labor and she did most of the cognitive. (There were no cases of the reverse.) More commonly, this narrative offered a convenient way to minimize the appearance of inequality. Because much of our interview focused on cognitive labor, many Woman-led couples were confronted with the ways they remained unequal despite their egalitarian ideals—a topic I will explore in more depth in chapter 3.[23] At the end of the interview, then, when I asked them to estimate their physical and cognitive labor allocations separately, they may have been eager to offer a counterpoint: *She does most of the mental stuff, but I make up for it elsewhere. Sure, I do all the thinking, but I delegate most of the acting to him!*

These findings suggest that understanding how a couple divvies up physical labor does not necessarily tell us how they allocate cognitive labor. Evidence of widespread physical labor inequality likely heralds even greater cognitive inequality beneath the surface. Further, we can't necessarily assume movement toward physical labor equality—for an individual couple or the population as a whole—implies movement toward cognitive equality, too. In my study, couples who shared cognitive labor nearly always shared physical labor, but the reverse was not true: couples who shared physical labor often remained woman-led in the cognitive dimension. Mind-use patterns appear more resistant to change than time-use patterns, for reasons we'll explore in later chapters.

Gender or Employment?

A worry lodged itself in the back of my mind soon after I started recruiting interviewees for this project: if I did find gender differences in cognitive labor patterns, how would I know they were a function of gender, rather than employment? Recall the economic theories of housework allocation I described earlier, which posit that the spouse who earns less or works fewer hours for pay will do more housework. On average, women married to men tend to earn and work (for pay) less, raising the possibility that what appear to be gender differences may instead reflect employment differences.[24] To counteract that worry, I went out of my way to interview couples with a wide range of income and hours configurations. There are at-home mothers in my sample, and at-home fathers, too. There are higher-earning women as well as higher-earning men, and several couples where partners' salaries and hours were roughly equal.

Fifty-five of the men in different-gender couples earned more and/or worked longer hours than their female partner. Fifty-one of those men (93 percent) also completed a smaller portion of the cognitive labor than their female partner. But in keeping with what other scholars have observed about physical housework, I found a very different pattern when I looked at the couples with higher-earning and/or longer-working women: 63 percent of these couples were *also* Woman-led for cognitive labor.[25] This asymmetry suggests that while economic factors may matter, gender does, too.[26] Men's higher earnings or longer hours were a near guarantee, at least in my sample, that they would take a backseat cognitive labor role; only a minority of women with a similar earnings or hours advantage did the same.

The interaction between gender and income is clearest when we look at the two extremes, comparing at-home mothers to at-home fathers. Sole-breadwinner women ceded many of the physical labor responsibilities to their husband. But they often shared in or even completed a majority of the cognitive labor. By contrast, sole-breadwinner men nearly always played a backseat role in domestic affairs, both physical and cognitive.

Gina, a researcher whose husband was out of the workforce to care for their three young children, described 8:00–9:00 p.m. as the time "when I think about everything that needs to be done" in the upcoming days: the schedule for tomorrow, school supplies to order, and so on. Years earlier, when the couple had only one child, her husband, Garrett, would "set the schedules a lot more." But, "now that there are many more moving parts," Gina considers the planning too complex for him to handle alone. Two of their sons have special needs, and Gina had learned the hard way that they "work a lot better with schedules. . . . We have to be really pushy about insuring that we have something to do," or meltdowns ensue. Garrett, she said, tends to be "time-blind." Thus, whether or not she is home to participate, Gina largely sets her sons' daily agenda.

Frank, an actuary, worked from a home office while his wife, Jill, cared for their three children. Frank left most of the daily planning and scheduling to

Jill because, he explained, "she knows the schedule of the kids, when she is going to be home. My schedule is not as routine, it varies a lot more." Together, Frank and Jill worked hard to maintain a "barrier" between Frank's paid work and family time: "The kids are not really allowed up [in my office]. Jill has been very respectful. She never knocks on the door even when I'm working. It's just like I'm not here. She has been extremely respectful of that." Even when he could "hear the kids raising hell" downstairs, Frank prioritized this strict separation. "I know Jill was sort of angry and upset with me for leaving her [to deal with the kids alone]" on the morning of our interview, he reflected, "but I felt like I made this decision, and we'll talk about it later. In the moment, I'm going to keep that boundary."

Frank took it for granted that his paid work responsibilities precluded him from paying close attention to the daily rhythms of family life, let alone trying to shape them. By contrast, Gina's sole breadwinner status did not absolve her of responsibility for cognitive childcare. She and Garrett were comfortable defying gender norms about which partner should work for pay and which should handle physical housework—she was the breadwinner; he did the bulk of daily chores—but their cognitive allocation remained heavily skewed toward Gina. In the next chapter, I'll begin to unpack the reasons cognitive labor allocation is particularly resistant to change, starting with a close look at the explanations couples give for their mind-use patterns.

CHAPTER 3

"IT'S NOT A GENDER THING, IT'S A ME THING"

The café buzzed with weekend chatter. Children babbled in strollers next to parents gossiping with friends; groups of spandex-clad bikers jockeyed for table space alongside grad students pecking at laptops. I snagged a small table near the register just before a White woman named Heather walked in, wearing black glasses that toed the line between serious and stylish. I was relieved to see her. Heather had wavered over email about whether life these days was too hectic for a research interview. She accepted, then declined, the invitation to meet before emailing once more to say she'd changed her mind and would participate. A few hours of adult conversation may have been the draw. Heather was nearing the end of a long parental leave from her research position, and her primary interlocutors had lately been a preschooler and an infant. While she and I sipped lattes and munched on muffins, her husband, Jeremy, was on childcare duty.

Later that same afternoon I'd meet Jeremy, a White man in his mid-thirties with poofy black hair and a winning smile. On weekdays, Jeremy worked in a lab, coordinating a staff of researchers and administrators. It was intense work, he said, but there were perks: "I went out for sushi twice with my boss this past week . . . and had this decadent meal. And I told Heather about this and she's like, 'Yeah, I haven't had an adult conversation in a month.'" When Jeremy wasn't in the lab or at the sushi restaurant, however, he invested in family time. "The second Jeremy gets home," said Heather, "he can barely get his jacket off or shoes off or his bag off his body before he's diving in. I mean he's really all in, like, all the time." On weekends, she explained, Jeremy takes their infant for "epically long walks" in her stroller. "You can't stop, otherwise she'll wake up. He just walks and walks and listens to audiobooks" for upwards of two hours most Saturdays, Heather noted admiringly.

Yet Jeremy admitted his involvement extended only so far. "The expression we have for it," he explained, "is that Heather sets it up and I knock it down. Like, she makes the list and then I execute the list, across every dimension of household management." Heather explained their dynamic using the same phrase ("I set it up; he knocks it down"), suggesting it was indeed a shared story about their relationship. "Ideally [the cognitive labor] would be 50/50 when I go back to work," she said. "Because it just has to be." Even as she said this, Heather recognized its improbability. "When I was working full-time and we had [our oldest child], I still did more. . . . At times, like even pre-kids, I wanted to say, 'Jeremy, can you just worry about this? I don't want to.'"

When I asked Jeremy about his ideal division of cognitive labor, he described their current allocation as "about right" before reconsidering, as if worried his contentment might come across as callous:

> I don't mean to answer my question by sort of guessing what Heather's answer was, but I could surmise she would say she wishes more of the mental [labor] was on me. . . . I think it's a burden, and that it feels really good for her when I take mental stuff off of her mental plate. . . . So I think ideally I would like to do more mental stuff, because I think that would make her happier.

Both spouses saw their current allocation as suboptimal, albeit for different reasons: Jeremy because it made his wife unhappy, and Heather because she found the work exhausting. Yet neither spouse believed change was likely. Why?

"Some of it is probably personality style," mused Jeremy when I asked why he and Heather divided the work as they did:

> Heather's a planner and is just constantly thinking about this stuff. And I—wouldn't say I'm a doer, necessarily, like I'm also a thinker, but I'm just more disorganized. And so I do really well with, like, "Okay, do this." Then I can do it. . . . So I think it's probably mostly personality type and how we've kind of always fit together as a unit.

Heather told a similar story:

> Over time we've understood just where we are, where our tendencies are. Jeremy is like, "I want to be helpful. Why don't you just put it on my plate? . . . These things don't bother me, or they don't occur to me, but . . . like, put it on my plate, and it's off your plate." . . . The platonic ideal of a marriage, where the division of labor is completely [equal], like of course

that's nice, but I do think that just doesn't lend itself to our personalities. I'm so much more uptight than Jeremy is.

When I left the café at the end of our interviews, I reflected on Heather and Jeremy's arrangement. There was a logic to the idea that the "planner" (i.e., Heather) would take on more cognitive labor. Why force anyone to do work poorly suited to their temperament? But something gave me pause. Individual personality had come up repeatedly in my interviews to date as an explanation for cognitive labor inequity. Yet in the overwhelming majority of different-gender couples, a woman's personality was said to drive her to do more cognitive labor, while a man's was described as an impediment to greater cognitive contributions. Had I stumbled on a cluster of "type-A" women, or was something more complicated happening?

Ultimately, I came to see this personality-centered explanation as the key narrative enabling Woman-led couples to resolve the contradictions between their egalitarian ideals and their unequal reality. Linking their cognitive labor allocation to *individual* difference obscured the gendered overtones of their arrangement. This narrative, which I call "personal essentialism," helped neutralize spousal conflict, but it also kept many Woman-led couples locked into mind-use patterns that conflicted with one or both partners' intentions.

The Magic Wand

Gender, as we saw in the previous chapter, was the best predictor of different-gender couples' cognitive labor division. This is not especially surprising, as this finding is consistent with a large body of research documenting the link between gender and physical housework.[1] A more interesting question is why and how this linkage has *remained* so strong even as opinion polls show attitudes and beliefs evolving toward greater—albeit complex—support for gender equality.[2] Many of my respondents experienced their own version of this clash between changing beliefs and stagnant behaviors. Toward the end of each interview, I offered a "magic wand" I promised could grant them their ideal division of cognitive labor. How, I asked, would they direct such a wand? Members of dual-income couples most often wished for some version of equality. "Oh my god, 50/50," gushed Kathleen. "Oh my goodness. I'd definitely put it at 50/50," Sheila enthused. "I would say, closer to 50/50," mused Jesse. "That's what you strive for." Several respondents used the word "obviously" in their explanation, as if they found it amusing I'd ask a question to which I surely knew the answer. "I would, I obviously want it to be, you know, a shared responsibility, 50/50," explained Alex. "It would obviously be even," Mindy offered.

But there was some variation in respondents' stated desires. A handful proposed an ideal where one partner (usually the woman) did most of the cognitive labor while the other (usually the man) compensated by doing more of the physical labor.[3] Ray initially suggested 50/50, before backtracking to this "offsetter" perspective:

> Well, the ideal would be 50/50. . . . Or, well, let me put it this way. Either 50/50, like we're both doing 50 percent of both the [planning] and the execution, or we reach an arrangement that works for both of us, where even if she's doing more of the executive-level planning, I'm doing a lot more of the executing, so it feels equitable.[4]

A few stopped short of wishing for perfect equality and instead hoped my wand would grant them a *less unequal* division. "I can't have too high of expectations," said Mandy, who estimated she was currently doing "99 percent" of the cognitive work. With the 50/50 ideal so far out of reach, she was willing to settle for incremental progress. "I would say maybe, like, I dunno, 75 percent [on me]?"

Though the majority of Woman-led couples expressed a desire for some version of cognitive labor equality, a smaller group did not. This response was concentrated among couples in which the female partner worked part-time or was not employed, and among women who could not imagine, even in this contrived, magic-wand scenario, their husband as capable of doing more cognitive labor. At-home mother Katie said she would retain "a good portion" of the cognitive labor she was currently doing because her husband worked long hours for little pay, and she was loath to add more to his plate: "Even though this pile [of household tasks she is responsible for] is as big as it is, I do feel like things are evened out. Especially if you take into account his work hours and stuff." Meanwhile, Melanie explained that "for [my husband's] personality and what he is, I think I'm fine handling [more cognitive labor]." Valerie was similarly skeptical of her husband's cognitive labor abilities: "I dunno, I watch him make decisions and I'm like, 'Did you think at all?!'"

These exceptions aside, most men and women in Woman-led couples expressed a desire for cognitive labor equality, or something closer to it. Yet their actions, as described in chapter 2, trended in a different direction: the female partner did a little (or a lot) more than the male partner. This contradiction might lead to skepticism about the sincerity of respondents' stated desires.

Were respondents telling me what they thought they *should* want, or what they *actually* hoped for? Likely, a bit of both. As sociologist and expert interviewer Allison Pugh reminds us, "People are contradictory: they have multiple and sometimes conflicting loyalties, goals, and commitments."[5] Trying to pin down someone's one "true" motive or belief is a misguided exercise. The desire for equality can coexist with the desire for efficiency or harmony or, as we'll soon see, self-expression. A more productive line of inquiry centers on how people juggle those competing desires and narrate the results, to themselves and others: if equality is an important goal or value, albeit one that may exist in parallel with others, how do they make sense of their failure to achieve it?

Conflicts between our actions and our sense of who we are usually generate cognitive dissonance. Much like its namesake musical chords, cognitive dissonance demands resolution away from discomfort and toward equilibrium.[6] We can reach that resolution by changing our behavior, changing our beliefs, or reframing the situation to remove the appearance of conflict between them.[7] Let's say I consider myself an anti-racist with a strong commitment to opposing structures of racial oppression. Yet when my supervisor repeatedly makes off-color comments, I stay silent—and feel miserable about it. To resolve my feelings of guilt, shame, and confusion, I could speak up and challenge my boss (change my behavior) or conclude that antiracism must not be all that important to me (change my beliefs). Finally, I could reframe the situation: my boss's comments aren't actually *that* racist, I might tell myself. And even if they were, I might reason that by staying silent rather than laughing politely, I do in fact register a mild form of dissent.

Individuals and couples trying to resolve dissonance between their ideal and actual household labor patterns often lean heavily on reframing.[8] In her seminal book *The Second Shift*, Hochschild terms these reframings "family myths."[9] Her interviewees Nancy and Evan Holt, for example, rely on the "upstairs-downstairs" myth. Nancy describes their allocation as if it is "half and half," but the "upstairs"—Nancy's purview—consists of "the living room, the dining room, the kitchen, two bedrooms, and two baths," along with the related labor of cooking, cleaning, shopping, and most childcare. Evan's "downstairs" territory, meanwhile, includes only the car, garage, and family dog.[10]

The Holts' myth of different but equal contributions obscures their labor imbalance, allowing Nancy, a committed feminist, to see their arrangement as a variation on equality. Thirty years later, in contrast, many of my interviewees openly acknowledged a gap between their ideal and actual cognitive labor allocation. Some described a narrower gap than I'd estimated, while others seemed to inflate the discrepancy. Brandi, in the latter camp, explained, "I don't wanna say he does nothing, but I do . . . almost all of it." Sheila, meanwhile, did not equivocate when asked what percentage of the cognitive labor she does for her household: "a hundred."

Men in Woman-led couples were also quick to acknowledge their partner's efforts.[11] "She's probably 75 [percent], I'm 25," mused Greg. "I would say [my wife] probably does 90 percent," Tommy explained. Other couples admitted to woman-led inequality in cognitive labor but argued, as Heather and Jeremy did, that it was offset by man-led inequality in physical labor. (As I noted in the previous chapter, however, this "offsetter" argument was rarely an accurate depiction of a couple's division of labor.)

In a minority of cases, one partner did seem oblivious to—or, perhaps, reluctant to name—inequities in their cognitive contributions. Donna suggested that she and her husband, Sam, are "about equal," whereas Sam immediately acknowledged his wife's larger cognitive role: "Oh, Donna definitely does more of that. I mean, like even grocery shopping, [I'll go, but] she'll write me a list. . . . She'll probably do like 75 or 80 percent [of the cognitive labor]." Jesse and Brenda reversed this pattern. Though she worried she was "not giving him enough credit," Brenda estimated she does roughly 70 percent of the cognitive labor, whereas Jesse felt they were "pretty even on the mental part of it." My own assessment of their allocation suggested Brenda's description was likely more accurate.

These cases aside, the modal respondent presented me with an intriguing puzzle. They desired cognitive labor equality, or something closer to it. They recognized they had not achieved this ideal. How, then, did they avoid or manage the cognitive dissonance we would expect to result? Put another way, what contemporary family myths uphold Woman-led couples' unequal division of cognitive labor?

"Not Because of Gender"

Most respondents pieced together multiple explanations for their cognitive labor allocation, which they drew on to differing degrees and in response to distinct interview questions.[12] But one thread in particular bound these disparate accounts together:[13] the conviction that gender was not the driver of their acknowledged labor imbalances.[14] In early interviews, I did not ask about gender specifically. Yet many respondents spontaneously repudiated its influence. "We're not shy about gender roles," insisted Todd. "We've seen [them], even in our own family, get crossed and changed in all sorts of ways. . . . We don't go out of our way to mix it up, but [we're] definitely in the realm of, 'Women can do anything, girls can do anything.'" Levi said dismissively, "I know the large gender blah blah blah structure, but I don't know why we specifically [divide labor] the way that we did."

Intrigued by these repudiations, I added a question to the end of each interview: what, if anything, did respondents believe gender had to do with the cognitive labor allocation they had just described? Respondents in Woman-led couples routinely acknowledged that their allocation might be mistaken for gender traditionalism by an outside observer like me. But, they clarified, it was not *because of* gender that they acted as they did.[15] "I think we have accidentally wound up in fairly gender-normal—I know there's a term—gender-normal ways," offered Kenneth. "I don't think either of us said, you know, 'You're the man, so you mow the lawn.'" Kathleen was adamant that "I don't think it's a gender thing. I just think, I don't think [my husband] has those ideas, and I don't have those ideas either." Scott explained that in contrast to his parents' "old-school thing," "I view [my wife] as, like, my partner, my equal. So it's not really, it's not a gender thing . . . I don't view any of it as gender-specific." Said Jennifer, in response to the same question, "There are no gender roles with us at all."

Others were more circumspect, yet still seemed uncomfortable with the idea that gender was anything other than coincidentally related to their practices. Amy and her husband, Kevin, a librarian and a doctor, respectively, stood out among this group. "There are some things where [we're] breaking a gender norm," offered Amy, and "other things where it's like, it fits the gender norm but it's not because of gender." Amy paused before continuing, clearly wrestling with something:

> Um, but then maybe more systematically it's because of gender, because Kevin felt empowered to be a doctor and maybe, like, did I want to be a doctor but then didn't do well in [organic chemistry]? I don't know. . . . That's a tricky one to answer. I don't think in a proximate way . . . he's at all thinking, "Well, I'm a guy so I don't need to clean the bathroom." Like, that's not happening. Maybe there's these very broad systemic things that were decades in the making that have led us to this same path of like, it's just easier for me to take care of the kids more.

Amy's verbal gymnastics reminded me of a phenomenon documented by scholars of "colorblind racism": while many White people disavow racial prejudice, their choices about where to live and send their children to school nevertheless reproduce racial inequality.[16] To resolve the disconnect, they reframe their choices as personal rather than linked to any broader social system. Amy seemed to be trying, and struggling, to accomplish something similar with gender inequality.

Amy's husband, Kevin, was similarly torn in his own interview. He seemed to be simultaneously imagining how his imbalanced arrangement might appear to my outsider eyes and struggling to reconcile that image with his egalitarian intentions:

> I think it's a complicated question. Because Amy is a librarian, and I'm a doctor, and you could go back seventy years and find couples where a wife is a librarian and the husband is a doctor. And you could claim that there's sort of [a] gender imprint in this world. . . . I don't know that that history would necessarily be applicable to our situation. I think in terms of our gender . . . stuff, um, I don't know, I can't put a percentage on it. . . . I would say it's a non-zero [role] that gender plays, but it's not 50 percent.

In the end, he concluded, theirs was a "true, true, unrelated situation": "Yes, I'm a doctor, yes, Amy is a librarian, yes, she has more flexibility in her time, but no, it's not necessarily a logic train of, these things were set up in a gender-specific way." Few respondents seemed as tortured as Amy and Kevin. But this couple's conclusion—that gender was not the *cause* of inequalities in a couple's cognitive or physical labor practices—was widespread.

Personal Essentialism

Merely repudiating gender's role is narratively and psychologically unsatisfying, unlikely to resolve nascent feelings of cognitive dissonance. Accordingly, most respondents gave an alternative account of their acknowledged cognitive labor imbalances. Molly unwittingly offered a tagline for the most common response: "I don't think it's a gender thing, I think it's a 'me' thing." Others offered less pithy variations on the same theme. "I'm not a dumb person," explained Shaun, but "I'm more spur of the moment." His wife, Jenny, meanwhile, was the type to always think two steps ahead: "That's just who she is." Mindy argued that "barring a fundamental change in [my husband's] whole being," he was unlikely to start managing household affairs on his own initiative rather than "having to be explicitly told to do something." In so many words, respondents like Molly, Shaun, and Mindy were arguing that cognitive labor was not simply a matter of what one did or did not do. Rather, it reflected who they were—their very essence, so to speak.

Essentialism—the practice of ascribing a set of innate characteristics to members of a group—has a long history.[17] Recall our earlier discussion of the "separate spheres" ideology, which features a classic case of gender essentialism: the belief that women's "natural" purity makes them ideal shepherds for children's moral development.[18] Clearly, essentialist beliefs need not be overtly negative; it hardly seems a slur to suggest women are more nurturing or have a stronger moral compass than men.[19] Yet embedded in essentialism, however positively framed, is the notion of inherent and unbridgeable difference. Belief in male superiority may have declined precipitously in recent decades, but for some people it has morphed into what scholars call egalitarian essentialism.[20]

Egalitarian essentialists posit that men and women are fundamentally distinct creatures who want different things. Many women would *rather* care for their children than work a stressful job, they argue, and they should be allowed to make that choice.[21] That's the "essentialism" component. The "egalitarian" part stems from the concurrent belief that innate gender differences in, say, nurturing abilities are not hierarchically related. Men's public-facing interests are no more important than women's domestic inclinations; they're simply different. From this perspective, gender gaps in employment, earnings, and household roles reflect innate gender difference more than women's continued subjugation.

Men Are from Mars, Women Are from Venus, a bestselling book I distinctly recall my parents discussing heatedly with their friends in the mid-1990s, exemplifies this perspective.[22] Author John Gray notes in the introduction that "men and women differ in all areas of their lives. Not only do men and women communicate differently but they think, feel, perceive, react, respond, love, need, and appreciate differently."[23] Historically, Gray argues, those differences were framed antagonistically, with the result that "one sex is generally viewed as being victimized by the other."[24] Gray's recommended alternative is to "create an understanding of our differences that raises self-esteem and personal dignity while inspiring mutual trust, personal responsibility, increased cooperation, and greater love."[25] In other words, the path to gender harmony lies in recognizing innate differences between men and women but treating them as value-neutral facts rather than evidence of one gender's superiority.

This version of essentialism was present but relatively rare in my data. It was somewhat more common among respondents without a bachelor's degree, who occasionally explained their labor allocation in terms of "male" or "female" preferences and responsibilities.[26] "If you're female, you probably enjoy shopping a little bit more than a guy does," explained Cassie. Taking out the trash, contended Amber, is "a man's job." She continued, "I just never, I just don't even ever think to take it out . . . I certainly can. I just prefer not to go outside if it's cold out. So a lot of times I'm like, 'Well, that's a man's job. You mow the lawn.'"

When college-educated respondents evinced gender essentialist logic, it was primarily in the context of parenting young children. "I just tend to devote a little bit more mental energy in general to a lot of this [childcare] stuff. Maybe that is also [related] to me being a mom. I like to think that doesn't play a role in the way we relate to each other, but I think it absolutely does," reflected Sharon. Her husband, Douglas, offered a similar perspective: "[Our infant son] takes up a lot of my energy—emotional, and physical, and mental. I feel like he takes up more of hers. She definitely is thinking about him and just all of his needs more than I am, just for the fact that she is who she is, and the fact that she is his mom." Sonya explained, "There's certain things I feel like gender plays [a role] in. Not a ton, I think there's almost everything that we all can do . . . I would say the differences are that innate ability for me as a mom to know when something's off with my children."

Yet overt gender essentialism was the exception rather than the rule. In its place, a logic I call *personal* essentialism dominated respondents' accounts. Personal essentialism combines a belief in the importance of innate individual qualities with a rejection of any connection between those qualities and gender. "I am who I am," argued Stacey. Darren explained, "My brain just naturally rejects . . . non-essential information." Colleen said, of her husband Ted's seeming inability to notice what needs doing around the house, "He's not programmed like that." Personality, nature, and temperament are central to this logic, but they are deployed as *unique properties of an individual, rather than hallmarks of their gender*. Recall Molly's tagline: "It's not a gender thing, it's a *me* thing." What's being essentialized in these examples is a person rather than a social group: Stacey, rather than "women"; Darren and Ted, rather than "men."

Despite this emphasis on individuality, two clear archetypes, whom I will call the Superhuman and the Bumbler, emerged. The main cognitive laborer in a couple was typically depicted as a Superhuman. She (and in Woman-led couples it is always a she) thrives on planning and can hold vast quantities of information in her head. Bradley referred to his wife, Denise, as "supermom" and "the type of person that's always going to do everything." "She is super-organized," said Trevor about his wife. "If I'm not organized," explained Kathy, in another couple, "I get anxious. And so just being on top of things, being organized, being a list-maker just keeps me nice and happy."

Superhumans solve problems before they become crises. "If someone invites us somewhere," said Shaun, "I go, 'Yep.' And she's like, 'Well, hold on. We have to go do [something else] at 9:00. How are we gonna meet up with them at 7:00?' 'Oh shit. You're right.'" The Superhuman also can't help but notice what needs doing: "If I see dust and stuff, it bothers me more than [my husband], like he can just not see it, let it go," offered Valerie. "I'm a perfectionist," explained April. "Maybe I notice [issues] more. My threshold for action is lower than his—so, deciding the bathroom needs to be cleaned or, you know, cutting [the kids'] hair." She's "proactive" about addressing problems, said Bradley about his wife. "She takes more initiative," suggested Ian about his. "She decides, okay, the vacation thing, or making the plans. She'll go online and look it all up. And I will do that, but she almost always takes the initiative before I do. . . . She will kind of get me in gear sometimes."

These same qualities could also be framed negatively. Eight women described themselves as a "control freak." One of these women, Jennifer, said that while she sometimes resented playing the Superhuman role, she also felt that "it's not [my husband's] fault that I'm, you know, a control freak." Denise explained that she is "a more kind of organized thinker" than her husband but also "a little neurotic about certain things." Tricia echoed this language, repeatedly describing herself as "neurotic," both in general and regarding certain tasks, like managing the budget.[27] Said Calvin about his wife, "She almost gets a little bit of, um, we call it agita. . . . Like she gets a little, almost panicky if she doesn't know the schedule." But whether framed positively or negatively, Superhumans' tendencies were described as largely outside their conscious control. They were also depicted as personal quirks rather than gendered traits.

The same was true for the Bumbler archetype, which was used to describe the secondary cognitive laborer in a couple. Jeremy, the Bumbler we met at the start of this chapter, dislikes "commercials with a woman who seems, you know, younger than her husband, and the husband is like this bumbling idiot who doesn't know what the laundry [is]." But he admitted some resemblance between these caricatures and his own life: "Heather's the thinker, and constantly doing meals and childcare stuff, and I'm just, I'm that bumbling guy who works most of the time."

Bumblers were passive where Superhumans were active, living "in the moment" while Superhumans continually looked ahead. These secondary cognitive laborers rarely took initiative, struggled to anticipate challenges, and routinely failed to notice the obvious until it was pointed out by a Superhuman. "My cognition is crap," said Bradley. "I probably put a lot more thought into everything," explained Valerie. "He's more like, 'Ooh, I like that truck 'cause it's pretty.' Okay. Does it run well? Like, let's look inside and let's look under [the hood], I'm more like that." Nicole believed she is "more aware of what's around me" than her husband, Luis: "Just for example, this morning [my daughter] lost her library card, but I remember[ed] seeing it last night on the couch. Which, I'm pretty sure my husband was sitting on the same couch, but he didn't see it."

Yet just as Superhumans' tendencies were sometimes portrayed as liabilities, Bumblers' foibles were routinely reframed as valued qualities. Bumblers were reportedly free from the anxiety that plagued Superhumans. Because they weren't continually attuned to next week or next month, they rarely stressed about hypotheticals. As a result, Bumblers were described as more "present" for their children and adept at calming a spiraling spouse. About her husband, Mandy explained, "he's a little bit more laid-back, I'm a little bit more, um, high-strung . . . I yell at the kids a little bit easier than he will." Denise testified, "I have a tendency to overschedule and be constantly doing something, and [Bradley] is much more relaxed. [If I stopped playing my role,] there'd be weekends, the kids would just hang out and play outside and they'd have a great time, whereas I'm like, 'Oh, we're gonna do this, and we're gonna do that,' you know?" Said Nina about her husband, "He's probably better at that than me, like being really present in the moment, which is, you know—'cause I'm doing all this mental thought stuff, and I'm like never quite fully present. Because I'm like, 'After this I'm going to do X, Y, and Z.'"

Neutralizing Conflict and Preventing Change

By this point, savvy readers may have noted the resemblance between the Bumbler and Superhuman archetypes and familiar gender stereotypes. Novels, movies, and television shows centered on different-gender couples or best friends frequently pair a Superhuman-esque woman with a Bumbler-like man.[28] One of my interviewees even alerted me to a folk song, thought to date back to eighteenth-century Germany, about this dynamic. In "There's a Hole in My Bucket," a woman named Liza asks Henry, presumably her husband, to fill a bucket with water.[29] But, moans Henry, "There's a hole in my bucket, dear Liza." Liza pragmatically suggests a patch, but Henry runs into problems at every step, and Liza must continually troubleshoot on his behalf. Straw too long? Cut it. Knife too dull? Sharpen it. Ultimately, Henry arrives at an impasse that ends the song where it began: "There's a hole in my bucket, dear Liza, a hole." Though we cannot know for sure, one assumes Liza ends up plugging this hole herself.

Liza and Henry are characters, but their power—and humor—comes from their familiarity. My respondent Nicole sounded like a modern-day Liza when describing failed attempts to get her husband Luis to cook dinner once per week:

> I told him . . . if you're planning to cook on Friday, let me know what you need, so if I go grocery shopping, I'll get it for you. [It was] just the actual cooking that I wanted [him] to get done. But then he will forget, and he wanted to make something and there was nothing in the fridge. . . . If he's missing something he can't cook that day, [and] I would take over.

Next, Nicole tried instating a new rule: if her husband was unprepared to cook, he was responsible for ordering takeout. "But then the budget started going. 'Cause that would mean, like, [takeout] dinner Friday, and sometimes we like to eat out on Sunday." In the end, Nicole retained primary responsibility for cognitive and physical food-related labor, with some resentment. "Sometimes I think he pretends he doesn't know [what to do], so he will have me helping him," she sighed.

Scholars and pundits refer to this dynamic as "strategic" or "weaponized" incompetence.[30] By repeatedly demonstrating ineptitude, men like Luis escape domestic responsibilities they would rather not take on. And women like Nicole eventually conclude that the hassle of directing their partner is not worth whatever time or effort they might have saved by delegating the task. (Strategic incompetence is not exclusively a male practice. Women have been known to practice strategic incompetence regarding male-typed household tasks, as we will see later.) But Nicole was an outlier in my data. While she ascribed some agency to Luis ("I think he pretends"), women more often attributed their husband's "incompetence" to his *nature* than to any nefarious intent.

This finding helps explain a pattern that initially puzzled me. When I began this project I expected to find angry women and embattled couples. After all, the prevailing narratives on social and popular media were of women filled with "rage" and "fed up" with men's domestic shortcomings.[31] Yet relatively few Woman-led couples I interviewed were actively trying to reallocate cognitive labor. To be sure, they bickered over particular tasks and grumbled half-heartedly about their partner's shortcomings. But spousal conflict and reallocation efforts were usually described as transient—that is, flaring up only occasionally before a swift return to the status quo—or as an early tension in the relationship that the couple had since moved beyond. Personal essentialist thinking seemed to be preventing or neutralizing cognitive labor conflict.

Kim, for instance, described fights with her husband—but almost exclusively in the past tense. Once her oldest child entered preschool, Kim recalled, her volunteer activities "really ramped up." As a result, "I needed more support." Kim felt her husband wasn't taking sufficient initiative at home, and the couple fought, until Kim eventually accepted that the arrangement that best "fits our personalities" is for her to be "kind of planning, making the lists" and her husband to offer willing assistance. "[He'll say], 'How do I help? What do you need? What do you want me to do?'" As a result, "I'm not as resentful about [being the planner] anymore. . . . Now I feel like, 'It's fine. I'll delegate. You just have to do it un-begrudgingly.'" Kim's husband had become more involved with physical labor, but she remained the chief cognitive laborer.

Like Kim, Colleen saw her husband Ted's "incompetence" as less a strategy of avoidance than a reflection of his nature. Colleen commutes nearly an hour to an office, while her husband Ted works from home. She freely admitted that in her absence, Ted handles the most critical daily tasks of feeding the children and pets and getting the former where they need to be for school and ballet. Anything beyond the daily routine, however, seemed to escape his notice. "I would prefer a world where Ted just recognizes things and then does them, but he's just not programmed like that," argued Colleen. A few days earlier, for instance, their daughters invited friends to sleep over. Ever since, the pump for the air mattress had been sitting in the middle of the living room: "I know exactly where it goes, and it's just as easy as walking it into the other room. But he wouldn't even notice it. He'll never see it. . . . Then the bigger things, like 'call to have the pool cleaned,' you know, 'schedule,' all that kind of stuff, he wouldn't think of it."[32]

As I described in chapter 2, Ted once responded to Colleen's frustration by suggesting she make him a to-do list. Though she initially resisted, Colleen eventually wrote one up. Ted's suggestion backfired, however, when this quickly became "a list of failures, because the things don't get done. . . . I was better when I just thought [Ted] was incapable of seeing the things. Now that you have a list, why don't you see the things? So then I just threw the list away." It is worth underscoring Colleen's final point: her conviction that Ted *could not see* things like the air pump lingering on the floor defused her frustration. If he was "not programmed" to proactively notice what needed doing, it would be unfair to blame him for his limitations. With a list in hand, however, this explanation was no longer plausible. Now, Ted's inaction appeared a failure of *effort* rather than a limitation of temperament. For Colleen, the latter was a more palatable explanation.

Colleen and Ted's list debacle nicely encapsulates the power of the personal essentialist narrative: if cognitive labor practices can be recast as a function of individual nature, then it is futile to expect change of your spouse or demand it of yourself. But not everyone bought into this narrative. Anita, for instance, was unwilling to throw away the metaphorical list. She had grown increasingly frustrated with her husband, Glenn, to the point where she was seriously contemplating divorce. Among other complaints, Anita was annoyed by what she interpreted as Glenn's deliberate shirking of responsibility. As an example, Anita pointed to a wobbly leg on the dining room table where we were sitting for the interview. "I've always [said], you know, 'That's broken, I'm gonna fix it' . . . Glenn would be like, 'Oh the table's [broken], yeah, alright.'" She looked away from the table, imitating Glenn. "It's always—I don't know if he's passing the buck, but it's always, 'Oh, Anita will do it.'" The problem, in Anita's eyes, wasn't that Glenn couldn't "see the things," as Colleen ultimately chose to believe of Ted. Rather, she believed he saw them and did nothing because he understood domestic affairs as Anita's responsibility.[33]

Bridget had wrestled with similar issues but ultimately concluded that her best option was to accept her husband for who he was. She estimated currently performing about 90 percent of the cognitive labor but said she would prefer to do 70 percent.[34] What, I asked, were the obstacles to reaching that 70 percent ideal? At first, Bridget talked about time and schedules. Between two full-time jobs, a toddler, and shared custody of Jimmy's children from a previous marriage, the couple had limited time to align on what needed doing. So, Bridget explained, she usually just managed it herself. But she seemed dissatisfied with this initial answer and continued musing:

> The other piece of that, I think, is just my ability to multitask versus his. Like I think his brain would have to change to be able to think about things in multiple realms [i.e., work and home] at once. . . . He is kind of present where he [is]. It is very easy for him to completely lose track of time and space in a way that is just not possible for me to ever do. That's just not how my brain works. So I think his brain would have to be different. Which is not a thing I'm committed to trying to change.

Like Colleen and unlike Anita, Bridget avoided sustained frustration in part by convincing herself that Jimmy's inaction was not under his conscious control.

In addition to neutralizing spousal conflict, personal essentialism seemed to discourage cognitive labor reallocation, even in the face of opportunities for change. This process is best illustrated by comparing couples' narratives about cognitive and physical labor. Whereas cognitive inequalities were most often chalked up to temperamental differences, physical labor inequalities were most often attributed to *circumstances*, such as partners' work schedules or children's unique needs.

"Kevin really works a lot of hours," explained Amy. "So he's just not home for the dinner prep hour, and he can't pick up a kid. . . . I just think [our labor allocation] is out of necessity." "Parent-teacher meetings? Um, I don't know why I end up always going," reflected Donna. "I think we both kind of want to go, but my work is just a little more conducive." Kenneth explained, "Picking up the girls from school, it's just, I'm [working from] home, so I do it." Said Harry, "If I'm being honest, I think [my wife] does more of the, just, like, handling the things that need to be done for the family. But I think that's also kind of born out of the circumstances, just because she's more available, working part-time as she does."

Interviewees framed their circumstances as only coincidentally gender traditional. Said Jody, "[Our allocation] is not so much gender, because we came from independent houses [before we married] where he, you know, cleaned his condo, he did the wash, he cleaned up. . . . So I don't think it's gender-related as much as it's just—everything comes down to our schedule, you know?" Jesse, who worked full-time while his wife, Brenda, a former teacher, cared for their two children, pointed to his higher income at the time of their eldest's birth: "A lot of the way we do things jumps off from simply, you know, at the time where we started having kids . . . there was one steady, higher salary than the other. . . . If that was reversed, or swung in the other direction, I think a lot of [our allocation] would actually jump off and head in different directions from that."

But couples often had more control over their circumstances than they acknowledged.[35] They made choices about what profession to enter, where to live, and whose career to prioritize in the event of conflict. Their circumstances were no more gender-neutral than their personalities. The difference, however, was that they understood their circumstances as contingent but their natures as fixed. This contingency meant respondents like Brenda, Jesse's wife, could easily conjure up a counterfactual world in which spouses' physical labor responsibilities were reversed: "If I'd had a job in a public school" rather than a low-paying parochial school before having kids, she hypothesized, "I'd be making more than [Jesse] with my degree, and then he'd be the one staying home!" Women working part-time, like Shaina, could confidently argue that "if I start to work full-time"—an eventuality she was hoping for—"I need my husband to do more [of the household tasks]." These were concrete possibilities, unlike changing a husband's "brain," as Bridget and several other women put it.

Several Woman-led couples had experienced a major circumstance change shortly before we met: the male partner either lost or voluntarily left his job. Suddenly, the hours or flexibility differentials that often justified an unequal division of physical labor were reversed. In such cases, most couples reported adjusting their physical labor allocation. In keeping with other research on gender and unemployment, these changes tended to be on the margins and did not eliminate, let alone reverse, gender gaps.[36] Nevertheless, there was often movement. Greg lost his factory job following health complications and was unemployed at the time of our interview. In the year he had been out of work, he took on a larger portion of the physical housework. But each morning before she left for the office, his wife, Jennifer, put together a to-do list for him, detailing the tasks she expected him to accomplish that day. The morning of our interview, the list instructed Greg to "'straighten up the house, set the pork up [i.e., defrost it] . . . clean the litter box.' . . . Stuff that she needs to be done around here."

Melanie's husband, Stan, had also recently lost a job and was channeling some of his newfound free time to housework and childcare. He had taken on a large chunk of the driving required to get their teenage children to and from various extracurriculars and part-time jobs, for instance. Melanie was reluctant to hand over any cognitive responsibilities, however. "He's trying to help," she noted, but that help was not entirely useful. If Stan was left to his own devices in running the household, Melanie suspected "it would be a disaster. I've done little things, like I left something on the stairs to see how long it would stay on the stairs, and it would stay on the stairs forever." She joked that "Stan probably doesn't know what grade all [our] children are in." Within the logic of personal essentialism, this arrangement—reallocate physical labor while leaving cognitive labor unchanged—makes perfect sense. Popular conceptions of personality and temperament emphasize consistency and stability. When Greg and Stan lost their jobs, they gained more time, but not more conscientiousness. Reallocation of cognitive labor was not within the bounds of what Jennifer and Melanie considered possible, and neither woman attempted it.

Personal essentialism emerges from my data as a successor to gender essentialism. In some ways, this represents progress. Few interviewees believed "women's work" and "men's work" were meaningful categories; many rejected the *Men Are from Mars*–style gender stereotyping of an earlier era. Yet the vestiges of these ideologies are nevertheless visible in the Superhuman and Bumbler archetypes, which were intended as individual labels but fell along gender lines. Gender inequality is not gone, just moving underground, where it is harder to recognize and combat.[37] Addressing the gendered distribution of cognitive labor means first bringing the logic of personal essentialism into the light where we can assess its accuracy: is this narrative simply a twenty-first-century family myth?

CHAPTER 4

GENDERED INVESTMENT, GENDERED DEPLOYMENT

Randall was frazzled when he answered the door on a wintry Thursday evening. Before I interrupted, he'd been huddled over his laptop, scrambling to meet a deadline for his job as a school administrator. But he gamely shut the computer and led me to a large dining table cluttered with the detritus of family life. The house was quiet: his wife was dropping their oldest child off at play practice; two younger kids were upstairs in their bedrooms doing whatever teenagers do on their phones; and the family dogs were settled at our feet under the table.

Some interviewees are slow to warm up, but Randall, who is White, launched quickly into his life story. His current status—married father of three, second-in-command at a nearby junior high—gave no hint of his meandering path through early adulthood. As a first-generation college student, Randall changed his major five times across two universities. In between college stints, he took time off to work in construction, serve in the military, and compete as a professional athlete. It was marriage that finally "focused me," Randall explained, curing him of his habit of "jumping from this to this."

Later that evening Kathy, Randall's wife of nearly two decades (also White), told me she took a similarly winding path through early adulthood. Coincidentally, she, too, had eventually settled on a career in education. Along the way, Kathy earned two master's degrees, taking a few classes at a time while acting as primary caregiver for the couple's two oldest children. "I found out I was pregnant [with my first] when I started grad school," she recalled. "By the time I finished, I had just had [my second child], so I felt like my professors were like, 'Oh my god, this girl's always pregnant!'" Upon graduation, Kathy found work first as an adjunct and then a tenure-track professor at a local community college. It hadn't been easy—she shuddered as she recalled an early encounter with a supervisor who warned her never to "play the mom card"—but ultimately Kathy felt she'd reached a state of equilibrium between paid work and family responsibilities.

Running a home with three teenagers, two dogs, two birds, and two careers is "an all-hands-on-deck kind of operation," explained Kathy. Both spouses recalled fighting over their division of labor when their children were young but said that in the intervening years they'd found harmony. Kathy drew on personal essentialist rhetoric to explain why: "We both went where our strengths are." She acts as "the planner" or, as Randall put it, "the foreman."[1] Whereas Kathy identifies as "a control freak," she lovingly referred to Randall as "a mess." "My entire success in life is based off to-do lists," she joked. "I always kid around with Randall, like, 'If I die, you've got to get married [again] really soon.' I don't even know. 'Cause it's just easy to have one person manage a lot of that. So, like the budgeting and the bill-paying and all that, I've got it down to such a science that he has relaxed."

Kathy and Randall's story bore a strong resemblance to Heather and Jeremy's arrangement, detailed in the previous chapter. It was a tale of labor allocation driven not by gender but by finding the right "fit" between person and task. Kathy is a "control freak," so she manages the family calendar. Randall is "so good at the home repair kind of stuff" that he takes the lead on DIY projects. This arrangement seemed perfectly logical to me as I sat across the dining table from Randall and Kathy in turn. It was only later, when I reflected on their story and compared it to those I was hearing at countless other tables, that I began to wonder.

To paraphrase an age-old question, are cognitive labor leaders born or made? Most of my interviewees, including Kathy and Randall, argued for the former. But I ultimately came to a different conclusion: cognitive labor leaders are largely *made*. In this chapter, I show how that happens and explain why it's most often women who undergo this transformation. Kathy and Randall's story provides important clues. Kathy, for example, was the undisputed family scheduler. Until very recently, she even made Randall's medical appointments for him. Yet one of Randall's core professional responsibilities was to manage the calendars of hundreds of middle schoolers. "I do scheduling for the entire [grades] seven to nine," he explained, along with coordinating parent-teacher meetings and events for the school's enrichment program. Randall also described himself as a stickler for timeliness, a relic of his old military days. I doubted he would have lasted long as an administrator or a soldier if his organizational skills were as lackluster as he and Kathy implied.

Consider, too, Kathy and Randall's career trajectories. There were notable similarities: both found their way to education after initial occupational dabbling, and both now earn roughly the same salary. But in the critical early years of parenthood, they had taken on more discrepant roles. Kathy had hardly been idle, going to school part-time while serving as primary caregiver for the couple's infants and then toddlers, but she was out of the paid workforce for about four years. To fit in time for her coursework, she organized a babysitting co-op with mothers in her neighborhood who agreed to swap childcare. Several of the relationships she formed with other women in the group continue to the present. Kathy was undoubtedly a skilled household manager, but I had to wonder whether her comparative advantage on the home front stemmed from innate talent or from differences in the way she and Randall invested in building up relevant skills and relationships.

In the coming pages, I reveal the social origins of the apparently individual "personality traits" said to drive cognitive labor inequality among Woman-led couples.[2] I argue that these seeming traits are better understood as skills. Men and women in Woman-led couples *invest* differently in building the domain-specific skills that facilitate cognitive household labor. They also *deploy* the more general capabilities they possess differently across the paid and unpaid spheres of their lives. Individual traits undoubtedly interact with these skills, placing upper and lower bounds on what is possible. Yet context—including gendered judgments about who is to blame when something goes wrong at home—plays a larger role than most Woman-led couples acknowledge. Over time, it seems, gendered behaviors help create and maintain the very selves they are said to reflect.

"He's Shut off That Part of His Brain"

Kara was among the many respondents who drew on the personal essentialist narrative to explain their mind-use patterns. She acts as chief cognitive laborer, for example, because "that's kind of how my brain works." But Kara also acknowledged an alternate possibility: "[My husband Joel and I] think about different things." Joel was more attuned to long-term concerns (next summer's travel, the couple's retirement savings), whereas Kara managed more immediate issues (scheduling with their nanny, tracking household inventory). Both were *capable* of handling the other's responsibilities if they needed to, she believed. But they largely didn't. Kara offered an analogy to explain:

> You know when you're in a new city how, if you're traveling with someone, one person just takes responsibility for being the navigator and the other person walks around blind? Sometimes, you're the navigator. Sometimes, you're the passenger. With different people, you take on [different] roles. So, I think because Joel's doing that long-term thinking, I've shut off that part of my brain a little bit, because I know he is taking care of it. I don't know if it works that way for him, but I think it's a little bit that way for the day-to-day, routine stuff. Because I am thinking about it, he's shut off that part of his brain.

Kara's musings came to mind when I began puzzling through the questions of how cognitive labor inequalities emerge and why they remain entrenched. Kara's navigation metaphor hinted at the importance of skills that are either actively honed or left dormant. Navigating the streets and transit systems of an unfamiliar city requires considerable effort. In the name of efficiency and harmony, traveling companions often designate one person as the directional lead. The navigator position may rotate from day to day or city to city: you lead today; I lead tomorrow. Alternatively, frequent travelers may determine that one person is better suited to a *permanent* navigation role.

This is the case in my own relationship. Whether we are biking through our neighborhood or traversing a foreign metropolis, my husband, Eric, nearly always charts our path. He prides himself on his directional sense, whereas I sheepishly acknowledge my tendency to get turned around in my own backyard. Given Eric's better sense of direction, we are both (as far as I know) content to make him perennial navigator-in-chief. Yet this narrative emphasizes some facts while obscuring others. For one, my husband has a long-standing interest in geography. He "browses" Google maps in search of interesting spots to explore and frequently eschews GPS navigation in favor of testing his instincts. Meanwhile, I spent childhood car rides reading books rather than road signs. As soon as the technology became available, I began turning on voice navigation, and I prefer to use it—just in case!—even for routes I know well.

In other words, Eric and I have invested very differently in building up our navigational skills. Or rather, one of us has invested, and the other has not. One might argue that our differences are a matter of innate talent or temperament. Indeed, there is likely some truth to this.[3] Eric's interest in charting new paths extends back to his early years, whereas my poor directional sense was noted by family members even in childhood. Yet consider this important counterevidence: I traveled extensively before meeting Eric, including to places where I did not have cell service and could not rely on turn-by-turn directions. Much of this travel was alone or with friends equally uninterested in navigation. When sufficiently motivated, it turns out I can way-find reasonably well. Though I start out hesitantly, over the course of a solo trip my directional skills gradually improve as I internalize landmarks and memorize important cross streets. As soon as I'm back with Eric and Google Maps, however, I subconsciously "shut off that part of my brain," as Kara might put it, and fall comfortably back into the passenger role.[4]

When I began investigating the origins of Woman-led couples' cognitive labor practices, I uncovered similar patterns. Much as Eric and I share a running joke about my navigational limitations, my respondents emphasized stark differences in partners' level of organization and attention to detail. Descriptors like "more efficient," "faster," and "better" characterized Superhuman women's performance of tasks ranging from coming up with a meal plan to finding a babysitter to picking out gifts. On some level, I agreed with their assessment: it did often seem "more efficient" for her to manage any given cognitive task. But when I broadened the aperture to consider other contexts (e.g., paid work) and a longer timeline, my perspective shifted. Her superior cognitive labor capabilities seemed less a foregone conclusion written into her very DNA and more the culmination of processes unfolding over years and reinforced by powerful social forces. In short, the longer one partner inhabits the "navigator" role, the more adept she becomes and the less plausible alternative arrangements—co-navigation, say, or taking turns—come to seem. Further, the fact that women so often become their family's navigator is far from random: our society provides them with both stronger motive and greater means for leading the way.

Gendered Investments

Mateo seemed in awe of his wife Leah's ability to manage their toddler's evolving diet: "I know the basics, but in terms of progress, each month [our daughter] kind of changes in terms of what she can eat and can't eat, and how you prepare it. I think Leah has all the knowledge." He further predicted Leah would "always be better at sensing what our daughter needs as a next developmental step. . . . My sense is she will always be ahead of me, mentally prepared to do the next necessary step in our daughter's development." Though Mateo described Leah's nutritional knowledge as if it were instinctual, Leah herself hinted at a more mundane explanation: "I'm at home alone with [our daughter] the whole week, and I read about it, what she can eat, and what is better." Leah used a generous maternity leave to educate herself on parenting best practices.[5] She was "always ahead" of Mateo because, quite literally, she had done the reading.

In the mind-use realm, as in most realms, practice makes perfect. One gets good at cognitive labor by, well, doing cognitive labor. In Woman-led couples, women like Leah earlier and more consistently spent time and energy cultivating relationships and accruing knowledge—such as how to manage an infant's changing nutritional needs—that aided their completion of cognitive household tasks. The result was women's greater capacity, which only further incentivized their continued responsibility for domestic affairs. When she "has all the knowledge," as Mateo put it, reallocation of cognitive tasks comes to seem impossible or ill-advised. In parallel, men's relative lack of investment resulted in their more limited capacity, which in turn justified their continued backseat role.

Because even simple cognitive tasks often draw on a web of contextual knowledge built up over time, the partner who started out in the navigator role typically stayed there. Respondents struggled to trade off on cognitive tasks even as they managed to take turns handling physical chores. To be sure, the latter also require knowledge and skill. But because these skills were less embedded in relationships and less dependent on deep understanding of the local parenting ecosystem, they were comparatively easy to transfer from one partner to another. Watch someone change a diaper or put on a onesie, practice a few times, and most people get the hang of it. By contrast, the knowledge required to effectively complete many cognitive tasks is harder both to summarize and absorb, contributing to respondents' sense of an unbridgeable gap in partners' abilities.

Gendered investment patterns were most prominent in the parenting realm, where women typically got an early "lead" in learning about child development and in cultivating stronger and more numerous parent-centered relationships. Of the days before her oldest child was born, Katie recalled, "I read a lot of books, more just . . . the practical side of things. Like what to— like, the different stages [of development] and stuff." She wasn't sure how her husband prepared to become a parent. "I don't know what he did, honestly . . . I don't remember having all that many conversations about it," she reflected, before recalling that they had attended a childbirth class together. It seems

Katie and her husband had assigned her primary responsibility for learning about parenting "by default"—to borrow a phrase from sociologist Jessica Calarco and her collaborators—rather than through explicit conversation.[6]

Their early investment in formal research related to parenting meant that women were quickly slotted into the role of "expert." Liz, describing the way she and her husband, Nathan, made parenting decisions, explained:

> He definitely defers to me with, like, "Is it okay for [our baby] to eat X?" . . . He'll say, "Is that okay?" And I'll say, "Well, the research says," or "My research I've looked into," or "The pediatrician [said]," or whatever—I kind of give him the expert info, and then we kind of talk it out . . . I feel like I present the expert knowledge—or, not the expert knowledge, but I've done the research for us as a couple. But then we make the decision together about what we're comfortable with.

In addition to reading, women built up their expertise by continually scanning their environment for relevant information they could apply to their own family life. "When we go out, I look to see what [other] parents have, to see what would make our lives easier," explained Desiree. Recently, she had noticed that other parents in their neighborhood had strollers that handled uneven ground well. She followed this observation up with online research and ultimately convinced her husband they should buy a second stroller. Similarly, Kendra joked that "my product research around here tends to be watching other kids and other parents." Last winter, for instance, she observed "kids wearing boots that have the handles on them. They are super easy to get on." She'd already purchased several pairs.

Women also tended to invest more heavily in forming social connections centered on family life, including ties to professionals (e.g., pediatricians, babysitters, and teachers) and other parents. These relationships gave them greater access to parenting tips, knowledge of community resources, and ability to coordinate with peers and service providers. Kara, like many women, acted as primary liaison to her son's nanny, who was often long gone by the time her husband, Joel, returned from the office. Joel explained, "Our nanny communicates almost exclusively with Kara. So if anything is coming from [the nanny] about our son, whether it's, 'We heard about this class,' or 'I think he's ready to try this new thing', that's almost—100 percent of the time that will come from the nanny, to Kara, to [me]." It would be difficult for Joel—and perhaps confusing for their nanny—to step into the middle of ongoing conversations for which he had neither the relevant context nor the interpersonal rapport Kara had built over years.

Similarly, many couples reported that although both spouses did their best to attend pediatrician appointments and parent-teacher conferences, women's participation tended to be more consistent, and thus their relationships with those professionals were stronger. Yvonne described hearing about her eldest child's academic struggles from his teacher, who advised her to "seek extra help for him." She couldn't imagine her husband attending parent-teacher conferences in her place: "He wouldn't even know what to ask the teacher, he wouldn't know what to tell them." While her husband could perhaps catch up eventually, doing so would require further labor on Yvonne's part—to bring him up to speed, and to tolerate the inevitable hiccups associated with a handoff of this kind.

In addition to cultivating relationships with the professionals who served their children, women described stronger and more numerous ties to parent-centered social networks.[7] Sam explained that his wife, Donna, collects the information required to make a parenting decision "because of her connection to the online community, [which] gives her more perspective on things. Like, sometimes she'll even bring it up and ask me what I think about something, and I'll say, 'Well, what did the moms' group have to say?'" When Sam and Donna were contemplating childcare options, Donna "would talk about looking at [day cares], and I would be supportive of her decisions, if that makes sense. . . . Like, if she would make a proposal about something, we might talk about it and arrive on the same conclusion." To clarify, I asked, "Donna was doing the first-step research and then sharing what she learned with you?" Sam elaborated, "I feel like we got a lot of information out of [the local first-time moms] group, and then she would share it with me, and then we'd talk about it, because people post on there [about] their childcare."

Women's cognitive labor capacity was also enhanced by in-person connections with peers. While explaining his wife's greater cognitive responsibility, Trevor noted that "there are things in Mindy's pile which I'd have more difficulty taking on." Pressed for an example, he continued, "Fixing playdates . . . and coordination with [other] parents about who will pick up, and things like that." Mindy, he explained, was an officer in the elementary school Parent-Teacher Association (PTA), which gave her insights into local happenings as well as connections with fellow parents in their neighborhood. Trevor acknowledged that Mindy had put in the work: "You gain knowledge, you build relationships, and she did not have that [before]. She started that, she worked on that, and that's how she got it." But he also suggested that doing so was in her nature, "in general, as a personality [trait]."

Outside the confines of formal organizations, networks of women shared parenting tips with one another. It was through friends that women learned how early one needed to join day-care center waiting lists (in some places, soon after conception). It was through friends and female relatives that women learned time- and sanity-saving parenting tips: size up on diapers to avoid messy "blowouts"; keep a stack of children's books to give out as last-minute birthday presents. It was through other mothers at drop-off that they got recommendations for the warmest snow pants or the best local swimming school. Such insider knowledge, channeled through informal connections among women, gave mothers a distinct advantage over fathers when it came to anticipating problems and opportunities and identifying promising solutions.[8]

The term "investment" implies conscious individual choice, and undoubtedly this is part of the story. There was nothing to stop men from reading parenting books, taking an active role at the parent-teacher conference, or making more of an effort to get to know the other parents they encountered on the playground. And yet, such personal decisions about how to allocate time and energy explain only a fraction of the patterns I observed: gendered social forces also channeled men and women in different directions and constrained their options. What we might call parenting "capital"—the knowledge and relationships that help individuals achieve their parenting aims—was both more easily attainable and more strongly incentivized for women than for men.

Consider the gender segregation of social networks and the gender typing of many parenting resources. In the digital space, several fathers mentioned their exclusion from parenting forums. Though fathers' groups existed, they were considerably smaller than parallel mothers' groups and thus perceived as less useful information conduits. Even groups with gender-inclusive names (e.g., "Parents of [city]") tended to be dominated by women. Tellingly, several queer interviewees described these forums as "dad-bashing groups," suggesting one reason men may have had a hard time breaking in.

Men also reported discomfort with or avoidance of physical spaces they experienced as feminized, which resulted in fewer opportunities to build relationships and learn from other parents. Playdates and birthday parties were seen as women's domain; even bus pickups were female-typed in some communities. When men did venture into these spaces, they—and by extension their wives—felt they were doing something transgressive. "If Scott is picking up one of the boys from the bus," explained Amanda, "he'll joke about, 'Oh yeah, I was just swapping recipes with the ladies at the bus stop' type of thing." She continued, in a mock fangirl voice, "I've had moms who are like, 'Oh my god, that's so wonderful, that's so great! You're so lucky. Oh, Scott, you're so good!'" Though the attention Amanda described was overtly positive, the sheer visibility of Scott's fathering behavior seemed to make both partners uneasy. Scott hinted at the limits to what he could accomplish in the parenting world without Amanda as buffer: "Sometimes, if there's a playdate or whatever, it's just kinda more gender-specific that the mothers [handle it]. . . . It would be weird if I was texting the mom to be like, 'Yeah, [our son] is going to come over.'"

An additional deterrent to men's investment in parenting-related skills and relationships was the fact that men and women were held to different standards.[9] Apparent "neuroticism" or maternal "gatekeeping" (i.e., controlling or restricting men's parenting opportunities) largely reflected women's expectation that they would bear a disproportionate share of any consequences associated with domestic problems.[10] Put another way, women's investment in family-related skills and relationships was to some extent an attempt at self-protection, while men's relatively limited investment reflected their sense that problems at home (with some notable exceptions, described below) would not, for them, be all that consequential. As we will see in the next chapter, these assumptions were well-founded.

Jennifer explained that her husband's efforts to take over some domestic tasks, particularly related to getting their daughter ready for school in the morning, were counterproductive:

> [It's] making my anxiety worse . . . because I'm a control freak. He would get up, and wasn't doing it fast enough, or efficient enough, whatever . . . I can do it much faster, and I'll just be done, and I know I can leave [for work], and I don't have to go, "Did he forget this? What if he forgot that? What if he didn't brush [our daughter's] hair? What if she smells when she goes to school?"

Tellingly, Jennifer was concerned about "efficiency" but also about the social consequences of her husband's carelessness. If her daughter was poorly groomed—"what if she smells?"—Jennifer feared it would reflect poorly on the family or, more likely, on Jennifer herself given her more extensive involvement in the school community and the general societal tendency to hold mothers accountable for their children.[11]

Bridget shared Jennifer's worries, in that she assumed she would be on the receiving end of opprobrium from others if the family failed to adhere to social conventions:

> There's a bunch of stuff around communication that I think it would be hard for me to cede [to my husband]. Not only around the sort of schedule stuff, but just like, he's not ever gonna remember when his mother's birthday is ... [or that] it's been six months since we've seen our friends. ... He's not ever going to remember the passage of time and the frequency with which you might maintain normal relationships.

Taking a less proactive role in maintaining their social connections "would be hard for me," Bridget admitted. "I care about it. I want to be a good neighbor and parent and kid and sibling and all that sort of stuff."

The role of gendered social expectations is clearest when we consider the domestic issues about which men were atypically "neurotic" and women more laissez-faire. An overgrown lawn was, for some men, the equivalent of a poorly dressed child for some women. Alex handles the gardening and yardwork for his household, though he admitted he doesn't enjoy mowing the lawn. "We did have a service do that for a little bit," he recalled, but they'd canceled it. "I'm really hung up on control. ... It's one of those things that I don't wanna ... give somebody else the control because I don't trust them." William shared a similar sentiment: "The state of the lawn is much more important to me [than to my wife]; Stacey's much more inclined to let it grow longer. I don't enjoy mowing the lawn, but I feel the obligation, the societal obligation to mow it, because we have snooty neighbors." Both Alex and William had internalized the notion that society—or, more narrowly, their neighbors—would hold them responsible for any landscaping inadequacies, and they invested accordingly in learning the ins and outs of mowing, fertilizing, and trimming.

In sum, men and women alike internalized gender-specific societal expectations and invested their time and energy in learning and forming relationships accordingly. Small initial gaps in partners' capacities widened over time as men and women ignored or attended to various habits of mind and interpersonal connections, in line with their understanding of which areas of family life were ultimately their responsibility.[12] These seemingly personal choices were facilitated by a range of structural and social factors: Leah was entitled to a months-long parental leave but Mateo was not; Donna had access to the collective wisdom of digital and real-world mothers who freely swapped childcare tips, but her husband Sam lacked parallel father-focused networks.[13] Regardless of their origin, however, these domain-specific skill and relationship gaps eventually came to be seen as unbridgeable—and, perhaps more consequentially, innate—gulfs.

Gendered Deployment

Men and women made differential investments in building knowledge, skills, and relationships directly relevant to managing family life. But for a second, more general set of capacities, the problem was less about differential investment than differential deployment: that is, men and women *activated* their existing capabilities in distinct ways. Superhuman characteristics—like being organized, proactive, and a good multitasker—overlap considerably with the set of capacities psychologists call "executive function."[14] Self-control, working memory, and mental flexibility, among the core components of executive function, are also core to many cognitive tasks.[15]

Consider the never-ending work of managing the family schedule. Though most couples had some sort of shared calendar, one partner was typically the primary manager. Success in this endeavor requires self-control: though few respondents find intrinsic enjoyment in their calendar work, they consistently update and review the family schedule. It requires working memory: to make the pieces fit, the calendar-keeper must memorize varied and ever-shifting constraints ranging from a spouse's commute pattern to a babysitter's availability. Finally, it requires mental flexibility: when conflicts arise, as they inevitably do, a good scheduler adjusts to the new reality and generates a creative work-around.

Though executive function and the abilities required of a cognitive laborer may not be identical, the former is a useful proxy for the latter because researchers have devoted considerable attention to studying whether executive function can be taught and how it differs by gender. Can a Bumbler learn to be more Superhuman? Are women naturally more organized than men? The broad consensus is that specific components of executive function can be improved with training and practice.[16] Gender differences are apparent in some individual components of executive functioning, but neither men nor women have a systematic overall advantage.[17] Further, findings of gender differences differ widely across studies and appear to depend heavily on measurement and testing strategies.[18]

This research conflicts with interviewees' focus on immutability ("I am who I am") and individual difference. Indeed, if I looked solely at their domestic

activity, men and women in Woman-led couples did appear to differ systematically in their capacity for planning, problem-solving, and processing complex
informational inputs. The catch is that *the same men who struggled to anticipate
domestic problems or follow a project through to its end frequently described success
in occupations requiring the very same skills they were said to lack at home.*

Nina, for example, described her husband, Julian, as temperamentally ill-
equipped for the frenetic multitasking and constant forecasting she relied on
to juggle home, paid work, and childcare. "If something is broken in the house
and Julian gets used to it, he will not consider it a problem," she explained. This
pattern predated their marriage:

> In his apartment before we got married, there was a hole in the wall, and
> [he and his roommates] just left it. They were just like, 'This is okay.' . . . It
> was sort of tragedy of the commons in that situation, where, like, no one—
> five roommates, no one felt the responsibility. If something is broken in our
> lives [today], in terms of a physical appliance or something, and he's gotten
> used to not having it, it filters out of his mind. Whereas for me it's an ever-
> present [issue].

In another couple, Trevor drew a contrast between his "super-organized"
wife, Mindy, and his own "deadline-challenged" and "scattered" tendencies. He
struggled with follow-through: "I'm in charge of laundry, so I will wash it, put it
in the dryer, but somehow I lose interest by then. Getting it from the dryer and
folding it, it slips my mind that that's also part of doing laundry." He described
himself as slower to learn new things, too: "In general, as a personality [trait],
I would say, it would be a lot more difficult for me to do things which my wife
is doing than for her to pick up things which I have been doing. Just overall, she's
better at that kind of thing, like picking up a new task and doing it."

It seems obvious that the guy who doesn't notice holes in the wall shouldn't
be in charge of managing home upkeep, or that the man with a tendency to
overlook deadlines should probably not be the calendar-keeper. But these particular men worked as a surgeon and a nonprofit founder, respectively—
positions that certainly rely on attention to detail and deadlines. Julian, the
surgeon, acknowledged the contrast between his professional and domestic
personas. It was "mostly time [availability]" that prevented him from doing
more of the cognitive labor at home, he began. "And then also—I mean with
the mental stuff I think Nina's much more attentive to all the things that need to
be done . . . I can mostly go a very long time before it hits me that now is the
time to deal with it." Quickly, he clarified: "I mean, in the home life. Not, like,

work." Nina made a similarly astute observation about this contradiction. "I'm also just, like, more of a detail-oriented person than Julian," she mused. "Except with regards to his career, where apparently he's . . . he's a doctor, so he has to . . ." Nina trailed off, changing the subject rather than dwell on this puzzling inconsistency.

"What do you think is different about your attention to those things in the work side [versus the home side]?" I asked Julian. He thought for a moment before speculating:

> I don't know. I mean, I think just being in a pretty busy job. I think in my work pretty consistently—I tend to try to prioritize basically all of that, and don't spend a lot of time with that [home] stuff. [Paid work] comes at the expense of, like, proactive work [at home]. . . . I think I'm likely fairly intellectually exhausted. I don't come home and think about what needs to be arranged for childcare.

Several other men acknowledged a similar contrast between paid work and home. Alan described himself as the "ideas guy" in his marriage and his wife as the "project manager" who figures out "what are we going to do and how [would] that actually work and, like, the nitty-gritty." But this arrangement is "funny," he admitted, because Alan works full-time as a project manager, and "that's partly what I need to do in my job, is get into the nitty-gritty." Steve likewise noted that his wife, Lisa, is the one to plan the family's leisure time, although, "Oddly, I'm a project manager by trade. But sometimes I don't want to plan for the weekend."

In some cases, the starkest contrast emerged between a man's domestic self and the self he brought to his hobbies or personal pursuits. Alex, an accountant, quit his job several months before our interview and was contemplating a career shift. Though he had taken on more physical household labor while unemployed, his share of the cognitive load remained largely unchanged.[19] Alex acknowledged that his wife, Mandy, "probably takes on more than 50 percent" of the cognitive labor (Mandy herself would later estimate that she does "99 percent"). But, he explained, "I think that's also, like, a combination of just how we are." He contrasted his own, more laid-back approach with Mandy's tendency to "put pressure on herself" to do everything well.

Earlier in the interview, however, when asked if he kept any to-do lists, Alex described himself as "much more of a planner" than his wife. He uses a paper planner that "breaks it down from quarterly goals to monthly to weekly to daily" as well as a to-do list app on his phone. Though he had relaxed the practice somewhat since leaving his job, Alex routinely spent Sunday nights "look[ing] back at the [previous] week and then plan[ning] for the upcoming week," both personally and professionally. At the time of our interview, those plans revolved around his job search, networking related to personal interests, beekeeping (which he tracks in a dedicated notebook), and backyard gardening (though it was winter when we spoke, Alex had already mapped out his garden beds for the next season).[20] Alex explained the contrast between his "planner" and lackadaisical tendencies this way:

> When it comes to the things that I don't care about, we'll deal with them when they come. And, we'll deal with them when that happens, or whatever. Or if it's something that I just don't view as important [as] Mandy does, I think that's probably where, you know, there's—where a lot of her extra mental—[why] she has more than 50 percent.

In other words, Alex selectively deploys his planning skills in service of aims he considers important. Few household management tasks made that list.

One might counter here that these men may rely on support staff to handle administrative tasks: doctors have nurses and receptionists; project managers have executive assistants.[21] However, the nature of modern knowledge work is such that all but the most senior executives must do much of their own admin.[22] Further, considerable education and prior work experience are required to reach the kinds of positions that come with administrative support; along the way, there is ample opportunity to hone one's planning and problem-solving skills.

It's also true that holding a job is not the same as being *good* at a job: maybe these men were disorganized and lackadaisical at home *and* at work. Though I cannot completely rule out this possibility, my data provide suggestive counterevidence. The educational and professional trajectories of Bumbler men more often hinted at success than struggle. Julian, for instance, graduated from an elite medical school before obtaining a prestigious residency in a competitive specialty. Trevor earned two master's degrees, founded and ran his own nonprofit organization, and juggled two jobs.

Even men who averred their disorganization in all facets of life seemed to exaggerate their limitations. Darren, a software engineer, described himself as "totally stress[ed]" out by long-range future planning. "It makes my wife feel in control, because she's planning," he explained, "and it makes me feel insane." Darren's wife, Sheila, manages the family schedule, along with completing most other cognitive tasks (she described her share of the cognitive load as

"100 percent"). But Darren's career path, albeit nontraditional, hinted at his capacity to manage complex projects, synthesize new information, and juggle multiple responsibilities. In his mid-twenties, he taught himself to program. Later, he was hired by a large company to do entirely different work but "begged" his way into the programming department. Once there, "I just sunk my teeth into it. I read books, I watched videos, I took training, like online training classes, from wherever I could find it." Over the years, he'd accumulated enough career capital to obtain a remote position that offered significant autonomy, well before Covid-19 made such arrangements commonplace. Alongside this full-time work, Darren apprenticed as a tattoo artist. He used an app to track his appointments and commissions, arguing that while this side gig made his life more complicated, it was worth it to have the artistic outlet. For someone "flying by the seat of my pants" at work and at home, Darren seemed reasonably adept at managing complexity.

Contrasts like these point to a pattern of differential *deployment* rather than differential *ability*. It was less that men like Darren were innately laid-back and more that different contexts brought out different sides of them. Why? Men who recognized the discrepancies between their work and home personas argued that by the time they finished with paid work, they had little mental bandwidth left. Like Julian, quoted earlier, who was "intellectually exhausted" by his day job, Jeremy described his project management work as "all-consuming": "I think that if I had the type of job that I cared less about . . . or that was less demanding in the background of my thinking at all times, then I would be more of a mental participant in this way [at home]. I think [my job] just crowds out a lot of this stuff, unfortunately."

This is a logical argument, if we imagine cognitive labor capacity as a tank that refills overnight or a muscle depleted with use.[23] However, when it was a *woman* who held a more demanding job—in terms of number of hours or schedule (in)flexibility—different logic prevailed. In a handful of cases, women's cognitively taxing paid work was referenced as further evidence of her inherent managerial prowess. Bridget, for instance, described herself as the "organizer" and her husband, Jimmy, as the "executer" in their relationship. By way of explanation, she added, "My [paid] job is basically to project-manage things . . . the dynamic in our relationship is very clearly a result of that." Rather than competing with her domestic responsibilities, Bridget argued that the professional skills she'd honed enhanced her domestic capacity.

Still, many women did experience their paid work as intellectually exhausting and a threat to their managerial role at home. But rather than accept this as an unfortunate reality, as men like Julian and Jeremy seemed to do, women in Woman-led couples viewed their occupational demands as a problem in need of a solution. They typically responded by making professional changes rather than by expecting or asking their husband to pick up the slack at home. This was true even of women who outearned their husband, sometimes by a significant margin.[24] Cassie, a telecommunications executive with an annual income more than twice her husband's, described herself as "a workaholic" who was formerly "consumed" by her job. Despite her intense career, Cassie did not cut herself much slack at home: "I was literally working [for pay] from, like, 6:00 a.m. 'til 9:30 p.m. and then would get up the next day and do it again. And [my husband] was working 'til 9:30 at night, so I would have to come home and still do everything that needs to be done when you're a parent."

Cassie remembered reaching a breaking point one evening when she was giving her six-month-old a bath. "My [work] phone was going off and was buzzing, and it's always numbers, numbers, numbers. And nothing happened to [my son], but he turned and I wasn't paying attention. And I was just like, 'I gotta get out of here, 'cause I'm not paying attention to my child while he's in the tub.'" Soon after this incident, Cassie switched from the commercial to the government division of her company, where work hours were considerably less intense. Though she had likely lowered the ceiling on her future compensation, Cassie now felt she had sufficient bandwidth to be an attentive parent. Intellectual exhaustion was not, in her mind, a valid reason to neglect her domestic responsibilities.

Cassie's story suggests the "facts" of partners' employment—hours, income, schedule flexibility—mattered less than the meaning couples ascribed to those facts.[25] While men's paid work was allowed to deplete their cognitive reserves, women's was not. This gender asymmetry meant that women in Woman-led couples often experienced more obstacles to their career growth than their husband faced. Sonya, for example, had been both primary breadwinner and primary cognitive laborer for most of her marriage. Despite her higher earnings, Sonya was clear that her husband Ray's career goals were the priority. Sonya kept her own ambitions more modest, in part because she knew she would need to preserve mental energy for domestic life. "I'm in middle management," she explained. "With the right support system, I probably could reach higher, but I also like to be around my children a fair bit. . . . With that understanding, we decided it was really important for us to see Ray's career goals through, because I don't really have a goal such as—one as important as his is." The couple's focus on Ray's career seemed to be the key factor keeping their hours and income differentials within reasonable bounds. Indeed, just before I interviewed them, Ray received a promotion that would equalize their salaries, whereas Sonya had bounced between jobs over the previous few years searching for a family-friendly firm. She remembered earlier periods when she felt frustrated and "wished Ray was the spouse that made more money and I was him. . . . In the height of our fights, I would say, 'You're the one with all the PTO [paid time off]. You take [the kids] to the doctor's appointment.'" Nevertheless, Ray's dream remained the axis around which the couple's decisions turned. Asking him to reserve more of his intellectual capacity for family matters would have threatened that dream.

It would be easy to dismiss men as bad actors weaponizing their incompetence to shirk responsibility, or women as too willing to give up on their professional ambitions. But this is at best an incomplete explanation. The same incentive structures I described in the previous section apply here: women are held socially accountable for most domestic outcomes. Meanwhile, men are more on the hook for a family's financial outlook, a fact that helps explain, if not fully excuse, what could sometimes seem like a myopic focus on their career.[26]

Men were also not the only ones who practiced selective deployment of their abilities. Women who demonstrated considerable skill in most other areas of domestic life, for instance, sometimes displayed a curious incapacity when it came to finances. Lisa, an at-home parent who managed her daughter's education and extracurriculars with exacting precision, laughed when I asked about the last home improvement issue her family had dealt with: "Oh god, I probably wouldn't know. So, that tells you who does that!" Holly, who described frustration with her husband Tyler's passive approach to household management, was more laid-back about finances: "He's a lot better at that than I am. So he's always running numbers in his head and thinking about finances . . . I'm just more on the, like, 'Let's make sure that [our daughter's] fed' and, you know, being a mom, and let him worry about the financial stuff." Tyler periodically presents her with a "breakdown" of their financial health, which Holly appreciates. "That's helpful. I just don't have the time or the brain space right now" to take a more proactive role, she explained.

———

When we link mind-use patterns to innate traits, we miss the critical role learned skills and honed capacities play in shaping how "good" one is at cognitive household labor. Men and women in Woman-led couples are not merely *responding* to personal differences when allocating cognitive labor. Rather, their choices are *creating and sustaining* those differences. When women invest in forming relationships with teachers or reading up on baby-weaning best practices, they hone capacities that come to look like instincts. When men deploy their problem-solving and planning skills at the office, they fail to recognize how those same skills might be useful at home. Yet these "choices" are only partially individual. Superhumans and Bumblers alike are also responding to a range of social forces that make it easier for women to acquire domestic knowledge and build family-centered relationships and that disincentivize men from using up their limited energy on domestic matters for which they are unlikely to be held accountable. These forces are not determinants, however. In the next chapter, we'll meet different-gender couples who build very different structures from some of the same materials.

CHAPTER 5

NONTRADITIONAL PATHS

Richard and Shannon, a White couple, live far enough outside the city that I opted to rent a car the day of our interview rather than navigate several trains and buses. I pulled up to the curb alongside a plastic neon figure holding an orange flag and entreating drivers to "Slow!" Richard answered the front door when I rang the bell, wearing trendy glasses and a T-shirt with an abstract drawing of a mermaid. He led me to a kitchen table where we sat surrounded by children's artwork and bins of health-food staples: arrowroot powder, psyllium husks, coconut sugar. Later, I would learn that his wife, Shannon, enjoys baking and, unlike her husband and two children, eats a primarily Paleo diet.

Richard was working from home that day but seemed in no hurry to return to his laptop. His job as a sales manager was not his passion, he explained. A decade earlier, Richard had been an aspiring filmmaker in Los Angeles; only after several unsuccessful years did he take a job at a finance company. He'd been in the corporate world ever since. His current sales job was "cushy" enough that Richard planned to stay as long as his employer offered schedule flexibility, which he would need if he was to continue doing the bulk of school pickups and drop-offs for his two sons.

Richard's wife, Shannon, also began a career in the arts before pivoting to a corporate role. Though she has occasional regrets about the path not taken—"Sometimes I wonder, what if I really applied myself? . . . What could I have done?"—she seemed more content than Richard with her accidental career as an operations manager. In the years she'd been with her current company, Shannon had risen through the ranks, including a recent promotion that put her in a "different and exciting and scary" new role. Her earnings had risen in parallel, but so had her hours: though nominally expected to work thirty-five each week, in practice she was routinely on call for more.

Shannon and Richard were one of a handful of Man-led couples—that is, different-gender couples in which the male partner completes more cognitive labor. Shannon estimated that Richard does roughly two-thirds of such work. "Other moms basically talk as if their husbands are useless. And Richard is definitely not useless!" she enthused. "He just thinks of things before I even realize they're an issue." But Man- and Woman-led couples were not mirror images of one another. Their differences simultaneously underscore the power of gendered social forces and illustrate alternative ways of navigating around them.

Both Shannon and Richard occasionally turned to the language of "personality" and "wiring" to explain their allocation. Shannon described their differences this way:

> Richard is more naturally organized and more naturally a planner. . . . And so I've just sort of stopped doing that. I mean, it's not that I'm incapable of it, I've had jobs where it's been a big part of my job. . . . But he just does things before I even realize that it needs to be done. . . . So I feel like, that those skills have atrophied in my personal life.

Richard offered a similar assessment. "I'm a highly organized person," he explained, "wired" to value orderliness.

But their accounts were not quite a gender-swapped version of the Bumbler and Superhuman archetypes. Instead, they demonstrated a more flexible and less essentialist understanding of how their "selves" related to their cognitive labor dynamic. Shannon recognized that she had let relevant skills "atrophy" in her personal life while continuing to deploy them at work, acknowledging her own agency: "Maybe part of it is [me] sort of trying to balance him, because he is so organized and sometimes tightly wound, and I'm just like, 'Ahh!' . . . We can't both be that way."

Further, although Shannon was the secondary cognitive laborer overall, she retained a particularly strong leadership role when it came to managing social relationships and the cognitive components of childcare. "The things that affect other people, parties and, you know, anniversaries and things, those are things that I keep in mind," she explained. Shannon manages most communication with other parents and acts as the primary liaison to their sons' school, including volunteering as a "room mother" for their older child's class. This would turn out to be a common pattern among Man-led and Balanced couples, hinting at the unique strength of cultural imperatives linked to motherhood.[1]

In this chapter, we take a close look at Man-led couples like Richard and Shannon, as well as different-gender Balanced couples (i.e., those who share cognitive labor roughly equally).[2] Revisiting the questions animating earlier chapters, we examine their mind-use patterns and the narratives they use to explain them, looking for clues about why, how, and with what consequences these couples have managed to chart an atypical path. My findings challenge the simplistic assumption that equality necessarily breeds happiness; indeed, several nontraditional couples were among the *least* satisfied I encountered. The most contented couples were those who perceived a match between their selves and their circumstances, while simultaneously believing in their own ability to shape and reshape their cognitive labor arrangement if need be. Regardless of their satisfaction level, however, nontraditional men and women alike noted the challenges involved in navigating the gendered social networks, parenting spaces, and accountability structures that steered most Woman-led couples toward cognitive labor imbalance.

A Distorted Mirror Image

In a narrow sense, Man-led couples mirrored Woman-led couples: his cognitive labor load was heavier than hers. Yet the reflected image was distorted in notable ways. For one, gaps between partners' cognitive contributions were smaller among Man-led couples. It was not uncommon for a woman in a Woman-led couple to lead eight, nine, or even all ten cognitive domains; the most a man in a Man-led couple led was six, suggesting there were limits to how uninvolved a woman could be. Whereas men in Woman-led couples were often detached from household happenings they weren't directly involved in (recall Darren's memorable assertion that "my brain just naturally rejects" information it considers non-essential), women in Man-led couples stayed relatively plugged in.[3]

This was true even in cases where he was a full-time caregiver and she worked full-time for pay.[4] I asked Rebecca, a hospital physician married to an at-home father, how familiar she was with her husband and two kids' daily schedules while she was at the hospital. "Pretty aware," she explained. "I check in throughout the day quite a bit, just to see how things are going. And then we always talk [about the] day with the kids. . . . So, I'm usually pretty cognizant of what they're doing through the day, and where they are." Meg, who worked in university administration while her husband, Bram, cared for their two young children, noted that she keeps tabs on Bram's daytime schedule via his paper planner: "If I wanna look at something real quick, I'll often just use [Bram's] computer. And his planner's sitting right there. . . . So I'll glance and see what he has going on for the week."

Women in Man-led couples were also more attuned to their cognitive labor imbalance, and more proactive about keeping it in check, than their male peers in Woman-led couples. Meg was acutely aware of Bram's heavier cognitive load—roughly 70 percent was on his plate, she guessed—and tried to alleviate both his stress and her own fear of not contributing enough. Though Bram was a paper-and-pen devotee, Meg convinced him to incorporate digital systems for household management so she could participate more easily. "There's a lot that I can do while I'm not at home," Meg noted. "You know, I can—I can think about stuff while I'm [commuting] and like, during my lunch break or whatever. I can do more of that kind of stuff." Meg recognized the limitations of her efforts to be helpful, however. "Even if I'm like, 'Oh, [our son's] shirts are getting too small,' and . . . I'll let Bram know . . . I can do that, but then it's not on me to think, 'Oh, well he needs new clothes, he needs bigger shirts.' That's stuff that's on Bram's list now." She sighed. "I don't know, it's something that I worry about and try to make better." Occasionally Meg asked Bram how she could help, but she disliked this approach because "I know it's not fair to ask him to manage me." Instead, she aimed to take over specific, one-time tasks that she could fully "take off his mind."

In addition to their overall sensitivity to their husband's contributions, women in Man-led couples tended to take a particularly active role in childcare-related cognitive labor.[5] This was true of Antoni and Siobhan. Antoni makes the meal plan and generates the shopping lists; he researches flights to visit family abroad and scopes out restaurants to try on upcoming date nights; he schedules medical appointments for both his daughter and his wife. Most exceptions to this pattern centered around the couple's preschooler Rory. A few years earlier when they were searching for a day care, the selection process "was all me," Siobhan recalled. Touring candidate centers was "a source of some frustration . . . because everywhere we went Antoni would be like, 'Yeah, I think this is fine,' and I would be like, 'Ah, no.' But he pretty much left [the day care] decision up to me, because he was like, 'Well, you're the expert, you have very strong feelings about this, I don't.'"[6]

Siobhan's parental leave ended before they'd selected a center, so she deputized Antoni (whose work schedule was more flexible) to visit candidates in her stead. "I would give him a list of criteria, a list of questions to ask," she recalled. "I would shortlist places that I wanted him to go and have a look at.

I would do all the background research." When Antoni finally toured a center that met Siobhan's criteria, they visited together to confirm his initial impression before enrolling Rory.

Similarly, while Antoni more or less dictated what he and his wife ate, both parents were heavily involved in managing Rory's diet. She'd been underweight since she was born, and Siobhan constantly worried she wasn't eating enough. At the infant stage, there was "a lot of stress" around breastfeeding; now, there was much handwringing over how much of her lunch Rory finished at preschool. "If she doesn't eat, I'm in a bad mood," Siobhan admitted.

This dynamic—male cognitive leadership, with notable exceptions related to managing children's lives—was common among Man-led couples. As Shannon, profiled earlier, made clear, her domestic priority was her children; she was comfortable neglecting many other aspects of household management: "My priority when I'm home is making sure the kids are set. . . . If I get home and the kids are fed and bathed and dressed and their meals are ready for tomorrow, I don't care if anything else gets done . . . I feel so drained so many days after my commute." Despite her busy work schedule, it was Shannon who volunteered at the boys' school and maintained the primary relationship with their teachers, even though Richard was the logistics point person in most other aspects of their lives.

To understand the discrepancy between their housework and childcare practices, it helps to remember that couples like Richard and Shannon or Antoni and Siobhan were not operating in a vacuum. Instead, they contended with many of the same social forces that steered most of their peers toward a woman-led division of cognitive labor. The weight of others' judgments and assumptions was particularly acute when it came to their parenting choices.

Carrie, whose oldest child was born midway through her PhD, began venting toward the end of our interview: "When we had kids, nobody asked my husband if he was going to quit his job to stay home! People asked me, and I'm like, 'I'm in year five of grad school! Do you think I'm really gonna [quit]?' . . . People asked me stupid stuff. And I think other people's assumptions—I notice other people's assumptions a lot." Though Carrie "hates the phone," for example, she is usually the one to field calls from friends wondering what to bring to a dinner party or the school nurse asking her to pick up a sick child. "People will call or only email me if [our daughter] has a party to go to or something like that," she explained, increasingly animated. "I think because I'm the mom, so I'm the social coordinator. But I'm like, 'I'm not the party planner in our house!'" Carrie also felt the weight of others' assumptions in situations far removed from her role as a parent or spouse. During a particularly frustrating business trip, "A bunch of the people from my lab up here went down [to another state] to work with another lab, and someone found out I had kids. He was like, 'Oh no, but who's feeding them while you're gone?' And I'm like, 'Uh, the same person who always feeds them!'"[7]

Siobhan, who worried that her daughter Rory was underweight, also experienced others' comments as an implicit critique of her parenting.[8] "It's really hard, because we've been subjected to comments from people all the time, like, 'Oh, she's so tiny for her age!' . . . You try to not let that affect you, but it's hard." Her husband, Antoni, attended most medical appointments for their daughter, but Siobhan decided to work from home the day of Rory's most recent appointment so she could attend. "The pediatrician—he's not very politically correct—was like, 'Oh, it's nice to see mom once in awhile at the visit!'" Aghast, I asked how she had responded. Siobhan laughed: "I said, 'Good to see you too.'" Though she made light of the experience, the doctor's comment stayed with her.

Shannon, too, had been on the receiving end of a service provider's negative judgment. Her husband, Richard, was the primary contact for their children's dentist and the one who received reminder texts about upcoming appointments. When Richard had a work conflict and Shannon brought their son to the dentist instead, she found herself chastised: "They were sending so many [texts] that Richard missed the one that said our son shouldn't eat beforehand. . . . The dentist was like, 'He wasn't supposed to eat.' She's like, 'Should *you* be getting these texts?' So, just rude about it."

Recall from chapter 4 how women in Woman-led couples felt pressure to ensure their child was dressed appropriately or that the family conformed to social norms around holidays and cards. Carrie's, Siobhan's, and Shannon's experiences suggest those women's fears were firmly grounded in reality: others might very well hold them to account for perceived neglect of their maternal duties.[9] Given the stakes, nontraditional women's relative emphasis on "social" tasks—cognitive labor related to managing their own and their children's relationships with other people and institutions—made a lot of sense.

Meanwhile, men in Man-led and Balanced couples also faced obstacles to their full participation in parenting routines. Dean noted his explicit discomfort with gatherings dominated by women. Gender, he argued, should not dictate one's household responsibilities. But Dean added a caveat: "I mean, other than maybe talking to other women, which is—I do go. I do take [our son] to the birthday parties a lot, and it's me and a bunch of moms. And that's one reason I don't like it. . . . If [my wife] goes, she'll talk to them, she'll get to know them. And I don't know them." Kurt reported, "I let Meredith deal with more of the social aspects with the kids. I tend to find that, around here, with the kids' birthday parties and things, the class parties, it's usually the moms. . . . I don't really wanna, you know, it's a comfort thing. I don't, like— I'm not comfortable." Phil's frustration was that his wife, Chelsea, had access to more information than he did. He joked that if Chelsea went on strike he would need to steal her iPad to get access to the local moms' group. "There is a dads' group," he admitted, "but it's not anywhere near equivalent."[10]

In short, Man-led couples were not simply a "gender-flipped" version of Woman-led couples. Rather, they blended elements of tradition and change, and most experienced some form of friction between their nontraditional practices and the norms and structures of the world around them. This was most acute in the parenting realm. Women struggled with others' negative appraisal of their involvement, consistent with my earlier argument that "maternal gatekeeping" behaviors partly reflect women's well-founded assumption they will be held more directly accountable for children's outcomes.[11] Meanwhile, men felt excluded from or uncomfortable within mother-centric parenting spaces.

Sharers and Splitters

Alongside Man-led couples like Shannon and Richard, who put more cognitive labor on his plate, were different-gender couples I classified as Balanced: both male and female partners shouldered roughly equal cognitive loads.[12] Though they achieved similar results, Balanced couples reached equality in two distinct ways. In one group, whom I'll call Splitters, each partner specialized in different areas of life, yet both spouses managed roughly equivalent cognitive portfolios. For a second set of Balanced couples—the Sharers—an unusually large proportion of the cognitive work was joint. Specialization was the exception rather than the rule.

Dean and his wife, Molly, fell more on the Splitter end of the spectrum. Dean played a leadership role for cognitive labor related to food, finances, maintenance, and logistics. He is the main calendar-keeper, for example: "I add [events] and check [the schedule] more than she does, because there have been a lot of times where something—like, I'm busy, and she doesn't know. I'm like, 'It's on the calendar!'" His wife, Molly, was not totally unaware of household happenings—she had access to their shared digital calendar and added personal events or family activities she planned—but both partners agreed Dean was ultimately responsible for keeping the family schedule updated.

Meanwhile, Molly managed cognitive work related to cleaning, shopping, and basic childcare. As was true in many nontraditional couples, Molly was also considerably more likely to handle social niceties such as remembering relatives' birthdays and picking out thoughtful gifts. "Gift-giving is her thing," Dean explained. Molly concurred: "I'm the birthday party person, usually. I'm the one who's more cognizant of when [the party] is and, like, getting the gifts and stuff like that."[13] She also handled their two children's wardrobes. If Molly went out of town, Dean explained, she would need to pick out outfits for their daughter before she left: "[Our daughter] has so many clothes, and I can't keep up with them, you know, what goes with what. . . . To me it's just overwhelming. I don't know where they are. I don't know what's supposed to go with what."

Though Molly and Dean had mind-use specialties, they were not operating wholly autonomously. One partner might do the anticipation and monitoring work, but the couple made many decisions together. Every few months, Molly explained, "We've gotta re-talk about [extracurriculars]: do we wanna sign our son up again for swimming and stuff like that?" Similarly, though Dean did more of the meal planning, he and Molly often texted back and forth during the workday about what he should make that evening. The main distinction between the Balanced Splitters and Man- or Woman-led couples was that among the former, partners' roles varied considerably from issue to issue rather than adhering to a global pattern of leader and follower: in some domains Molly did the legwork, and in others Dean took point.

The Splitters' divide-and-conquer approach contrasted with the comparatively inefficient practices of Sharers like Annette and Craig. "A lot of our decisions seem to be common," Annette mused. Indeed, I could not identify a leader or follower in most household domains. Neither Annette nor Craig was more likely to make a meal plan; instead, they agreed on a dinner template—at the time of our interview, fish served with grilled vegetables—and whoever stopped by the grocery store first would confirm with the other that the usual menu was fine. Both partners were on text threads and email chains with friends and family: "Usually we include the other one in every communication for [arranging social plans]," Annette explained. If Craig was scheduling something with his family, he might send the first email, but "I'm in CC, and then we check in: 'Have you heard from someone else that maybe just replied to you?'" Both Annette and Craig attended all pediatrician appointments, and when it came time to schedule the next one, "We both get our calendars out and make sure that it seems that we can do that day."

Sharers did not, of course, do everything together. One partner typically anticipated an upcoming issue and brought it to the other's attention. Annette initiated a discussion about finding a new nanny; Craig set up a system both partners used to keep track of their daughter's changing diet. However, the identity of the initiator varied even within the same topical domain. When I tried to ascertain who the family meal planner was, for instance, I initially found Annette and Craig frustratingly evasive. "We're a little bit of a day-to-day family," Annette explained:

> So, quite often Craig would pick up that night what we were going to be eating for dinner. . . . It's always around the same theme, but once again usually it's, we have an idea of what we're going to be doing. Usually in the morning we're going to check in about that and say . . . 'Do we do fish and veggies as usual?' 'Sounds great.' . . . Usually we check in in the morning and have more of a discussion of, is it a typical night or is it something special?

When the spouses described similar dynamics across multiple domains, however, I came to accept them at their word.[14] In comparison to most other couples, Sharers had an unusually fluid cognitive labor allocation.

The diverse experiences of these Balanced couples suggest there is no one path to equality. Further, they challenge the easy binary of "equal" as good and "unequal" as bad. For instance, you might guess that the Sharers were happiest. Indeed, in a recent study, sociologist Daniel Carlson found that couples who share physical tasks tend to be more satisfied than those who divide and conquer.[15] My data suggest a somewhat more complicated relationship between satisfaction and sharing cognitive labor. For Annette and Craig, sharing seemed to reflect their mutual respect and joint investment in domestic life. Yet for other Sharers, the same behavior took on a more adversarial tone as spouses jockeyed for authority.

Sharers Chelsea and Phil were both cognitively involved in most domains, but this seemed to be because neither trusted the other to handle things independently. They'd recently purchased a new car, recalled Chelsea, and both spouses were involved. "This was gonna be a car that I primarily drove, but Phil knows more about cars and cares more about cars than I do," she explained. But, she added, "I have some strong opinions of my own." When it came time to shop:

We both sort of knew the type of car we wanted to get, but you know, I think I was leaning toward one [model], and he was leaning toward another. We test drove them both, we had a ton of discussions about the pros and cons of each, and really, like, we did tons of research. Probably—maybe we over-researched it, but at the same time, a car is a big thing, so it's tough to over-research. And we really went back and forth. I ended up deciding on the car that he recommended . . . but I really feel like this was not a case of him convincing me, this was a case of me coming around to it on my own.

Though Chelsea summarized the experience as "a case where we really made the decision together," her description made it sound more like two independent decision makers had somehow come to the same conclusion.

Intentional and Unintentional Pathways

Whenever I mention the Man-led and Balanced couples I interviewed, ears perk up. Women who feel overburdened by their own cognitive responsibilities are especially interested in understanding who these "unicorns" are and how they ended up with a nontraditional cognitive labor arrangement. What's different about couples like Annette and Craig or Chelsea and Phil that enables them to buck the status quo? Demographically speaking, I noted more *similarities* than differences between the nontraditional couples and their Woman-led peers. Most came from relatively traditional families of origin featuring a mother who stayed at home or worked part-time or inconsistently during their childhood. Most were highly educated but not substantially more so than their Woman-led peers.[16] Nor were their gender ideologies distinct: the majority of both groups eschewed gender traditionalism and held up household labor equality, or something close to it, as their ideal.[17]

Nearly all Balanced and Man-led couples did, however, share one important characteristic:[18] the female partner equaled or exceeded her husband in terms of the income she earned and/or the number of hours she worked for pay.[19] Nontraditional men earned less than the average male respondent ($77,500 versus $100,000), whereas nontraditional women earned considerably more ($99,000 versus $65,000). Nontraditional women were also more likely to work full-time for pay than the average female participant (93 percent versus 69 percent).[20]

At first glance, these figures support economic theories of housework allocation, which predict that regardless of gender, higher earnings and longer hours will translate into a lower housework load.[21] Yet, as I noted in an earlier chapter, most women in this more powerful economic position—63 percent, to be specific—*also* completed most cognitive labor for their household. It seems that women's career "success" was an important prerequisite for cognitive labor balance or male leadership, but not a guarantee. What, then, was different about the minority of higher-earning (and/or longer-working) women who completed a smaller proportion of cognitive labor? Further, did nontraditional women's relative career success *lead* to cognitive labor equality, or did cognitive equality facilitate their career success?

To begin answering such questions, I looked beyond the numbers to the broader arc of each nontraditional couple's trajectory, paying particular attention to the narratives they used to make sense of their experiences. This qualitative analysis revealed two types of nontraditional couples, each of which was roughly split between Man-led and Balanced. In one group, exemplified by Man-led couple Ronald and Carrie, the presumption of equality or even man-led imbalance emerged early in the relationship and shaped the couple's decisions at key turning points. In a second group, exemplified by Balanced couple Kurt and Meredith, nontraditional outcomes were more accidental than intentional: these couples did not plan for an unconventional allocation but responded flexibly when circumstances nudged them in that direction.[22] Though these two groups' cognitive labor practices looked similar, there were striking differences in how they *felt* about their cognitive labor allocations.

Carrie and Ronald, a White couple, were firmly in the first, intentional group. Carrie leads an organization facilitating connections between academic scientists and potential industry collaborators. She had been on both sides of this equation in previous iterations of her career, first as a lab scientist and later as a biotech startup leader. Before that, though, Carrie was the oldest child of parents she calmly described as "a disaster." Though her parents eventually divorced, she speculated that "they'd probably be happier if they [had] split up when I was younger." Carrie identified one of their major problems as a skewed division of labor: "My mom did everything, and my dad complained about stuff and then sat on the couch." To illustrate her father's domestic incompetence, Carrie recounted an early memory of a trip to the grocery store. "You know, like, Thanksgiving, where you forget something last-minute? [My mom] sent him to the grocery store to pick something up, and . . . he tried to take me or my sister—I was ten and she was five—to help him find the things at the grocery store. Which, first of all, he speaks English and he can read, so I don't understand."

Carrie was not far removed from this context when she met Ronald midway through college. They grew up in the same county and crossed paths in high school but didn't begin dating until both were enrolled in different universities several hours' drive apart. Carrie was surprised when Ronald proposed marriage two years later, before either had graduated. "I think he's just much more traditional than I am," she explained. "I wasn't super, like, 'yay, pro-marriage!' 'Cause my parents were kind of a disaster, as I said. So, I wasn't like, 'The thing I want to do is get married,' you know?"[23] Nevertheless, she accepted his proposal, and the pair wed shortly after commencement.

Ronald, a journalist-turned-communications director, described his own upbringing with considerably more fondness than Carrie. "I had a fabulous relationship with my dad," he recalled, citing the many hours they spent tinkering together in the garage during Ronald's childhood. He was similarly positive about his mother, whose career ascendance—from classroom teaching into local and then regional school administration—Ronald described with pride. "I can't remember a time where my parents didn't both work," he reflected.

Ronald corroborated Carrie's memory of the couple's origin story but added considerably more detail, including the exact day they met and the back-and-forth required to arrange their first date. Though Carrie called him "sentimental," Ronald seemed driven by logic as much as feeling. "I surprised her [with the early engagement]," he explained, because he felt "I had got an amazing thing here; she is amazing, I would be lucky to spend my entire life with her."

Fast-forward two decades, and Ronald and Carrie now live with their two teenage children in a cozy townhome. Both spouses work standard full-time hours and earn well into the six figures, though Carrie's salary is roughly 20 percent higher than Ronald's. Ronald acts as the primary cognitive laborer: he is the family chef and menu planner, travel arranger, social coordinator, and financial manager. He interfaces with service providers and keeps a closer eye on the family schedule. Carrie and Ronald are roughly equally involved in the cognitive aspects of caring for their children, while Carrie keeps a closer handle on cognitive labor related to home maintenance, cleaning, and laundry.

Ronald and Carrie laid the groundwork for their nontraditional approach early on in their relationship. At each major turning point they faced, the presumption of equality (on Carrie's part) or prioritizing her needs (on Ronald's part) steered their decision making. Carrie graduated from college a year before Ronald, for instance, but deferred her plans for graduate school because "I thought it would be more fair if the two of us got to choose a place together, rather than, if I moved someplace then he'd be stuck following me as opposed to us kind of going together." Meanwhile, Ronald recalled his effort to mold his own career around Carrie's professional interests:[24]

> Part of the reason I went into journalism is because Carrie wanted to become a tenure-track professor, and to solve the two-body problem was gonna be next to impossible . . . I was looking for [a career] that played to my strengths that I enjoyed [and] would find rewarding, but that was 100 percent mobile so I could follow her where she needed to go.

Ultimately, Carrie left academia, and both partners pursued careers they had not foreseen in college.

Despite their atypical path, neither Ronald nor Carrie struck me as particularly radical. Indeed, at one point Ronald veered into gender essentialism: "I think there are things that women just are better in tuned to do," he speculated, before quickly adding, "Obviously it's a spectrum, and there are guys who are better." Carrie reported her frustration with the way working mothers were treated and noted how light her domestic workload was in comparison to many of her female peers. Still, she seemed to regard these as societal curiosities rather than personal motivators. The couple's intentionality, it seemed, was more personally than politically driven. Ronald sensed early on he would need to demonstrate his differences from Carrie's father in order to convince her to marry and, later, have kids. "I spent a good chunk of the early part of our relationship paying for the sins of her father," he explained. His primary strategy was to pursue what he called "sweat equity": "Sweat equity is, it doesn't matter what either person does, what actions they're doing. There needs to be a perception from the other that there is an equal level of sweat being put in."[25]

Both Ronald and Carrie sometimes drew on the language of personality to explain their cognitive labor allocation: "He's a bit more sentimental," Carrie said of Ronald. "I'm just more neurotic and logistical than she is," explained Ronald about Carrie. "You know, there are those people who just, like, love that nitty-gritty detail? That's not her."[26] But their use of this trait-based discourse differed in subtle ways from the personal essentialism deployed by Woman-led couples. Both partners retained a strong sense of agency. Carrie was emphatic that "I'm not the person who likes to fill out a spreadsheet. I just am not . . . Ronald is better at detail-y things, anyway." That said, "I can finish things when I need to." Ronald concurred. "I tend to take the lead on all logistics," he offered. "Again, it's because Carrie just really dislikes dealing with all that crap. She's perfectly capable. She'll do it when she has to."

In short, both Carrie and Ronald seemed to believe their current arrangement was a good fit given who they each were. Yet they *also* felt they had the power to shift if it stopped working for either of them. Their economic circumstances—Carrie was the primary breadwinner—may have facilitated the couple's Man-led allocation. But those circumstances were not a coincidence; early on, Ronald proactively molded his own career ambitions around Carrie's.

Though neither Carrie nor Ronald seemed surprised by how their domestic life had shaken out, this was not the case for a second group of nontraditional different-gender couples. Where Ronald and Carrie set out on an unusual path early on, other couples—and particularly the men in those couples—started out with more gender-traditional expectations before circumstances pushed them onto a different trajectory. Kurt and Meredith, White parents of two elementary schoolers, were among this group. When I arrived at their home on a Friday evening, Kurt and his daughter greeted me at the door. He led me to a couch situated in the front window before apologizing and asking if I'd mind waiting while he put dinner for the kids (chicken nuggets) in the oven. His daughter kept me company in the meantime, providing extensive commentary on the family dogs barking at my feet.

When Kurt finished in the kitchen, he began a story with clear echoes of Richard's, featured at the start of this chapter.[27] Upon graduation from college, Kurt's twin dreams were to work in law enforcement or build guitars. He had trouble finding work in either field, however, and instead took what he expected would be a temporary job at a firm where he'd previously interned. Nearly fifteen years later, he remained with the same company, though he had switched roles within it. His income was modest (and only 60 percent of his wife's) and he displayed little passion for the job, yet Kurt had no plans to move on. "My time is more valuable than, you know, than the paycheck," he explained. He appreciated the relative flexibility of his hours and the proximity of his office to his children's school, which enabled him to be the on-call parent most weekdays.

While Kurt and I spoke, his wife, Meredith, remained in her basement office even as the clock inched past 6 p.m. on a Friday. Her apparent dedication to her work as a mortgage underwriter accorded with Kurt's description of her as "a strong-willed workaholic." "She's down[stairs] working right now," he explained:

Technically she doesn't have to be. But more than likely she'll be on her computer tonight until whenever you have her come up here [for the interview], and then probably she'll jump back on until 10:00, 11:00 at night . . . I'd like to think that my job allows me to kind of compensate for the hours that she's more or less forced to put in because of the volatility of her industry.

When Meredith did emerge from the basement to speak with me, she largely corroborated Kurt's assessment. But she also offered more context for her "workaholism." The oldest of seven children, Meredith had visceral memories of her financially precarious childhood. As she watched her parents scramble to make ends meet, Meredith resolved to build a more stable future for herself. Self-reliance became her priority: "I knew that if I was going to be successful, I needed to work hard. I knew that there was no fortune coming my way."[28] Meredith opted to pay her own way through an associate degree rather than "gamble that my parents would fill out the student [financial aid] forms"; ultimately, she left school for full-time work just a few credits shy of a bachelor's.

By the time Kurt and Meredith met through their church, Meredith was confident in her financial future. She recalled telling Kurt during a rocky period in their courtship, "I'm building a life for myself, and you really have a choice, you know? I'm not looking for a person to provide for me, I can provide for myself . . . I am a full person, a whole woman, and I have my own retirement plan, like, money in the bag." Meredith's take-it-or-leave-it attitude contrasted sharply with Kurt's gradual acceptance of his unexpected familial role. When the couple was expecting their first child, Kurt had been contemplating moving to a job at a larger company. Ultimately, he opted to stay where he was, since professional advancement would have meant more travel—a requirement he didn't think would be feasible once their family expanded. By this point in their marriage, "I knew Meredith was never going to just stop and quit working." Meredith recalled halfheartedly offering to "quit my job and be a stay-home mother," since she felt Kurt's "traditional values" initially led him to expect her greater housework participation.[29] Kurt called her bluff, she remembered: "He's like, 'Come on now.' He knows." Over time, Meredith felt Kurt had "morphed into" a more contentedly domestic role.

Yet Kurt acknowledged the gap between the future he'd once imagined and the life he was now living: "There is a level of frustration for me because, again, you know, there's that whole installment of, 'I'm a man, I'm supposed to be a provider of the family.' Yet I see Meredith much more invested in her work than I am." Kurt was proud to be a more involved dad than his own father had been and said he was happy to do more than 50 percent of the household's physical work. He was less pleased, however, with their cognitive labor arrangement: "I would like to see her handle some of, more of the, you know, the mental and cognitive. 'Cause I do feel it's a little off-balanced." Specifically, "some of the recognition things I would like to not have to [do]. Like, tell me something's broken, let me know that, or notice that something's broken . . . and then convey that to me so that I can deal with it. . . . And then the scheduling thing, I would definitely like to see her take a more active role in."

Although Meredith was the driving force behind the couple's arrangement, she, too, sometimes struggled to reconcile her situation with the alternative reality she desired. "I have this dream," she confessed, of being able to "slow down and work less." She fantasized about moving into a lower-pressure industry and devoting more time to her children, but work always got in the way. "I value my children and value the time with them, but I find myself gravitating more toward what is necessary or what feels urgent"—usually, her paid work responsibilities.

Conflicts, both internal and interpersonal, arose among couples like Kurt and Meredith when their own or their spouse's "self" was understood to deviate from an implicitly gendered mold, or when they felt circumstances forced them to go against their nature. Because Meredith, a self-described planner, felt she needed to devote her energy to securing her family's economic future, she frequently watched from the sidelines as her husband fumbled through domestic matters she would have approached differently. Meanwhile Kurt, the self-described "passive" spouse, longed to be as "absorbed" by his career as Meredith was by hers but instead found himself saddled with the work of keeping the family machinery in constant motion.

Kurt was clearly frustrated by what he saw as Meredith's myopic focus on her work, which left him to pick up the pieces. "Meredith is more of the person who forgets to charge their phone and puts it in their purse and it's dead," he explained, "and you're in the emergency room trying to get ahold of somebody and can't. So . . . all of her family, my family, if they need to get ahold of her, they usually go through me." Kurt also resented Meredith's tendency to "get stuck in [her] routine and kind of overlook that something needs to be, you know, fixed or replaced or resolved." Meanwhile, Meredith depicted Kurt as the Bumbler to her Superhuman. "I'm a planner by nature," she explained, hinting that she felt she could do a better job with some of Kurt's cognitive responsibilities, if only she had the capacity to do that work alongside her paid labor.

When we spoke, both partners remained frustrated by an incident from earlier in the day: Kurt had arranged for an exterminator to visit and asked

Meredith, who was working from home, to be ready to let him in. The exterminator was late, and Meredith missed his call. For Kurt, this was an example of Meredith's single-minded focus on her job. "Work differently absorbs her time," he sighed. For Meredith, it was an illustration of Kurt's lackluster planning skills: "You have to give windows for things to happen, right? Like, life isn't always how you plan it. . . . You hope that it's going to go this way. But if not, you always have a contingency."

Where Carrie and Ronald held less essentialist views on the relationship between their personalities and their labor allocation, Kurt and Meredith felt more constrained. As Kurt put it, "You have to kind of work with people's strengths." Like many Woman-led couples, he and Meredith believed a person's nature dictated their household role. Unlike such couples, however, Kurt and Meredith also perceived a mismatch between their socially prescribed role and the one their employment circumstances pushed them toward. They had responded adaptively to her career success and his career stagnation, but neither seemed especially thrilled with the outcome.

Equality does not in itself ensure happiness, it seems; rather, as others have noted, satisfaction is most likely when desires and behaviors are aligned.[30] Man-led and Balanced couples who did not intentionally set out for equality wrestled with an uncomfortable disjuncture between their expectations and their reality. They felt stuck in an arrangement they hadn't quite chosen but couldn't see their way out of. Meanwhile, more intentional couples like Carrie and Ronald remained focused on their own agency. They believed that personality mattered, but they were less "essentialist" about it. In this way, they resembled many of the queer couples whose stories I present in the next chapter.

CHAPTER 6

"WHICH OF YOU IS 'THE WOMAN'?"

Though Olga claimed to be sleep-deprived, I wouldn't have guessed it. She grew increasingly animated as our interview progressed, her curls bouncing each time she moved to illustrate a point. Olga's charisma and humor were palpable; it took little imagination to picture her as a prosecutor delivering cross-examination. The heterosexual enterprise was a recurring target of Olga's sharp wit. She rolled her eyes when I asked what, if anything, she'd set out to do differently than her own parents: "I have found my parents' example to just be irrelevant. I don't think of how we divide labor or do anything in the house based on, what did my mom and dad do? . . . Neither my wife nor I have to do things the way our moms did, because then who would do any of the stuff our dads supposedly did?"

Olga was clearly frustrated by others' tendency to map heterosexual frames onto her relationship with her wife, Andrea. Recalling the process of wedding planning, she said, "Everybody used to ask us how we were splitting up the wedding duties. Kind of implying that one of us would be doing all of it. The implication of the question was always like, 'You're both women, so which of you is 'the woman'? Which, we get that a lot. And the answer is both."

Given Olga's disdain for different-gender couples' inequality, I was somewhat surprised when she estimated doing "a majority" of the cognitive labor in her household, "something like 55 to 60 percent." Andrea put Olga's share even higher, at "maybe 75 percent." Olga described her specialty as "big, kind of run-to-the-finish-line, it's-all-on-your-plate-at-once stuff," much of it cognitive in nature. Andrea, meanwhile, focuses on the "small, day-to-day stuff that adds up over time" or, put another way, "the stuff that just kind of needs to be done almost every day. The neatening up, the putting stuff away."[1]

I spoke with Andrea right after Olga's interview concluded and was struck by the contrast between the two White women. Where Olga radiated energy,

Andrea exuded calm. Olga delighted in long diatribes and humorous asides, but Andrea's conversational style was matter-of-fact with few embellishments. This may have been situational. When we spoke, Andrea, who had given birth to their daughter, was nearing the end of maternity leave and seemed eager to return to her job as an attorney. Caring for an infant had been harder than expected, and she was recovering from a severe case of postpartum depression. Olga had tried hard to lighten Andrea's load. "Basically any decisions that we made in the first three months [after the child's birth], anything that I could make myself responsible for, I did," Olga explained. "As much as humanly possible, I made myself the primary contact or tried to make myself responsible."

Because terms like "Man-led" and "Woman-led" are unhelpful labels for same-gender couples, I refer to spouses like Olga and Andrea, who divide cognitive labor unequally, as Imbalanced queer couples.[2] The majority of queer couples (72 percent) I interviewed fell into this category; I classified the remaining as Balanced. But while cognitive labor inequality was a common thread between Imbalanced queer and Woman-led couples, it took different forms in each group. The average gap between queer partners' contributions was smaller, for one, which meant the distinction between Balanced and Imbalanced queer couples was often a matter of degree rather than kind.[3] Further, most queer respondents took on a combination of cognitive tasks that were male- and female-typed among their Woman-led counterparts. To Olga's point about wedding planning, there were few cases where one partner clearly took on the "woman role" and the other the "man role."

Though equality was held up as a strong shared value by many Imbalanced queer couples, relatively few seemed dissatisfied with their unequal mind-use practices. Partly this was because they engaged in ongoing dialogue with their partner about those practices. "We talk about this all the time," Olga said when I asked her to estimate the proportion of cognitive labor she and Andrea each perform. "This is not something that is abstract." Through this dialogue, they came to understand their cognitive allocation as both mutually chosen and well-suited to their individual natures and current circumstances.

Olga seemed to veer into personal essentialism as she explained why their allocation worked so well:

> I don't think we could change how we do things without changing who we are . . . I would like to carry a little less of the mental burden, a little less of the, "We need to make sure we get the contractor by this date, or else this

thing won't be done." . . . I would like to not worry about that. But I think that's so ingrained to who I am. And to make Andrea someone who does worry about that would so change who she is.

But two things were different about the personality narratives deployed by Imbalanced queer couples. First, the traits they described rarely mapped onto the Bumbler and Superhuman archetypes common among Woman-led couples. Olga, for instance, described herself as improvisational, more "off-the-cuff, figuring things out as I go," whereas Andrea is "the most systematic person you're ever going to meet." I initially pegged Olga as a Bumbler and Andrea as a Superhuman based on remarks like these. But Olga surprised me by subsequently describing herself as the more "pragmatic and detail-oriented" partner, as well as the chief cognitive laborer. I asked her to clarify: wouldn't Andrea's systematic, disciplined approach lead her to be the more detail-oriented, forward-thinking one? Olga thought for a minute before answering:

> You know what it is? It's that Andrea's a lot more a professor. . . . She has sort of a more professorial—she likes to be in her head space, thinking, working on work products. So it's not head in the clouds, per se, but she doesn't want to—not "doesn't want to" . . . it's not her preferred place to be focusing on the nitty-gritty. Whereas I'm very . . . I know I just made myself sound like an idiot. I can also think about things deeply! But I want to be moving and doing and just crossing things off a list . . . I don't know, they're not as inconsistent as I made them sound.

Second, many queer respondents believed they could adjust their existing cognitive labor allocation if they wanted to. When I offered Andrea a magic wand that could grant her an ideal division of labor, she responded, "If Olga had a magic wand—or, I guess it's your magic wand. . . . But if you were granting her what she wanted, and if she wanted me to take on more of the mental load, I think I've got the capacity for it." Contemplating how their labor patterns might change as their daughter grew, Andrea speculated:

> I mean, I guess it could be that the small things of caring for the child, the everyday things, are what I do. And then the bigger issues are what she does. But I don't know that it'll necessarily be like that . . . I guess the point is, we're both very capable people, and it's sort of how we end up assigning things. So, we'll figure it out. We'll sort of talk about what the aspects are and think about what makes sense.

Andrea's belief in her own and Olga's ability to shape and reshape their cognitive labor patterns was largely hypothetical at this point. However, I found that queer couples further along in their parenting journey had indeed managed to keep inequalities in check by thoughtfully managing the way each partner invested in and deployed parenting-related skills.

In this chapter, I first describe queer couples' mind-use patterns before delving into the narratives they use to explain those patterns and, finally, the unique ways they develop and deploy their cognitive labor–related skills. Their stories affirm the challenge of perfectly splitting cognitive responsibilities. But together with the Man-led and Balanced different-gender couples described in chapter 5, they also point to a less essentialist way of understanding the relationship between who we are and how we practice cognitive labor.

"We Each Have Our Things"

Olga and Andrea were one of thirteen Imbalanced queer couples, a group that included roughly equivalent numbers of same-gender female and male couples and encompassed a wide range of cognitive labor allocations. Some Imbalanced couples, like Dustin and Paul, were markedly unequal. Paul manages a theater company, which requires him to work "definitely more than the thirty-five [hours per week] that's on my offer letter." Dustin, meanwhile, acts as primary caretaker for the couple's kindergartener and occasionally picks up part-time paid work. Though Dustin is the (mostly) at-home parent, Paul does the bulk of the family's cognitive labor—about 75 percent, he guessed. "Paul's much more of a planner," Dustin explained. "I'm more active in general," argued Paul. "And also, if I'm at a computer, which I am a lot during the day, sometimes it's easy for me to have a moment where I, you know, detach from work brain for twenty minutes, and I'll be able to easily turn around and look for electricians, you know, and make a few phone calls." Whatever the reason, Paul is the one to find the summer camps, organize the playdates, make plans for the long weekend, troubleshoot issues with their health insurance, and keep track of the car maintenance schedule. Dustin, however, is the primary physical laborer for their household. He does the school pickups and drop-offs, most of the shopping, and the bulk of the laundry, among other tasks.[4]

Most Imbalanced couples, however, looked more like Kristy and Lori: Kristy carries a slightly larger cognitive load overall, but Lori is nevertheless involved in many cognitive tasks.[5] Lori described Kristy as the primary household scheduler, for instance: "She writes things. She has her work calendar that's digital, but she also has her paper book that she keeps all of her stuff in, all of her to-do lists and whatnot. She's much better at daily and weekly maintaining that kind of stuff, making sure that we don't forget." But Lori noted that she is rarely surprised by something Kristy scheduled, since the spouses talk frequently about short- and long-term planning. Similarly, though Kristy does most of the meal planning and inventory management, she and Lori typically sit down together to make a grocery list. Because most Imbalanced couples were, like Lori and Kristy, neither perfectly equal nor vastly unequal, the differences between Imbalanced and Balanced queer couples were often subtle.

Balanced queer couples, like their different-gender counterparts, reached equality in distinct ways. Eliza and Tara were Sharers: both women were cognitively involved in most household domains. However, this did not mean they worked together all the time. The spouses trade off meal planning and cooking on a weekly basis, for instance: one week, Eliza is fully in charge; the next week, it's Tara's turn. Both partners are responsible for scheduling, but one handles medical appointments and the other manages the school calendar. Eliza preferred to have a mutually agreed-upon allocation; when they did not, she noted, they sometimes duplicated their efforts:

> There was, not a lot, but there was some conflict leading up to [planning their child's birthday party]. It was almost as if we were both trying to divide the work, but not really having any explicit conversation about how we were dividing it . . . I had been the one to send out the invitation. I was tracking the RSVP, so I thought I should be the one to say how many people we needed to serve food to. Then Tara had calculated her own number, and it was lower than what I thought we needed, and so then that was another little conflict. . . . We just hadn't talked about it in years, because we hadn't thrown a party in years [due to the Covid-19 pandemic]. . . . We were probably both trying to keep track of it, all the components, in our head, and that's probably what made it stressful and [caused] the conflicts.

Notably, the problem here was not that role ambiguity led one partner to shoulder a heavy load while the other slacked off. Rather, both partners stepped up to lead, hinting at the possibility that this kind of cognitive work was considered desirable—a source of power rather than a mere burden.[6]

Patrick, part of another Balanced couple, offered a different theory about why Tara and Eliza may have struggled with the birthday party planning. He argued that a clear delineation of household responsibilities is particularly important for same-gender couples. While gender acts as a convenient heuristic for different-gender couples, he and his husband, Travis, did not have societal defaults to fall back on: "Because we're both men, and there's no mom in the picture, every single [childcare] task, we had to figure out who's going to do it. There was no norm, and no biological necessity."[7] As a result, "everything is a negotiation, or everything is like a relationship management issue . . . I feel like that's a privilege that we have as two guys; we don't get stuck into social norms."[8]

Unsurprisingly given Patrick's philosophy, he and Travis were Splitters: each man had discrete responsibilities, but the spouses' workloads were roughly equivalent. "Everything related to food, everything related to the car, that's just 100 percent Patrick's wheelhouse," Travis explained. Travis himself was more likely to handle cognitive labor related to home maintenance issues, cleaning and laundry, and shopping.

A third Balanced couple, Linda and Billy—a cisgender woman and transgender man, respectively—deployed a similar Splitter approach. "We each have our things," Linda explained. "Like, we know, 'oh, you're logistics, and you're this.' So things are not surprising. For example, if my family's talking about 'Hey, you guys wanna do X, Y, and Z?' I'll chime in, 'Well, Billy's logistics, he'll take care of that.'" Linda described herself as the "events" person: "Like, 'hey, we want to go out this weekend, what do you wanna do?' Linda is gonna figure out what that is."[9]

Whether Balanced or Imbalanced, most queer respondents' cognitive specialties included a combination of tasks that were male- and female-typed among different-gender couples.[10] Patrick handled cognitive labor related to the family car, but also to meals. Vanessa led maintenance along with cleaning. Joshua led finances and maintenance, but also food and shopping. Even the Imbalanced queer couples who noted similarities between their own relationship and traditional gender roles simultaneously complicated those roles. "Leslie is a little more, maybe a little more masculine than I am," explained primary cognitive laborer Katrina of her wife. "So she tends to do some of the more—she just tends to do some of the more masculine things." But, Katrina continued, "Leslie also does some of the more traditionally defined female things as well," including planning most meals and prompting the family to clean on a regular basis.

Leslie and Katrina did not use the term "butch" or "femme" to describe themselves, but both women described Leslie as a more stereotypically masculine and Katrina a more stereotypically feminine person. This differentiation was somewhat unusual; more commonly, respondents went out of their way to note that they and their partner had similar gender presentations. Among female couples who did hint at a butch/femme dynamic, the femme partner was not always the primary cognitive laborer.[11] Indeed, Lindsay described her cognitive leadership role as a function of her more *masculine* qualities. "I have a more domineering, controlling, traditionally male approach," she noted, "where I'm just like, get it done, you know? . . . [My wife, Pamela,] has a more traditionally female approach, less solution-oriented."

In another Imbalanced couple, Brent explained, "It's the joke, I guess . . . that [my husband] Victor is more of the financial, he's the breadwinner, kind of the man of the house, and I'm the one that's a little bit more hands-on with [our son] and the cleaning and the organizing and the taking care of things and making sure that we're presentable in public." But while Brent saw himself in the "mom's role," I assessed the couple's cognitive labor allocation as slightly skewed toward Victor. Victor handles finances and maintenance but also logistics and managing their son's engagement with the external world.

Regardless of their gender configuration, the *content* of queer couples' cognitive labor looked virtually identical to what I observed among different-gender couples. Same-gender female couples dealt with tricky home maintenance issues; same-gender male couples planned playdates and sent thank-you cards.[12] One exception was the cognitive labor required to become a parent in the first place, which was uniquely extensive for queer couples. To be sure, some different-gender couples struggle to conceive. But the elaborate cognitive work of figuring out *how* to have a child was something nearly all queer couples faced.[13] Same-gender male couples debated whether to adopt or hire a surrogate and navigated complex legal regulations that varied by state. Same-gender female couples had to figure out which partner would carry and how they would acquire sperm, as well as navigate the ups and downs of IVF (in vitro fertilization). Olga, always ready with a quip, summarized the challenge: "It's the actual worst to have a kid when you don't have a sperm and an egg in the same relationship."

Developing Shared Narratives

Equality and fairness emerged as strong values among queer interviewees, whether Balanced or Imbalanced. Yet, like their Woman-led counterparts, most Imbalanced queer couples found an equilibrium state in which they made peace with the gap between their ideal and actual cognitive labor allocation. Unlike their Woman-led counterparts, however, it was not typically personal essentialism that helped keep the peace. Instead, their satisfaction resulted from the conviction that their patterns were mutually chosen and that they fit each partner's idiosyncrasies without being set in stone.

Skylar's response to my question about his ideal cognitive labor allocation was typical of Imbalanced queer respondents: "I like the idea of 50/50," he explained. "If you're able to think, 'I do this, I do exactly half of the work, and you do half of the work,' then I think it just feels good. Then everyone can do their thing." Anthony told a similar story in response to the same question: "I'd probably make it 50/50 on both [of us], just sort of from an equity perspective, feeling like, 'Hey, we're both contributing roughly equal amounts to the household.'" Riley's perspective differed slightly, in that they valued fairness as paramount and argued the ideal was for each partner to contribute equitably, "proportionate to people's assets and needs and abilities."

Nevertheless, most Imbalanced queer respondents acknowledged a gap between equality (or equity) and their current allocation. "I'm probably going to say [cognitive labor is] 80/20 me," estimated Vanessa. Her wife, Whitney, agreed: "I think that Vanessa holds more of the mental load overall in the household, 'cause she just has to manage a lot, a lot more things than me." But when I asked if she would change anything about their cognitive labor allocation, Whitney took a long pause before answering. "No. I think, it takes me a second to think about it, because there's moments where I'm like, 'I wish she would do this!'" On the whole, though, "I'm okay with it. Yes." In another couple, Joshua described his share of the cognitive labor as "probably 60 percent." Surveying the results of the card-sort exercise, he noted that his pile of responsibilities was larger than his husband Erik's: "I win. Or, I lose. I don't know how to think about it." He, too, paused when I asked if he'd change anything about their allocation: "That's a very good question. Sorry. I'm pausing . . . I think I have minor frustrations, but no."

Many queer respondents could name individual tasks they wished their partner would take on or recall occasions they felt overwhelmed by their workload. Katrina wished for Leslie to take more responsibility for managing their daughter's social life, for instance, while Leslie wished for Katrina to help more with meal planning. Yet few couples reported prolonged battles or serious labor-related grievances. "What we have going here is working for us," concluded Katrina. Similarly, Leslie granted that "I think it's very fair, to be honest with you. Like I said, sometimes we argue about it, and you feel like it's not fair, but I think we both try really hard to make sure that it is fair, and that we're both pulling our own weight."

How did Imbalanced queer couples reconcile their egalitarian ideal with their unequal reality? One factor seemed to be the favorable comparisons they drew between themselves and different-gender couples. Scholars studying couples' justifications for housework inequality have noted the importance of a carefully chosen comparison point.[14] For different-gender couples, the reference is often one's parents. *At least I do a lot more than my dad did*, a man might tell himself. *At least I get more help than my mom did*, a woman might say.

For the Imbalanced queer couples I interviewed, different-gender couples—either specific friends or a more open-ended evocation of heterosexual culture—provided similarly favorable comparisons. "I think part of the good thing about being a queer couple," explained Karen, "is that we can just kind of decide if there is something that—like, I like doing the dishes. . . . But it's not a homemaker type of thing. It's not like I have to do the dishes because I'm the woman in the relationship." Lori said she and Kristy "feel really lucky" not to have strong gender stereotypes to contend with. "There's a lot of frustrating things about being a two-mom family, and this one seems like a huge bonus, to not have to deal with that." Joshua observed that "almost to a person" among his heterosexual friends, "it's not even. The men get patted on the back for being involved fathers. And it's like, okay, great. You're doing better than your dad did, but it's not even . . . I think [my husband and I] are able to be more equitable, because we don't have that."[15]

In addition to these favorable comparisons, Imbalanced queer couples reached equilibrium through ongoing dialogue with their partner about their division of labor. In the process, they created shared narratives about both the "facts" (i.e., who was doing what) and the reasons for their allocation, coming to see their patterns as mutually chosen but not fixed.[16] "We're so communicative about this, all the time," explained Olga. "I start apologizing to Andrea, like, 'Oh my god, you've been doing too much. I'm so sorry.' And she always says, very genuinely, 'No, I think you're doing more than I am right now.'" When I asked Derek how his partner's career shaped Derek's thinking about his own work, he said, "We were just talking about this, this morning. . . . He works many small jobs, piecing everything together, really hustling. It's a lot of energy. It's a very inefficient way to earn money." As a result, Derek prioritizes stability and flexibility in his own work and takes on a larger share of the domestic labor.

This spousal communication did not typically take the form of a premeditated plan for dividing labor. Like respondents in Woman-led couples, queer respondents often recalled that responsibilities had been "organically" allocated or simply "fallen into place" without explicit discussion when the partners moved in together. But most queer respondents also described ongoing dialogue in which they reflected on, and in some cases decided to adjust, their labor patterns. "Like the good lesbians that we are," joked Kristy, "we talk about everything. There is nothing left unsaid for the most part." Around the time of our interview, for example, an article about "mental load" went viral. "We both read it," said Lori, "and [Kristy] was like, 'I think that's you [carrying the load], not me.'" Since then they'd been working on making incremental adjustments. Kristy explained:

> We were reading [the article] and kind of laughing at ourselves, because I think Lori carries more of the emotional load, and I think that it's a little bit self-inflicted, and a little bit that I need to step up and take more because she feels like that. Like for packing. I pack in thirty minutes, and if I forget something, it doesn't bother me. . . . And she takes hours to pack and has lists. And if she forgets something, it's deeply distressing for her, regardless of how necessary the item is. . . . She gets more stressed out about packing because she sees that I'm not thinking it through enough, and so she feels like she needs to pack for both of us. So we've talked about how to have her let me help, and what kind of things I can do to help her with the stress of getting ready to [travel]. I'm trying to say, "I will do our son's packing, and I will think through each of the things." And, "What do you need me to check in with you [about] so you're not stressed out that I forgot something?"

I was struck by the complexity of Kristy's analysis, which emphasized both partners' contribution to the problem. Lori needed to be "willing to let go and let someone else help," and Kristy needed to "step up and take more." When similar dynamics came up among Woman-led couples, the dialogue was not typically so productive, in part because they framed their patterns as evidence of unchangeable traits rather than solvable problems.

To be clear, it was not that different-gender couples didn't have discussions about household labor. But their discussions tended to be more tactical than strategic. For example, Eddie, a cisgender man partnered with a cisgender woman, explained:

> We're not very organized in that way in the house, in terms of delegating responsibilities to each other. We try to work together to be organized enough to delegate tasks to the kids, but with each other we just kind of, *do*, you know what I mean? If she needs help or if she needs me to do

something, it's like, "Hey, do this." Or if I need her to do something, it's like, "Hey, do this." So, yeah, we rely on each other a lot, but I don't think that we really think about it.

With big-picture discussions few and far between, men in Woman-led couples often relied on their ability to "sense" their partner's mood and adjust their own behavior accordingly. "I'm kind of always trying to perceive where she's at," explained Bradley, "and if I can tell she's got too much on her plate, I'm going to vacuum downstairs" or pick up another task. Women in Woman-led couples were more likely than men to describe reflective conversations. Often, however, these were conversations with female friends and family rather than their partner. When I interviewed Kendra immediately after I spoke with her husband, Troy, she admitted she'd been eavesdropping on parts of his interview: "I know I wasn't supposed to be listening, but when he said, 'This is really refreshing to think about [our dynamics] in this way,' it kills me. . . . How do you not think about that? It's not just people my age, it's my mom, and my mom's friends, they are all having the same thoughts." I asked her whether she'd talked with Troy about these issues. "We have talked about it," she admitted. But nothing really stuck. "I think our approaches are so different," she mused. Ultimately, she'd concluded that "nobody is going to change their stripes at this point."

In addition to talking more openly with each other about cognitive labor–related issues, queer couples tended to have a more optimistic take on the question of whether one could "change their stripes." It wasn't that they viewed personality as irrelevant. As Olga, quoted earlier, put it, the lead cognitive laborer role was "ingrained to who I am." Others echoed this sentiment when asked to speculate about the reasons for their unequal division of cognitive labor. "It's grounded in personality, probably," guessed Derek. The allocation "plays to our natural strengths," suggested Cody. A desire to plan ahead was "just how I'm wired," explained Paul.

As was true for Woman-led couples, queer respondents' belief that cognitive labor was an outgrowth of one's personality sometimes discouraged reallocation efforts. This dynamic was especially acute for Riley and Cameron, among the most imbalanced queer couples I interviewed. Riley, who is nonbinary, does most of the cognitive labor for their family of four. Their husband, Cameron, admitted that "I can't organize a schedule or, you know, keep a to-do list to save my life." Later, Cameron mused in amazement that Riley "has somehow this magic timeline in their head that says, like, 'Okay, in order for us to do this here, then we first have to do this and this and this and this, and before we can do this, we need this and . . .' Yeah, my brain isn't as skilled at that." Offered an opportunity to magically achieve his ideal cognitive labor allocation, Cameron seemed doubtful: "Does your magic wand work on my brain?" He'd like a 50/50 split, he said, but that would only be possible "if you fix my brain."

This belief—that to take on more cognitive labor Cameron's brain would have to be "fixed"—mirrors the perspective of many women in Woman-led couples, who argued that changing their husband's brain would be a prerequisite for reaching mind-use equality. Yet there were also subtle distinctions between queer respondents' personality narratives and the personal essentialism I observed among Woman-led couples. Recall that among the latter, two archetypes—the Superhuman and the Bumbler—emerged. These characters, though not explicitly gendered, map neatly onto existing gender stereotypes. The Superhuman conjures images of the all-knowing, all-seeing mother; the nagging wife; the brains behind male brawn. The Bumbler, meanwhile, connotes the clueless sitcom dad; the childlike husband; the charismatic but ineffective male politician.

Like their Woman-led counterparts, queer couples relied heavily on the assumption that one's nature should dictate one's cognitive labor role. But the "selves" queer respondents described were often amalgamations of Bumbler and Superhuman, coupled with idiosyncratic characterizations I couldn't map onto any archetype. "Our brains operate completely differently," testified Joshua. For instance, "Our memories are perfectly opposite. Erik will remember anything somebody told him about their life, and I will forget that somebody had a kid. But then I know our credit card number by heart and he, however many times he has to punch it in, he'll just never remember a number." Other queer respondents offered similarly hard-to-classify statements about their distinct natures. "I sometimes joke that Patrick thinks in time, and I think in space," said Travis. "So I'm in charge of how things look, I make aesthetic decisions . . . I know where everything is supposed to be in the apartment, and where it usually is. And Patrick does not. But he knows when everything is happening and how long it takes to get there." Vanessa described Whitney as focused on "the moment-to-moment stuff, and . . . the very long-term," while Vanessa managed everything in-between.

These patterns—ongoing discussions about their division of labor, through which queer couples developed nuanced narratives about spousal difference—were not universal. A handful of respondents in Imbalanced queer couples were markedly dissatisfied with their cognitive labor allocation and seemed unable to agree on either a shared explanation or a path to change. Riley and Cameron were in this camp, the former frustrated by their exponentially larger cognitive load, and the latter embarrassed that he couldn't seem to get his brain to work as he wanted it to. Ultimately, though, the spouses' shared belief that it was Cameron's temperament that kept him from completing more cognitive work seemed to defuse the tension, much as a related narrative helped many Woman-led couples accept their status quo.

Lindsay and Pamela, however, were mired in ongoing conflict. Their struggles seemed to stem from a lack of collaborative discussion and from Pamela's belief that change was not possible given who they each were. In response to my question about what Lindsay imagined was on Pamela's to-do list, Lindsay began venting:

> I have no idea. I think this is actually a thing in our relationship that we continually need to work on. Which is, I feel like I do everything and Pamela feels like that's not true and that things are pretty equal. So I don't actually know what's on her list family-wise. Like it feels to me like—and this is where I think the gap comes in—that she doesn't have anything on her list family-wise. . . . Other things on my list are "pay the bills" or "transfer the money," like, I do all the financial stuff. I also manage all the vendors. We have these home maintenance people that I need to call, and I need to get the toilet fixed and this kind of thing. Yeah, I don't think she has that stuff on her list. I don't know what's on her list.

Lindsay was frustrated by her heavy workload but also by what she saw as a lack of productive communication between herself and Pamela. I asked Lindsay whether the couple had made any conscious decisions about how to allocate tasks. "No," she admitted:

> This is just sort of how it's fallen into place. Honestly, I would like to have those conversations more, but it's a sort of a pain point in our relationship that I feel like, "Oh, I do so many more things than you do. I spend so much more time doing things than you do." And she's like, "That's not true." And then we end up arguing about it, and then it goes nowhere.

When I spoke to her the following afternoon, Pamela mentioned that the spouses had recently begun seeing a marriage counselor, in part to deal with labor-related conflicts. Pamela recognized that Lindsay "manages a lot of the logistics" and "back-of-the-house" work for their family, but she attributed their uneven cognitive loads to Lindsay's "strong project manager energy":

> She'll just like, bring that [energy]. It's tricky. I hate it. I hate doing that kind of thing. And I often get feedback from her that I have not done it well. So, I was like, "Great, you do it! I hate it." But then there's some resentment that comes with that, because I think she feels like she's doing a lot more than I do. And we have talked about [that] at length in therapy.

Lindsay shared Pamela's assessment of the spouses' differences, which—unlike most Imbalanced queer couples—roughly mapped onto the Superhuman and Bumbler archetypes: "I'm good at remembering and planning and organizing, and Pamela is not."

Lindsay's ideal compromise would be for Pamela to do 100 percent of the physical labor and herself to do 100 percent of the cognitive labor. Lindsay hadn't broached this possibility with Pamela, however: "I don't know that she would agree with it. It's a really good topic of conversation. . . . [Our allocation] comes up only at times of conflict, I think that's really the issue." In the absence of more "neutral" discussions about how they divided labor and why that worked for them, Pamela and Lindsay had not managed to generate a common narrative. For slightly different reasons, both seemed skeptical that reallocation was likely or even desirable given their differences.

Pathways to (In)equality

When I examined mind-use inequalities among Woman-led couples, I found that partners invested differently in building relevant skills and relationships. Over time, small gaps snowballed into seemingly unbridgeable differences. Imbalanced queer partners also invested differently. But rather than one partner investing and the other largely opting out, each partner tended to make comparable investments, albeit in different domains of domestic life. Further, skill gaps were more commonly recognized as such, rather than interpreted as evidence of partners' distinct—and unchangeable—temperaments.

This was true of Erik and Joshua, a White couple with a toddler at home and a second child on the way. Erik, a product manager, began apologizing as soon as he joined our video call. It was 8:30 p.m., and he'd been in the middle of bathing his daughter when he remembered our appointment. (The following day Joshua, an entrepreneur, would tell me that in fact he'd been the one to remind Erik about the interview.) She had splashed water all over Erik's work clothes, and now here he was in a T-shirt, taking the call from bed—horribly unprofessional, he apologized, but hoped I would understand.

I didn't mind in the slightest, but given this first impression I was not terribly surprised when Erik's and Joshua's interviews both confirmed Joshua as the primary cognitive laborer for their household. In the lead-up to parenthood, Joshua recalled, "I basically did all the gear. I'm the researcher of the two of us." Erik concurred: "I knew that Joshua was going to do all of this comprehensive research, of his own accord, and that I would just Google what is the best one and put that on the registry. So, that [he would manage it], I think, was pretty clear." It was Joshua, too, who had read the parenting books and summarized them for Erik, and Joshua who was primarily interfacing with the couple's surrogate, who was due to deliver their second child in the fall.

Joshua and Erik's story includes clear echoes of the differential investment dynamics that characterized Woman-led couples. Joshua's cognitive workload was larger than Erik's at least partly because he spent considerably more time and energy on tasks like learning which companies make the best strollers or how often and by what channels their surrogate preferred to communicate. When a new gear need arose, then, Joshua was clearly in a better position to meet it. If an issue with the surrogate came up, Joshua was undoubtedly the best person to broach it.

But there were parallel areas of responsibility in which Erik had invested in building his capacity and Joshua remained relatively ignorant. "We assumed [going into parenthood] that I would be more of the organizational person, with clothing and laundry," recalled Erik, "and he would probably be more of the food person. . . . He's often the research daddy. I'm clothing daddy, he's food daddy, et cetera, that's our shorthand." Though Joshua's product research was painstaking, Erik described him as frustratingly "laid-back and relaxed" in other circumstances. Joshua concurred:

[Erik] is clothing daddy. And that began even before our daughter was born. He definitely got the hand-me-downs from friends, washed them, sorted them, the whole thing. He also wanted to work with an organizer because, again, he cares about things being orderly and I don't. He got everything sort of set up in its proper place.

Rather than one partner investing a lot and the other a little, Joshua and Erik each invested in accumulating knowledge and relationships related to some aspects of domestic life while neglecting others.[17]

Similarly specialized investment patterns were common among Imbalanced queer couples, though some took pains to keep their skill differentiation in check. Olga and Andrea had recently hired an au pair, and in preparation for her arrival the agency asked them to complete extensive paperwork. They planned to tackle it together, Olga explained:

> There's a lot of inefficiencies in this marriage, I'm realizing as I talk to you. There's no reason that we both need to do every part of the [paperwork]. But I think we both like to, this is kind of one of our "value" things. I don't think we like having separate spheres . . . I think we just both really like to know what's going on. I like to feel very in control of my space, and I think Andrea does, too. And the best way to do that is to just share control and be really cognizant of what is happening because I'm picky, and maybe Andrea's picky, too.

For same-gender female couples, the feminized nature of parenting infrastructure facilitated such parallel investment: neither partner was at a clear advantage in building relationships with other mothers or accessing parenting resources overwhelmingly directed at women. Kristy noted that she and her wife were both members of a local mothers' group on Facebook, "which is unique when you are a lesbian couple, because both of the moms are on it. . . . Some people use it as a bit of a venting forum, but they also post a ton of, 'Hey, I learned this about X.' So there are lots of articles, blogs, et cetera, about sleeping, eating, everything." Though Kristy admitted Lori was "more diligent" about reading the posts, both women used the forum as a resource. Similarly, Olga noted that she and Andrea were each able to tap into their networks of female friends before their daughter was born: "We both called friends who had been pregnant and were young parents and got advice."

In addition to their differential investment, it was common for Woman-led couples to practice differential deployment: that is, for the man to reserve the bulk of his mental bandwidth for professional pursuits. This kind of differential deployment was rare among queer couples, and virtually absent among same-gender female couples. This might be in part because partners in such couples typically had comparable earnings. In cases where there was a wider spread, however, it was typically the *higher*-earning woman who played the lead cognitive labor role, consistent with prior scholarship showing that the currencies of power are not identical across all relationship types.[18]

A few male couples had established a career hierarchy in which one partner went all-in on his career while the other acted as lead parent. Notably, however, they remained cognizant of this as a choice that cost *both* partners dearly: one had to temper his professional ambitions, while the other missed out on closeness with his children. Though Cody, a psychologist, and his husband, James, a lawyer, both worked for pay, they were clear that Cody was the primary caregiver for their two elementary schoolers and James was the primary breadwinner. But Cody and James, both White men, stood out for their mutual recognition that this division was the product of deliberate choices that set off a chain reaction of consequences, none of which had been inevitable at the start of their relationship.[19]

Cody exuded a complex mixture of resignation and wistfulness as he reflected on the decisions he and James made about how to structure their lives together: "From the beginning, we were very aware of how much more flexibility there would be for me in my career path than for him [in his]. . . . From very early on, we said I would be primary caregiver and he would be more of the primary breadwinner." James, a more exuberant presence, concurred. He recalled the months before their eldest child's birth, when the couple lived in a minuscule apartment with a refrigerator in the living room and made a pivotal decision:

> We said, "This is going to be hard, to raise a—or multiple—kids in this kind of space." So then we had this very conscious conversation about my having the ability to earn significantly more than I was earning. [By] doing work that was not necessarily satisfying or nourishing but was financially nourishing, and therefore [helping] to achieve our other life goals. This was a very planful, "Okay, you're going to be primary caregiver, I'm going to be primary earner." [Cody] will [also] earn, and I will [also] caregive. But we would have these primaries.

James was in a particularly reflective mood, perhaps because we spoke during a period of professional transition for him. "I don't know that I would necessarily change anything about [what we did]," he mused:

> Although now having lived it, I've learned some of the additional emotional and other elements to it, that I wasn't necessarily expecting when we pushed off from shore. . . . I'll just say that one of the things that's hard for me is that—not to turn this into a therapy session—but the kids will, I'll be standing right there, and Cody will be in the living room. They'll scream, "Daddy!" I'm Pop, and he's Daddy. They'll want him for something, and I will say to them, "Guys, I am right here. You can ask me anything."

Though this broke James's heart, just a little, he believed the kids' affinity for Cody was more a function of Cody's greater time and energy investment than a referendum on James's parenting abilities. "Sometimes I feel like I have fewer opportunities to do the groundwork that is necessary to shift [the dynamic]," James explained. "It's not like the kids know that we made a decision that he would be primary caregiver, and I would be primary earner. But that is a muscle that gets built up over time." James's muscle analogy was remarkably similar to the way I'd come to think about cognitive labor as driven by a set of skills that could be practiced and perfected, rather than an inborn capacity some had and others lacked.

After an interruption from a colleague, James continued, succinctly summarizing the cumulative effects of his and Cody's respective focus on professional and domestic growth: "Anyway, these decisions then have reinforcing consequences, such that if I'm responsible for 75–80 percent of our income, which I have been . . . then the job is such that until . . ." He trailed off briefly before concluding, "It takes a long time to turn the ship at sea." Later, he specified some of the "reinforcing consequences" he had in mind:

> In some ways, my story's been the same story for fifteen years. I've been doing the same job, basically the same way, and earning at a high level. But also not being available. A result of that has been not being available for things. So, for instance, [Cody] develops the relationships with the teachers, because he's present and I'm not. He's going to be able to go into school, and volunteer on a school day.

Whereas members of Woman-led couples typically argued or implied that their labor allocation was more or less inevitable given who they were, James's focus on skills and relationships helped him maintain a sense of agency: "We chose this, right? Nobody forced me to take this job. Nobody forced us to have kids. Nobody forced us to have *two* kids. Nobody forced us to do surrogacy. . . . Nobody forced us to buy a second home. All the things we've done, we did— this was a plan, and we did it." Despite the cumulative weight of those choices, James remained optimistic that he and Cody could alter, though perhaps not fully reverse, their course going forward. In fact, the day we spoke James had just given notice at his corporate law firm and was making plans to move to a nonprofit. Cody was preparing to expand his private practice, with the anticipation that James would be more available on nights and weekends and have more schedule flexibility overall. Though neither man was expecting to close the domestic capacity gap that had widened over nearly a decade, they were hopeful about narrowing it.

Queer couples' cognitive labor practices, narratives, and trajectories both reflect and refract the patterns I documented earlier among Woman-led couples. Particularly striking was how, like their different-gender counterparts, queer respondents frequently drew a straight line between their individual natures and their cognitive labor practices. Yet the "natures" in question did not coalesce into a clear taxonomy of types. Perhaps this will change over time as queer parenting becomes both more common and more socially visible; clearer social scripts may emerge that render extensive dialogue between partners less necessary. But for now, as Patrick, quoted earlier, put it, "Everything is a negotiation." I nodded along with him before asking, "Is that exhausting, to have to negotiate, or decide everything proactively?" Patrick was dismissive but kind: "I've never felt exhausted by it. But I can imagine it getting exhausting, especially if you don't get along with your partner. I'm super lucky." Though Patrick and his husband, Travis, might indeed be "lucky," it struck me that they had surely played a part in creating that luck for themselves.

CONCLUSION

Desiree and I sat side by side on a brown sectional in her living room. Danny, her husband, had taken their infant outside, but no one had bothered to turn off the rocking bassinet, which continued to sway rhythmically as we spoke. Desiree sighed as she recounted a recurring conflict with Danny:

> Sometimes when we are arguing, I have to remind him that even though the stuff I'm doing is "easy"—I'm not out there mowing the grass—I'm actually doing a lot of stuff. . . . Making sure the baby has all his stuff, all his diapers and stuff like that. Or paying the bills. Organizing stuff for the house. Making sure appointments—like, keeping track of everything, pretty much.

In households across the country, people like Desiree are hard at work. They are solving problems, or preventing them from arising in the first place. They are sorting through a glut of information and advice to determine the best path forward. They are reminding others to follow through on their commitments. Their efforts, though not always apparent to observers, are critical to their family's functioning. And these invisible laborers are overwhelmingly women.

When we exclude non-physical forms of labor from our understanding of housework, we fail to recognize the full scope of gender differences in family life. Cognitive labor emerged from my research as a ubiquitous, highly feminized dimension of household labor that is poorly captured by the time-based measures we normally use to measure such work. In the majority of different-gender couples I interviewed, women carried a heavier cognitive load, and one that was disproportionately weighted toward relatively high-burden but low-benefit activities.

This largely invisible inequality helps prop up its more visible counterparts. On the one hand, so long as cognitive responsibility remains firmly in women's hands, men's physical labor contributions will also be limited. Far more couples *talked* about offsetting inequality in these two dimensions (e.g., she plans, he executes) than actually achieved it. Rightly or wrongly, many women agreed with my interviewee Colleen: "If I make the list, then I already had to think about it, and I might as well just do it." Cognitive and physical labor may be distinct dimensions of household life, but they are closely tied. On the other hand, even if time-use patterns do change, mind-use patterns will not necessarily follow. When men did take on additional physical work, sometimes following changes to their employment circumstances, women often retained the associated cognitive labor: providing detailed instructions about what to pack in a child's lunch, offering reminders that the trash hadn't been taken out, suggesting the purchase of a specific gift for an upcoming birthday. Movement toward greater physical labor equality does not necessarily imply movement toward greater cognitive equality.

Of course, these insights beg a further question: *why* is cognitive work so stubbornly feminized? The personal essentialist narrative, a logical extension of cultural scripts that tell us our personality and preferences are core to who we are, offers an important clue.[1] Many members of Woman-led couples described their unequal cognitive contributions as a reflection of partners' distinct natures. In the aggregate, those natures were highly gendered: women were depicted as Superhumans, men as Bumblers. In individual households, however, they were experienced as deeply personal and thus impossible to change.

This narrative is appealing in part because the "gender revolution" of the past half century has disproportionately focused on behaviors. We've repeatedly told women they can do anything they want—with "do" often defined primarily in terms of careers. This is important but incomplete work. "Doing" gender involves habits of mind as well as action.[2] Yet the range of acceptable *activities* for men and women appears to be expanding faster than the range of acceptable *selves*.[3] Perhaps this is because behavior is understood as subject to conscious control in a way thought, attention, and perception are not. Thus, the latter may be seen as truer manifestations of one's essence. And in turn, the social costs of nontraditional ways of "thinking" gender may be even higher than the costs of nontraditional ways of doing gender.[4]

When they recast gender inequality as personal difference, Woman-led couples downplayed their own agency and overlooked opportunities for change. But this is not primarily a story of self-deception. Rather, it is a tale of creative—if largely subconscious—problem-solving. The personal essentialist narrative provides a way out for couples squeezed on both sides: by social norms and personal values that point toward equality, and by structural constraints that render that equality exceedingly difficult to achieve.

Man-led, Balanced, and Imbalanced queer couples were not immune to the siren song of individual personality; however, many found alternative ways of relating to it. Often, that meant holding onto a looser, less essentialist version of the personality narrative, one that acknowledged the role of skills alongside traits. Social and cultural forces alternately enabled and constrained their non-traditional paths. For Man-led and Balanced different-gender couples, women's relative career success emerged as a necessary—but not sufficient—condition for a nontraditional cognitive labor allocation;[5] however, gendered account-ability structures and parenting networks placed limits on how far such couples could stray from the status quo. Meanwhile, queer couples took advantage of their unique relationship to familiar gender binaries to carve out arrangements that relied less heavily on personal or gender essentialism. Though they did not typically land on precise equality, their commitment to discussing their labor arrangement with each other, coupled with an openness to future change, meant any imbalances were acknowledged and regularly revisited.

Toward a Sociology of Mind-use

To fully understand how gender operates among contemporary families, we need an expanded sociology of household labor that accounts for mind-use alongside time-use. My findings suggest that a disproportionate focus on ac-tions we can easily see and measure with a stopwatch prevents us from under-standing major sources of inequality within families. While there are countless questions for Housework 2.0 scholars to take up, I see three topics as particu-larly pressing: consequences, measurement, and variation.

First, what are the consequences of a heavy cognitive labor burden? We already know that women experience higher levels of stress and anxiety, lower relationship satisfaction, more limited career growth, and reduced political participation compared with men.[6] While the causes of such gender dispari-ties are multifaceted, women's disproportionate cognitive labor burden may be an important ingredient. As I argued in chapter 1, cognitive labor is taxing—particularly when it is complex and abstract, as the most feminized cognitive tasks tend to be. It also carries an opportunity cost: when a woman's brain is constantly pinging with thoughts about who needs to be where when, or what needs to be purchased for whom, she has less mental bandwidth available for concerns related to her employment, or national politics, or her hobbies.

My study was not designed to measure such effects, but emerging research is beginning to connect the dots between cognitive burdens and gender gaps in other domains. For example, sociologist Reilly Kincaid has shown how mothers' decision-making responsibility contributes to a disruptive "spillover" of family life into their paid employment.[7] Sociologists Richard Petts and Daniel Carlson find that mothers' performance of cognitive labor during the Covid-19 pandemic was negatively associated with their psychological well-being.[8] And political scientist Ana Weeks identified cognitive labor load as one driver of the relationship between gender and interest in political affairs.[9]

Studies like these represent an important step in the development of a sociology of mind-use, demonstrating the importance of this topic for people interested in population health, economic growth, and political engagement, among other issues. But to move this nascent field forward, we need to address a second question: how can we best measure cognitive labor load at scale? Unfortunately, we cannot simply add cognitive labor as another category for time-trackers to record or include a new survey question asking respondents to estimate what proportion of their household's cognitive labor they complete. As I've shown, time-use and mind-use are only loosely related, and the experience of cognitive labor is difficult to translate into counts or percentages. To accurately measure household contributions in multiple dimensions, we will instead need to augment time-use measures with new tools better suited to capturing non-physical household contributions.

What might such a mind-use measurement tool look like? One approach, currently pursued by several scholarly teams, is to develop a cognitive labor inventory similar to the one I employed in my interviews, comprised of tasks carefully chosen to represent diverse substantive domains (e.g., cooking, maintenance) and forms of cognitive labor (e.g., anticipation, decision making).[10] Respondents specify who in their household completes each task, and researchers then sum up their responses to determine which partner is the primary cognitive laborer and roughly what proportion of such work they complete.

This is a promising strategy. Its focus on specific tasks rather than overall patterns avoids the pitfalls associated with asking respondents to summarize dispersed behaviors. Relative proportion (i.e., this task is something I "usually" or "mostly" do), rather than counts or time estimates (i.e., I do this X times per day or spend X hours per week), is closer to the way people actually process cognitive labor. This tool is also simple enough to be incorporated as a module in large-scale surveys with relatively limited marginal cost, increasing its accessibility to researchers who depend on secondary data.

Still, the inventory method is not without flaws. Descriptors like "usually" and "mostly" are open to interpretation, and individuals may have very different ideas about what it means to share a task.[11] When I debriefed the card-sort activity during interviews, for example, I asked participants to explain why they had classified some tasks as shared. Some gave themselves or their partner credit if they had *ever* done a task or even if they could simply imagine doing so in the future. Others were much more selective about assigning joint credit. Still others struggled to translate an idiosyncratic allocation into categorical terms: if Partner A is *currently* doing all the meal planning, but Partner B used to, who should get credit? The cognitive inventory format is also susceptible to the biases that always accompany retrospective self-reports, such as a tendency to nudge one's answers toward perceived social norms or into alignment with personal values and identities.[12] A respondent committed to egalitarian practices, for instance, might err more on the side of reporting "shared" tasks.

A second approach to measuring mind-use would build on the accumulated wisdom of time-use researchers and instead aim to record what people do— or, in this case, think—in real time, rather than ask them to summarize after the fact. This could take the form of a log or diary in which participants record their cognitive activities over the course of the day, analogous to the decision logs I asked Phase 1 interviewees to complete. Detailed, specific instructions developed via extensive testing would be necessary to produce reliable results. Cognitive labor is an unfamiliar concept for many, and cognitive work may not be registered as such by participants. Capturing anticipation and monitoring work, which are simultaneously the most female-typed and the least visible cognitive subtypes, would likely be most challenging. This diary approach would also be considerably more resource-intensive than the inventory, requiring more effort from respondents to complete and from researchers to evaluate. Nevertheless, I suspect that if executed well, the diary method would ultimately yield more accurate results, much as time-diary data has proved more accurate than survey data in the study of physical household labor.[13]

A third critical question is how cognitive labor patterns—what people do but also how they make sense of those behaviors—vary across diverse populations. My sample, while carefully crafted to answer my research questions, is neither random nor representative. I spoke with millionaires and the just-scraping-by, with people born in the United States and those born an ocean away, with White and Latinx and Black Americans. Still, most of my respondents are middle- or upper-middle-class, native-born, and White. The relative privilege of this group likely insulates them from forms of cognitive labor others must routinely contend with: preparing their children for, and protecting them from, racism; applying for and maintaining eligibility for public benefits; navigating byzantine immigration requirements.[14] Further, as sociologist Dawn M. Dow and others writing in the Black feminist tradition have shown, definitions of "good" motherhood, and of the relationship between an individual household and a broader community, vary across racial and ethnic groups in ways that likely impact dominant narratives about cognitive labor (in)equality.[15] I eagerly await the future research that will unpack this diversity in more depth than I can here.

The Road Ahead

Every now and again, someone asks me about the ideal solution to the problem of cognitive labor inequality. What, they want to know, is the end goal? My vision is not, to some questioners' surprise, that every couple divide their cognitive labor 50/50. Though it sounds nice in theory, in practice such an outcome would ignore the incredible diversity of circumstances, preferences, skills, and beliefs that characterize individuals and couples. Instead, I imagine a future in which each couple aligns their ideal and actual divisions of cognitive labor and, in the aggregate, gender ceases to be the best predictor of mind-use patterns. In this dream world, there would be just as many Man- as Woman-led couples. Cognitive labor would also have a smaller footprint overall: that is, family life wouldn't be quite so mentally taxing.

We are far from that future, but I remain optimistic. Concerted effort at all levels of society, from individuals up through the federal government, could disrupt the status quo and bring about a more equitable and less onerous cognitive labor future. Three general strategies should guide our collective next steps. First is *recognition*: social change rarely occurs without the committed efforts of those who have named a problem, deemed its persistence unacceptable, and mobilized a powerful coalition to work toward change. This process is well underway in the case of physical household labor: activists, scholars, and policymakers have identified housework as important labor, despite its unpaid status, and documented its unequal distribution across society.[16] Their advocacy has helped many others hone their awareness of the unpaid and underappreciated labor keeping families, and by extension society, running.

There are promising signs that awareness of household labor is broadening beyond its physical forms. When I began this research in 2017, I met few people who had heard of cognitive labor or one of its near-synonyms. Seven years later, as I finish this manuscript, most of my interlocutors are at least somewhat familiar with the concept. What changed? Several articles (and at least one comic) spread like wildfire across the internet, giving many readers the language to describe a familiar but previously unnamed experience.[17] Major media outlets began to routinely cover cognitive labor–related issues as part of a pandemic-era spike in conversations about domestic life.[18] New subgenres sprang up on social media to explain, complain about, and poke fun at gender inequalities in physical, emotional, and cognitive labor.[19]

The next step is to open this burgeoning conversation to more diverse voices. For example, with notable exceptions, cognitive labor inequality remains a feminized topic.[20] Women—and especially women partnered with men—are the ones most often writing and speaking about these issues publicly, reading about them online, and discussing them with friends and acquaintances. This is understandable given that women are the most obviously disadvantaged by the status quo. However, there is a long history of so-called women's issues being siloed, trivialized, and ultimately ignored.[21] A bigger tent is more likely to catalyze meaningful change. We especially need more male voices among the ranks of scholars, policymakers, and laypeople discussing the problem and pushing for change.

Widespread recognition, though an important prerequisite, cannot be the endpoint. Once aware of the phenomenon, we need to *reimagine* it, acknowledging that it could be otherwise. The recognition of physical housework as work did not immediately ignite activists' ire. They needed to first question the long-standing assumptions that linked women and domestic work in most people's minds. They needed to reframe "specialization"—an arrangement in which men focused on careers and women on homemaking—as inequality and conjure up alternative arrangements that could keep families fed and clothed at less cost to individual women.[22]

In the case of cognitive labor, reimagination is likely to be an uphill battle. As documented in chapter 3, many of the couples I interviewed struggled to picture meaningful change to their cognitive labor arrangement. Though many of them acknowledged their allocation as suboptimal, they told themselves that their power to disrupt it was limited because doing so would require changing who they were. Though this reflects a limited and inaccurate understanding of how and why cognitive labor inequalities emerge and persist, its power comes from its resonance with widespread cultural narratives.

To move forward, we will need to walk a fine line between restoring agency to individuals and couples and blaming them for their cognitive labor problems. The self-help genre is full of admonitions to men, women, and couples that subtly (or not-so-subtly) imply that inequality is their fault, and thus their problem to solve.[23] Lower your standards, we tell women. Is it really that important to write a thank-you note or sign your child up for three different sports? Drop the ball, we urge them. If it matters, someone else will pick it up. Step up, we implore men. Be a co-manager in your home, not a helper. None of these recommendations is inherently problematic; indeed, I offer versions of several below. What's problematic is their implicit premise: that the issue lies primarily with what individual men and women are doing (or not doing). What's problematic is the failure to acknowledge the broad array of structural and cultural forces that constrain those individuals' options and channel their actions.

We cannot ignore the individual household, but nor should we assume the problem of cognitive labor inequality is primarily of its making. We must also look to social policies designed for the increasingly rare breadwinner/homemaker family.[24] We must consider the rampant inequality that makes parents fearful for their children's future.[25] We must acknowledge the array of cultural messages describing men and women as irreconcilably, categorically distinct beings and "personality" as individual and fixed rather than social and malleable.

Only once we've collectively acknowledged the problem and envisioned alternatives can we move toward the third strategy, *reducing* cognitive labor loads. Here, I envision a two-pronged approach: First, work to lessen the overall footprint of cognitive labor in families' lives. In our hyper-capitalist, privatized society, much of the work required to maintain families is placed squarely on the shoulders of individual households. If institutional actors—local and federal governments, employers, schools, and so forth—took on more of that load, or at least minimized their own contributions to it, individual families would be less burdened. Second, we need to redistribute the remaining mind-use burden more equitably within households. To reach that imagined future in which gender is a poor predictor of cognitive load, many families will need to redistribute load away from their female members.

To do so, they will again need the support of a wide range of institutional actors. I once spoke with a business reporter who asked me, somewhat skeptically, whether there was anything employers could do to help solve the household labor inequality problem. "It's not like companies can force couples to divide housework more evenly, right?" he asked. Though perhaps technically true, this perspective overlooks the critical role played by employers—and many other actors beyond the household—in shaping a couple's options and forcing them to make difficult choices that ultimately reproduce gender inequality.[26]

With the three principles of recognition, reimagination, and reduction as a strategic blueprint for reducing cognitive labor inequity and overload, I turn now to a discussion of specific tactics. In keeping with my argument that individual households are not solely responsible for, nor capable of independently changing, the status quo, I begin by describing the actions that policymakers, cultural tastemakers, and members of other powerful institutions can take. Second, I address the organizations, particularly employers and schools, that directly shape families' daily lives. Finally, I speak to individuals and couples who are dissatisfied with their existing mind-use practices.

Institutional Tactics

While policymakers cannot specify how labor is allocated within a family, they *can* reduce the total cognitive effort required to maintain a household and raise children. Such changes are likely to disproportionately benefit the women who bear much of the existing cognitive load. Policies that reduce economic inequality, protect workers, and directly support families—so long as they are designed with an eye to simplicity and ease—will be most helpful. For women, yes, but likely for society, too, in the form of improved population health and greater economic productivity.

Ample evidence shows that parenting has become more resource-intensive in recent years. Contemporary parents spend more time, money, and, likely (though this is difficult to document quantitatively), mental effort on caregiving than previous generations.[27] Scholars attribute this intensification to rising economic inequality, among other factors.[28] No longer confident their child's future will be better than their own, many parents—especially mothers—are working harder than ever to ensure their children get good grades, excel in the right extracurriculars, and ultimately attend the best possible college. Greater assurance that society will care for all its members, signaled by a commitment to reducing inequality, could go a long way toward assuaging parents' anxiety and in turn reducing the perceived need for high-intensity parenting.

Policies that more directly support families are also essential.[29] The largely privatized nature of crucial services such as early childcare puts undue burden on individual families, cognitively as well as financially and temporally. Consider the cognitive labor involved in securing high-quality, affordable childcare: identifying candidate centers well in advance, running the numbers to figure out which are affordable, completing paperwork to prove ongoing eligibility for subsidized programs, and so on. For older children, consider the challenge of finding and maintaining before- and after-school care and coverage on snow days or when a child is ill. For even the most economically privileged couples in my sample, such work had a large cognitive footprint, much of it borne by women. Making it easier, as well as cheaper, to obtain comprehensive, affordable childcare should be a key policy priority.

Initiatives that protect workers are likely to have a similarly positive, if slightly less direct, effect on families' cognitive burdens. The challenges involved in "balancing" work and family responsibilities fall most heavily on women's shoulders.[30] Policies that counter overwork, require employers to give advance notice of schedule changes, and support workers' rights to collectively advocate for their own interests would leave caregivers with more time and space to attend to domestic matters without fearing employment penalty. For dual-income couples currently forced to prioritize one partner's career while the other picks up the slack at home, these changes could open up new possibilities.

Policymakers should also, perhaps under the purview of an expanded Paperwork Reduction Act, conduct a "cognitive audit" of existing and proposed programs to ensure they do not unnecessarily add to families' cognitive load.[31] Though social programs such as SNAP (colloquially known as "food stamps"), EITC, and TANF provide low-income families with free or heavily subsidized resources, they often demand nonmonetary payment in the form of what some scholars call "administrative burden"—that is, time and mental energy spent navigating byzantine bureaucracies.[32] Programs that provide similar benefits with less hassle should be prioritized. Efforts to reduce the individual burden associated with cognitive tasks like preparing tax returns, filing medical claims, and sharing health information across providers would also benefit families across the income spectrum.

In addition to political and policy change, a more equitable cognitive labor future depends on cultural change. Though the precise definition of "culture" is difficult to pin down, I refer here to the set of broadly available narratives, norms, and schemas that help people make sense of their lives, interpret others' behavior, and determine their best course of action.[33] Changing culture is not a straightforward endeavor. Nevertheless, one starting point is for those with a public platform—celebrities, influencers, media outlets, and the like—to avoid perpetuating outdated gender stereotypes.

Paradoxically, even "female empowerment" messages can subtly reinforce notions of gender difference and underline archetypes of female Superhumans and male Bumblers. While this genre may be overtly flattering to women and girls, it also acts as one more thread in the cultural fabric that establishes women as managers and men as their hapless domestic assistants. Even cultural objects with no obvious connection to gender can inadvertently prop up essentialist ideas. The widespread and largely unquestioned championing of individuality and personal authenticity, for instance, helps reinforce the idea that "who we are" is a stable fact rather than a socially mediated construct. To borrow the language of psychologist Carol Dweck, we need more cultural support for a "growth mindset," in which people are encouraged to see traits and skills as more a function of effort and practice than of innate capacity.[34] We also need more cultural products that celebrate complexity and contradiction rather than sorting individuals into discrete "types." For example, the proliferation of personality tests, including in schools and companies, subtly encourages test-takers to categorize themselves in static rather than dynamic and situationally defined ways.

Organizational Tactics

Though coordinated, societal efforts to support families, reduce inequality, and combat personal and gender essentialism may be the ideal, our current political reality suggests such sweeping changes will be slow in coming. In the meantime, organizations and the individual decision makers who comprise them have an important role to play. I focus here on two kinds of institutions, both of which interface directly with families and thus have clear opportunities to intervene productively: employers and child-serving institutions (e.g., schools, childcare centers, and summer camps).

My research adds to the growing consensus that inflexible, unpredictable, and "greedy" work harms families and exacerbates gender inequalities.[35] The old model of a single breadwinner supported by a full-time caregiver at home is no longer tenable. Nor is the notion that the "ideal" worker is one who is constantly available, never distracted, and single-mindedly devoted to meeting the company's needs.[36] Adding cognitive labor to the equation reveals that physical presence in the home is not a prerequisite for completing household labor and that "caregiving" means much more than feeding and bathing. Likewise, while parenting may be most physically demanding in the early years of a child's life, cognitive parenting demands remain high well into the teenage years.

This means employers must acknowledge the reality that employees with caregiving responsibilities—to say nothing of employees simply trying to care for themselves—likely comprise the bulk of their workforce and require support to carry out both their cognitive *and* physical caregiving duties. This is not just a matter of altruism: companies interested in recruiting and retaining diverse talent, particularly female talent, must develop policies that support rather than oppose such activities or risk losing out on valuable human capital. Any policy that enhances workers' flexibility, increases the predictability of their workload, or reduces the need for overwork is likely to be helpful toward that end.

For example, giving shift workers advance notice of schedule changes and salaried workers visibility into upcoming busy periods would allow them to avoid last-minute scrambles to find childcare or enable them to coordinate more effectively with a spouse.[37] Offering flexibility in terms of where and when employees work and thoughtfully scheduling important meetings to avoid school pickup and drop-off times can help mitigate the effects of a mismatch between school and work hours, lessening the need for individuals to construct and maintain a complex web of childcare arrangements. Ideally, such policies will be made available to all rather than take the form of individual accommodation, and managers will be trained to notice and combat the stigma often associated with uptake of such provisions.[38]

For schools, childcare centers, and related organizations, the twin objectives should be to reduce the cognitive demands imposed on caregivers and to avoid reinforcing gender stereotypes about parents' roles. On the former point, parent-serving organizations should aim to streamline communication: a weekly school newsletter compiling all relevant information is easier to manage than a daily assortment of flyers, emails, and social media posts. Organizations should also look for opportunities to soften the blow associated with misaligned work and school or camp schedules, whether by providing low-cost before- and after-care or thoughtfully aligning drop-off and pickup times across the schools in a district. They should encourage teachers to carefully consider the cognitive costs of parenting requests, such as dressing children in special costumes or sending them to school with homemade snacks. At the very least, such requests should be communicated well in advance, so parents have sufficient time to prepare.

Schools and related organizations can also reduce the cognitive costs they impose on parents by making it easier to submit required information. Rather than require caregivers to input the same data year after year, digital forms could be prepopulated with information from the prior year. Instead of completing a unique health questionnaire for every extracurricular or summer camp, parents could complete one standard form easily shared with multiple organizations.

School personnel cannot mandate father involvement any more than employers can require male employees to share housework equitably. But they can scrutinize their formal and informal policies regarding parent interaction. For instance, recent research suggests that when both mother and father contact information is offered, schools are more likely to communicate with women.[39] In my study, several female respondents (chiefly those in Man-led couples) expressed frustration that despite being listed as the secondary contact, they were the frequent recipient of calls from their children's school. Meanwhile, men reported discomfort with parenting spaces they perceived as feminine. By carefully monitoring their language and imagery for gender inclusivity and actively recruiting fathers to volunteer as "Classroom Parents" or PTA representatives, schools can do their part to combat the notion that mothers are the ideal school liaisons. Those in volunteer leadership roles— PTA leaders, moderators of online parenting forums, and the like—would benefit from a similar audit of their gender inclusivity.

Individual Tactics

As a sociologist, I'm trained to situate individual experiences within the context of broader social patterns. This bias toward the systemic provides a crucial counterweight to the individualism I've critiqued throughout these pages. It shows us that we are not alone in our struggles, that it is not our fault, and that the problems we face are bigger in scope than we ever imagined. Yet recommendations for policy changes and institutional overhauls are likely cold comfort to readers currently struggling with cognitive labor overload or imbalance, readers who cannot afford to wait for the systemic changes I call for above. Without blaming them or placing responsibility for change solely on their shoulders, I want to speak directly to those readers.

If you feel overloaded by cognitive labor or suspect your partner may be, what can you do?[40] The first step, perhaps counterintuitively, is to simultaneously depersonalize the problem and recognize your own agency. On the one hand, acknowledge that your struggles are the product of myriad social forces that stack the deck against those who aspire to cognitive equity. If you are a woman carrying a heavy cognitive burden, it does not necessarily mean you are a "control freak." If you are a man with an unduly light burden, it does not always follow that you are a slacker. If you are part of an Imbalanced queer couple, you are in good company. Acknowledging the role of social norms, gender socialization, inadequate social provisions, and other barriers to equality can reframe your struggle as a joint mission against powerful external forces rather than a head-to-head spousal battle.

On the other hand, recognize that you may have more room than you think to maneuver around those obstacles. When I asked study participants about their ideal cognitive labor allocation, many told me what they wanted and why it was impossible in the same breath. Their pessimism was typically rooted in essentialist thinking about the fixedness of individual natures or current employment circumstances. This does not mean you should ignore your preferences or set aside considerations related to finances or health. Just because a preference is socially constructed does not mean it isn't "real." The economic and cultural forces discouraging gender equality are *definitely* real. Nevertheless, apply extra scrutiny to the assumption that one partner is innately better suited to cognitive household tasks or that the patterns you've fallen into are irreversible.

Next, clearly articulate your individual and joint goals.[41] What are you striving for? A certain level of fulfillment in your career, a home that feels comfortable and welcoming, children who are healthy and happy? Keep these guiding principles in mind as you consider the cognitive, physical, and emotional tasks you want to prioritize or let go of, and as you articulate your ideal allocation of each dimension of household labor. While 50/50 across the board may seem like the "right" answer, it is unlikely to be the ideal division for all couples. If you do aspire to 50/50, consider whether you'd rather emulate the Splitters or the Sharers: would you prefer to identify a clear leader in each domain and let them do their thing, or do you hope for close collaboration across the board?

Reflecting independently on your own goals and ideal workload *before* coming together with your partner may help each of you gain clarity regarding your preferences. When you do compare notes, you will undoubtedly encounter points of misalignment. One partner values a clean, tidy home; the other couldn't care less about their surroundings. One partner strongly aspires to an equitable division of labor; the other is happy doing less than half the work. Confronting these differences is often painful, but the alternative—simmering frustration, disappointment, or resentment—is likely worse.

With your shared vision established, take inventory of your current practices: who is doing what and, importantly, how is it affecting them? Where possible, ground your discussion in concrete events rather than vague generalizations. I am skeptical of existing tools that purport to quantify partners' relative cognitive loads, but consider keeping your own version of the decision diary my interviewees completed: have each partner log the family-related decisions they make or contemplate over a specified period. You could do a similar exercise for the physical tasks each of you completes. After collecting the data, compare your logs and debrief. Be sure to discuss your *subjective experience* of each task as well as your observations about overall workload. You may find that you don't mind some of the same tasks your partner can't stand, and vice versa. Perhaps there are tasks on the list both of you agree could be simplified, automated, or eliminated altogether because they don't clearly contribute to shared goals. The responsibilities neither of you enjoys—but at least one of you deems important—are the ones to allocate most carefully.

If, like many couples, you identify a mismatch between your ideal and actual allocation, develop a plan for bringing them into alignment. For some couples, particularly those at an earlier stage in their relationship, a complete overhaul may be effective. For most, however, I advocate starting small and allowing momentum to build with each success. For instance, begin by transferring one relatively low-stakes cognitive task or domain from one partner to the other. By "low-stakes," I mean that both partners are prepared to tolerate the mistakes, inefficiencies, and pushback from others that often accompany a reallocation. Most low-stakes tasks are not especially public-facing: for many couples, the relatively private work of making a meal plan or arranging travel will be easier to reallocate than handing over communication with your child's teacher or responsibility for planning extended family gatherings.

Expect this reallocation to be slow and occasionally painful. As I argued in chapter 4, cognitive labor is a function of skills and capacities that develop with repeated practice. Reallocation requires an upfront transfer of knowledge and, in some cases, relationships. For both partners, patience is critical. A skill gap that emerged over years is unlikely to close overnight. Expect a period of inefficiency: it probably *would* be faster for the usual partner to complete the work, but presumably other values, like equity, or maximizing both partners' mental health, are also important considerations if you've gotten this far. Be prepared to face others' implicit or explicit judgment, particularly where you are going against a strong gender norm—for example, as a man planning a child's birthday party, or a woman deferring to her husband on scheduling matters. Ideally, these judgments will soften over time as gender becomes less predictive of household roles; in the interim, mentally preparing yourself for pushback can help ensure you hold steady when it inevitably comes.

For the partner taking on a new cognitive task, it may be helpful to look to other contexts for inspiration: what skills do you deploy in your professional life that may be applicable at home? For the partner handing over the reins, remember that many roads lead to Rome: don't assume a different process will inevitably lead to an inferior product, and allow your partner the time and space to experiment and make the work their own. Take stock periodically, assess what worked and what didn't, and try again with another task, slowly working your way toward your ideal cognitive, physical, and emotional labor allocation.

None of this change—political, organizational, or personal—will be easy. But if we are serious about creating a world in which one's gender is a poor predictor of both mind-use *and* time-use, it's work worth doing.

ACKNOWLEDGMENTS

It is daunting to attempt a comprehensive list of all the people who have supported me over the approximately eight years this book was in the making. Add in the decades before I even dreamed up this project—but was nevertheless building up the skills, perspectives, and life experiences that made a work like this possible—and, well, I must admit defeat before I begin. To those of you I've inadvertently neglected, please know that my memory is much more limited than my gratitude.

This book would not exist without the many interviewees who gave so generously of their time. As these pages show, they faced extensive demands on their time and attention but still gave up precious hours to share the intimate details of their lives with a stranger. I hope they feel this work does justice to their experience.

I'm grateful to the Harvard sociology faculty who saw potential in me, despite the fact that when I entered graduate school I had never taken a single sociology class. In particular, my co-advisors Sasha Killewald and Jocelyn Viterna were early champions of me and my work. Their encouragement was often the push I needed to aim higher than I would have thought possible; their constructive criticism inspired me to polish and refine my ideas. Michèle Lamont helped me deepen my thinking and engage with a wider range of scholarship; Mario Small taught me what it meant to be a qualitative researcher; Mary Brinton pushed me to write more clearly.

My broader academic community, at Harvard and elsewhere, shaped my scholarly development in important ways. Kathleen Gerson deserves a special shout-out for adopting me as one of her own and remaining an unflagging source of encouragement over the years. I'm also grateful to the many scholars whose mentorship and feedback propelled me forward in critical moments, including (but far from limited to!) João Biehl, Caity Collins, Sarah Damaske, David Deming, Christina Ciocca Eller, Patrick Ishizuka, Jane Jones, Kathleen

McGinn, David Pedulla, Joanna Pepin, Leah Ruppanner, Maya Sen, Chris Winship, and Jaclyn Wong.

My graduate school classmates buoyed me with laughter and camaraderie and answered countless questions I was too embarrassed to bother my professors with. Particular thanks to my cohortmates Victoria Asbury-Kimmel, Elena Ayala-Hurtado, Nicolette Bardele, Leah Gose, Holly Hummer, Andy Keefe, Jasmine Olivier, Cresa Pugh, Ethan Raker, Channing Spencer, and Joey Wallerstein for their friendship. I benefited immensely from the mentorship of peers just ahead of me on the academic ladder, including Laura Adler, Eun Se Baik, Allie Feldberg, Kelley Fong, Hope Harvey, Hanna Katz, Barbara Kiviat, Robert Manduca, Olenka Mitukiewicz, Derek Robey, Adam Travis, and Alix Winter. Thanks also to Nino Cricco and Lilly Yu for making me laugh often and only occasionally making me feel old.

I am immensely grateful to have landed at UW-Madison, where the Sociology Department welcomed me with open arms. My "official" mentors, Jess Calarco and Christine Schwartz, not only answered an endless stream of questions about navigating academia and the tenure track, they both read a full draft of this manuscript and provided invaluable feedback. Chloe Hart and Eunsil Oh have become great friends as well as valued commentators on early chapter drafts. Many others have provided informal—yet invaluable—advice and support. I'm especially grateful to Fabien Accominotti, Max Besbris, Marcy Carlson, Monica Grant, Eric Grodsky, Chaeyoon Lim, Jenna Nobles, and Lauren Papp. Meg Bea, Michaela Hoffelmeyer, Malia Jones, and Tawandra Rowell-Cunsolo kept me moving forward on research when other responsibilities threatened to take up all my time. My AP peers—particularly the Sociology/Psychology/GWS crew—provided precious solidarity throughout the transition to Madison. So Yun Park's research assistance has ruined me for life: I fear I will never again find someone so meticulous, forward-thinking, or kind. I'm grateful for her support with citations, proofreading, and fact-checking. Connie Meyer took my often-vague instructions and turned them into illustrations that perfectly matched my vision.

The staff at Harvard and at UW have gone above and beyond to make my job easier, leaving me more time and bandwidth to focus on what I do best. Particular thanks to Jessica Matteson, Pam Metz, and Nicole Tateosian at Harvard, and to Toni Schulze and Erin Skarivoda at UW.

I'm grateful for the ideas42 colleagues who introduced me to concepts that ultimately inspired this research, particularly Anthony Barrows, Jon Hayes, and Josh Wright. Margo Beth Fleming, Jess Lander, and Rita Rosenkranz generously shared their knowledge of the publishing world, which turns out to be very confusing.

At Princeton University Press, Meagan Levinson was an early champion of this project, helping to convince me that it was possible to write a rigorous *and* accessible book. Though I was sad to see her go, I was comforted by the support of her colleagues Erik Beranek, Eric Crahan, and Christie Henry. Rachael Levay stepped in just in time to steer me through the peer review process and has been instrumental in helping me bring this manuscript over the finish line. I'm also grateful to Akhil Jonnalagadda and Katie Stileman for helping me get my message to a broader audience; Ali Parrington for shepherding this book from Word document to physical object; Jenn Backer for meticulous copyediting; and the many others working behind the scenes at PUP to make my authorial dreams a reality.

Generous funding from several organizations made this research possible. At Harvard, thanks in particular to the Weatherhead Initiative on Gender Inequality, the James M. and Cathleen D. Stone Scholarship in Inequality and Wealth Concentration, the Center for American Political Studies, the Graduate School of Arts and Sciences, and the Shapiro Graduate Student Fellowship at Harvard Radcliffe Institute.

Some of the ideas presented in these pages previously appeared in the *American Sociological Review* (vol. 85, no. 5, pp. 806–29 and vol. 84, no. 4, pp. 609–33), and I'm grateful to the editors and reviewers of those articles for helpful feedback.

Last, but certainly not least, I thank the friends and family members who love me, sustain me, and remind me about the importance of life beyond the academy. Some of those friends even took the time to read and comment on parts of this manuscript; special thanks to Chloe Bordewich, Erin Kendall Braun, Christine Call, Krisia McDevitt, Eleanor Meegoda, and Gregor Schubert. I'm grateful to Mitra Salasel for her sage public relations advice and to Rachel Drapper for many thought-provoking conversations about household labor. And to all those friends who have checked in on my book progress, enthusiastically shared my work with their network, and just generally enriched my life over the years: you are amazing.

My family's support has been critical to shaping the person I am. My grandmothers, Joan Daminger and Helen Taylor, have been some of my staunchest supporters. I know that my late grandfathers, George Daminger and Bill Taylor, would have been over the moon to see their granddaughter in print. My sister Jordan Mancini is one of the strongest, most thoughtful people I know.

Among her most important contributions, together with my brother-in-law Christian Mancini, has been bringing my niece Mila into this world. Watching Mila grow, even from afar, has been one of the greatest joys of the past few years. I am endlessly grateful to Leslie Leventhal for raising the best person I know and for welcoming me into her family with great enthusiasm and love.

My father, Ken Daminger, was both my earliest writing teacher and the first to suggest I might make a good professor someday. Our early battles over syntax were critical for helping me develop my ear for language. My mother, Michelle Daminger, was, like so many of the women I write about here, the chief emotional, physical, and cognitive laborer for our household growing up. But of course, she is so much more than that: creative crafter, empathetic listener, and generous soul.

Winston will never read a word of this book and couldn't care less about it—except insofar as my writing habit limits our fetch time—and that is why he is the best.

Finally, Eric Leventhal: how immensely grateful I am to the winds of fate (er, algorithms) that brought our paths together, and how proud I am of what we've been able to build over the years. It can't be easy being in a relationship with someone who spends her days studying the problems with different-gender relationships, but you manage it with grace and humor. Thank you for reading my work and providing thoughtful counterarguments. Thank you for your commitment to living out our very own Balanced partnership, though it often means swimming upstream. Thank you, above all, for seeing all of me, and loving me anyway.

METHODOLOGICAL APPENDIX

Inspiration

Though I entered graduate school with a long-standing personal interest in gender, I'd never considered studying it. I was surprised, then, when my first-year PhD coursework introduced me to concepts like the "second shift" and the "motherhood penalty" and something sparked in my brain.[1] That spark contained indignation, and perhaps a touch of anger, but curiosity predominated. I filled page after page in my research notebook with questions, many of them a variant on one central puzzle: why haven't women's experiences of household life changed all that much in the past thirty years?

Coincidentally, I was required that same semester to conduct a series of interviews for a qualitative methods course. Mario Small, who taught the course, encouraged his students to take an inductive approach, letting our intuition and interest guide our early research. In that spirit, I began interviewing parents about how they decided where to send their children to school. I thought this might tell me something important about economic inequality; instead, I began obsessing over pronouns. Specifically, my respondents' widespread use of the first-person plural: "we" toured four schools; "we" asked friends for advice; "we" decided to stick with the local neighborhood public school. Whether partners were interviewed together or separately, they largely narrated the school choice process as a collective endeavor. But when I pressed for more detail, I learned that this communal language obscured considerable gaps in men's and women's contributions. Typically, *she* initiated the search, made a schedule of open houses, and canvassed friends and neighbors about their opinions on local schools. Couples might make a final decision together, but they often did so based on *her* preparatory work.

At least in this small sample, women seemed to be expending considerably more effort on the decision-making process. I wondered: at what cost? My prior work for a behavioral science firm had introduced me to the notion that humans have limited bandwidth—our brains can only process so much at any given time. Cognitive tasks like focusing our attention, preserving items in short- or long-term memory, and making careful choices are taxing, particularly under conditions of time or resource scarcity.[2] Though behavioral scientists did not necessarily label such decision-related efforts "work," I wondered what would happen if we reframed the myriad decisions parents made each day as a form of labor and applied a sociological lens to the study of such efforts.

I dove into the literature to see what other sociologists had to say about the phenomenon I was then calling "decision labor." My search turned up several related concepts, including invisible labor, hidden labor, emotional labor, mental labor, and household management.[3] Each of these nodded to the incompleteness of an action-focused conception of housework, yet none captured the phenomenon I was interested in with sufficient nuance and specificity. Scholars who did talk about household decision making usually treated it as an indicator of power, the assumption being that the partner who gets their way has "won" the negotiation.[4] I suspected that labor and power could coexist in complicated ways. And so, I set out to design a study that would elucidate the underexplored dimension of household work I eventually labeled "cognitive labor," hoping in the process to shed new light on familiar questions about gender inequality in family life.

Studying the Invisible

From the start, I knew I would need to rely on qualitative methods to answer my emerging research questions. Since I wasn't entirely sure what cognitive labor entailed or how pervasive it was, I couldn't confidently draft a set of standardized survey questions, let alone rely on existing survey data. I was initially torn, however, between drawing on participant observation or in-depth interviews. On the one hand, I was concerned that respondents would struggle in an interview to recreate their thought processes, given the absence of cognitive labor from most people's vocabulary. Further, I knew that self-reports of household labor were, like any self-reported data, subject to a range of biases affecting their accuracy.[5] On the other hand, I worried that the internal nature of cognitive labor would render it difficult to observe; to bring it to the surface I would need to be more intrusive—and potentially disruptive—than I'd like as I followed participants about their days. Ultimately, I chose interviews for two primary reasons: first, I came up with a strategy I hoped would render self-reports more accurate, and second, I was increasingly interested in understanding not just what individuals did, cognitive labor–wise, but also how they made sense of those patterns—a question better suited for the interview format.[6]

The primary strategy I landed on for rendering the invisible visible was to modify a long-standing technique for "observing" individuals' behaviors when physical proximity was impossible or impractical: asking research participants to complete a written log or diary in which they track their activities in real time. Time diaries are more accurate than generalizations in capturing individuals' daily activities; food logs are similarly preferable to questionnaires as a measure of dietary intake.[7] These tools are effective in part because they help reduce—but of course cannot prevent altogether—the biases triggered by generalization and aggregation, such as the way that unusual and recent events are often disproportionately salient in memory.[8] Because I was more interested in mind-use than time-use, however, I asked each participant to keep a record of all of the family-related *decisions* they made over the course of a day. By this point, I knew the phenomenon I wanted to capture extended far beyond decision making; nevertheless, I expected a decision to be the closest thing to a concrete, visible outcome I was likely to find. In the interviews, I planned to work backward from this salient outcome to uncover the preparatory and follow-on efforts linked to each logged decision.

My second strategy for rendering the invisible visible in interviews was to recruit couples rather than individuals but to interview partners separately. This approach has several advantages. First, outside observers are unreliable narrators of others' behavior, let alone others' thoughts and feelings. Because I wanted to understand how cognitive labor was divided between partners, I expected it to be particularly important for each major player to report on their own thought processes. Second, this approach helped ensure that men's voices would be present in my data. Too often, studies of family life, or of "work-family balance," are populated solely or primarily by women. As I would soon learn, this may be partly a recruitment challenge: mothers were easier for me to reach and more likely to express interest in a "parenting" study. Thankfully, many of these women were willing to recruit their male partners.

Defining the Sample

Among the most painful parts of designing a small-sample interview study are the inevitable trade-offs required. The populations of interest and possible dimensions of comparison are often legion, whereas resources are frustratingly finite, particularly for graduate students just starting out. Though I ultimately conducted three rounds of data collection over five years, gradually broadening the demographics of my sample, there are still many questions about how cognitive labor patterns and narratives vary across populations that will need to wait for future research to answer.

For all three phases of data collection, I focused on recruiting cohabiting romantic partners living with at least one child under fourteen years old. Because my primary interest was in the relationship between gender and cognitive labor allocation, I wanted to speak with couples who had merged their lives to some extent and were operating as a shared household. I also wanted to speak with people in a relatively similar phase of life. I chose parents of young children because prior research has associated parenthood with a shift toward gender-traditional behaviors and extreme time pressure.[9] Focusing on this population would, I hoped, give me a unique window into how such gendering happened; further, I expected this demographic would have a particularly heavy—and, thus, particularly salient—cognitive load.

In the first round of recruitment (Phase 1, 2017), I narrowed down even further, to college-educated parents of children five years old or younger. I expected a college-educated group to be among the most progressive in their gender beliefs and was curious to see whether and how that translated into their cognitive labor practices.[10] However, I also expected these parents to be particularly subject to the intensive mothering and concerted cultivation parenting logics associated with the middle class, making them an interesting case for understanding the effects of contradictory imperatives.[11]

In Phase 2 (2019–20), my goal was to understand how the patterns I'd initially uncovered might generalize beyond this narrow and privileged slice of the population. Specifically, I sought out parents of older children (roughly ages 5–14), in hopes of understanding how cognitive labor patterns shifted as children entered new, more socially connected life stages. I also recruited participants from a wider range of educational backgrounds, aiming for a roughly equal split between respondents with and without a bachelor's degree. This operationalization of social class backfired somewhat, as I ended up with quite a few couples in which one or both partners lacked a BA, even as the couple's income was well above the U.S. median. Despite my best efforts, I succeeded in recruiting only a handful of truly low-income couples, a challenge I reflect further on below. This phase of research convinced me that I was not documenting an exclusively upper-middle-class, elite phenomenon; however, it did not enable the broader social class comparison I had originally envisioned.

Technically, I did not require that participants in Phases 1 or 2 be in a different-gender partnership; however, the vast majority of those who participated consisted of a cisgender man and woman.[12] In Phase 3 (2022), I completed one final round of interviews with LGBTQ+ couples, very broadly defined as couples who self-identified as queer and/or consisted of something other than a cisgender man and woman, parenting a child or children under fourteen. I wondered how couples operating outside a heteronormative framework would deal with the problem of dividing up cognitive labor. My expectation was not that gender would be irrelevant for these couples but that its significance might differ from what I'd observed among different-gender couples.[13] The requirement that the couple have a child—albeit not one necessarily conceived together or genetically related to either of them—made recruitment challenging, but I felt it was an important variable to "hold constant" across all three rounds of data collection.

Recruiting the Sample

I recruited Phase 1 participants (N = 64; 32 couples) primarily (roughly 75 percent of the sample) via posts on email listservs and social media groups dedicated to parents living in a large northeastern metropolitan area. The remaining 25 percent of the sample came via referrals from my extended network or from prior participants. Digital parenting forums serve as important vehicles for sharing information about local resources and crowdsourcing solutions to parenting challenges. Though some forums had moved toward more gender-neutral language, my primary recruiting channels had "moms" in their name. Anecdotal evidence (coupled with research on other parenting forums) suggested they had a primarily female membership.[14] Unsurprisingly, then, in nearly all cases it was a woman who made initial contact with me and then either connected me directly with her husband or communicated with me to schedule an interview on his behalf. Toward the end of the recruitment period, I specifically sought stay-at-home or "lead parent" fathers in order to ensure rough comparability in the employment statuses of men and women in the sample, and I did some recruiting via online groups catering specifically to this population. In these cases, it was typically a man who volunteered for the study and then recruited his partner.

With any self-selected sample, it is important to question whether—or, more likely, how—those who volunteer to participate might differ from the underlying population. To avoid priming potential respondents about gender or the division of household labor and to reduce the likelihood that only parents with strong feelings about such issues would volunteer, I advertised the project as a study of "how parents make decisions." Thus, while this may have resulted in a group with an unusually strong interest in parenting, I have no reason to believe their beliefs about gender or housework were particularly unique. However, I worried that the requirement for both partners to partici-pate might lead me to screen out some high-conflict couples; indeed, several women expressed initial interest but withdrew after failing to secure their hus-band's participation. Thus, in Phases 2 and 3, I relaxed the requirement that both spouses participate while continuing to strongly encourage it.

To recruit Phase 2 participants ($N = 74$; 44 couples), whether individuals or couples, I began by posting on online channels, the same medium through which I found Phase 1 respondents. This strategy was again successful, but only for recruiting college-educated respondents. To find less-educated respon-dents, I pursued partnerships with nonprofit organizations serving low-income families, attended parent open houses for school districts serving a diverse population, and networked with friends-of-friends who were well-connected in local immigrant communities I knew to be socioeconomically diverse—all in the same northeastern metro area where I'd conducted prior interviews.

When these strategies proved only moderately successful, I decided to add a second research site in the county where I grew up. Through personal and family connections, I secured agreement from the superintendents of two school districts to share flyers about my study with all their elementary and middle school students, as well as to post a digital announcement on their parent forum. Though this was a secondary consideration, one benefit of adding this additional site was that it helped me test the hypothesis that my Phase 1 findings were somehow linked to respondents' location in a major city associated with progressive politics. The towns I recruited from in New Jersey are in a county that went for Trump in 2016 and have a distinctly suburban, and in some parts even rural, feel.[15] Ultimately, 59 percent of the Phase 2 sam-ple came from the New Jersey site.

I was able to speak with both members of 32 couples (73 percent) in the Phase 2 sample. There were notable asymmetries in the gender of the unre-cruited partner. Of the 13 men who initiated contact regarding the study, 12 successfully recruited their partner. Of the 31 women who volunteered, only 20 were able to recruit their partner. I collected basic demographic informa-tion about the uninterviewed partner from each respondent and asked a few questions about their partner's reluctance to participate. The most common explanations offered were that the partner was "too busy" or this kind of in-terview "wasn't their thing." Out of the 12 different-gender couples from whom I only interviewed one partner, all but one were Woman-led for cognitive labor, often by a wide margin.[16] I found more variety among these women than I expected in terms of their level of conflict or dissatisfaction regarding labor allocation. A few were indeed quite frustrated with their husband's limited involvement in cognitive and physical household labor, but the majority appeared similar to women whose husbands I did interview, in that they acknowledged their allocation as suboptimal but did not report actively engaging in trying to change it.

In Phase 3 (N = 34; 18 couples), I recruited LGBTQ+ couples via a wide range of channels, including my extended social network, social media groups dedicated to queer parents, and nonprofit organizations serving queer families. I spoke with both members of 16 couples (89 percent); in the remaining two couples I interviewed only one partner. Finding queer coparents of young children proved especially challenging.[17] Partly in response to this challenge and partly because I was conducting the interviews in early 2022, at a time when many people were still limiting their in-person interactions, I opened up the geographic range to anywhere in the United States and conducted all interviews via Zoom or a similar tool.

The resulting sample is comprised of 172 individuals representing 94 couples. Their demographic characteristics are presented in table 8.1. Notably, the sample is socioeconomically quite privileged, with a median household income of $155,000. There is also limited racial diversity: the vast majority of respondents were White (84 percent) or Asian (8 percent). Only a handful of respondents each identified as Black, Latinx, or multiracial. In both research sites, I suspect my own identity as a White, Harvard-affiliated researcher was a barrier to recruiting a more racially and socioeconomically diverse sample. In New Jersey, an additional factor was the lack of racial diversity in the school districts where I recruited.

In the data analysis phase, I looked for racial/ethnic differences but was unable to detect any; however, given the very small sample size of racial and ethnic minorities in my study, as well as the fact that my interview guide was not designed to uncover racial/ethnic variation, this should not be seen as the final word on the matter. Indeed, other studies, though not specifically focused on cognitive labor, show that certain racial groups must manage difficult dynamics their White counterparts rarely face, including anticipating and responding to racist acts and managing the consequences of systemic oppression.[18] Gender ideologies, particularly beliefs related to mothers' employment, also differ across racial-ethnic groups, with potential consequences for cognitive labor patterns that I was unable to capture here.[19] National origin

TABLE 8.1. Demographic Characteristics of the Sample

Gender		Educational attainment	
Cisgender man	43%	HS/GED	6%
Cisgender woman	54%	Some college	5%
Transgender or nonbinary	3%	Associate	4%
Race/Ethnicity		Bachelor's	23%
Asian	8%	Graduate/Professional	62%
Black	2%	Employment status	
Latinx	3%	Full-time (35+ hours)	75%
Multiracial	3%	Part-time	16%
White	84%	Unemployed	9%
National origin		Household income*	
U.S.-born	88%	Median $155K	
Other	12%	<$100K	20%
Age		$100K–$200K	48%
Average	38	>$200K	32%
Range	28–59		

*Calculated at the couple level; N = 94. All other statistics calculated at individual level; N = 172.

did emerge as a tentative source of difference in my data: foreign-born respondents were overrepresented at both extremes of the cognitive labor distribution. Again, however, the small numbers necessitate caution and call for further research.

The Interview Process

Once I secured agreement to participate from both partners (Phase 1) or at least one partner (Phases 2 and 3), I scheduled the interview(s). Because my primary goal was to make participants comfortable, I avoided prescribing a location and instead offered respondents the choice of several: their home, workplace, or a café or library conveniently located near work or home. Most often, respondents invited me to interview them in their home; secondarily, they picked a café or library. Only a handful of interviews were held at respondents' workplaces. Often, I interviewed partners back-to-back on the same day so they could trade off on childcare: one spouse spoke with me while the other supervised their child(ren), and then they switched roles.

One obvious downside of conducting interviews in homes is that respondents might self-censor for fear of their spouse or child overhearing. In most cases, however, the non-interviewing spouse made themselves scarce for the duration of the interview, either taking the children outside, going upstairs to work from a home office, or making dinner in the kitchen while we spoke in another part of the house. If a partner happened to be passing through during the interview, I sometimes reordered my questions to save a potentially contentious topic (e.g., about conflict, or how fair they thought their labor allocation was) for the moment they disappeared again.

Yet there are also advantages to home-based interviews for a study like this one. Entering respondents' homes exposed me to many more "context clues" than I would get in a neutral public space. At home, I could observe the interviewee's casual interactions with partner and children and make note of calendars or meal plans posted on the fridge. Respondents also seemed to find environmental cues helpful, either to illustrate a point ("You see how messy this place is?") or to jog their memory in response to a question.

In a handful of cases, eavesdropping spouses spontaneously offered commentary on what the interviewee had said, or the respondent explicitly called for their spouse to come answer a question—often, to confirm a fact they were having trouble remembering, such as the year something happened or the order of events. I found this back-and-forth instructive, as I could listen to partners hash out their sometimes divergent perspectives in real time as well as observe who served as the primary "memory" for a topic.[20] On two occasions, a miscommunication led to me interviewing both partners simultaneously. While these interviews offered a fascinating look into the way partners co-constructed narratives, they also affirmed my decision to conduct separate interviews, as I found that one spouse tended to dominate the other in the discussion, such that it was difficult to ascertain their independent perspectives.[21]

I conducted all Phase 3 interviews via Zoom or a similar videoconferencing platform, due to their timing (early 2022) and the geographic range necessary to find a sufficient number of queer coparents. As others have noted, virtual interviews have both benefits and drawbacks.[22] The convenience of not having to travel likely made it possible for me to speak with people who might otherwise have felt an in-person interview was too much to fit into a busy life. It also made it easier for me to conduct interviews during the workday, when interviewees could take a lunch break without having to worry about childcare, or later in the evening after the children were in bed. One downside, however, is that these virtual interviews may have hampered my ability to observe body language and environmental cues and to build a level of emotional rapport

Start	End	Issue/Decision	Outcome	Setting	Others Consulted
8:45 AM	8:48 AM	What to feed daughter for breakfast	Told husband to give her Cheerios	At home getting ready for work	Husband in charge of breakfast; asked me what to feed
9:30 AM	9:35 AM	Son needs new shoes	Made a note about going to mall this weekend	Was at home dressing son and noticed shoes were tight	N/A

FIGURE 8.1. Decision diary format and examples provided to participants.

that's only possible via physical proximity. While I do not believe the virtual component impaired my ability to collect good data, future research is needed to compare data quality across physical and virtual settings.

The content of each round of data collection was similar but not identical. Phase 1, for example, included preparatory work: a few days before we were scheduled to meet, I emailed respondents and requested that they keep a log of all the household- and child-related decisions they made over the course of a twenty-four-hour period. I encouraged them to define "decision" loosely (i.e., to include planning-related activities, unresolved questions, and ideas they were mulling over). Figure 8.1 shows the format of the diaries, as well as the two examples I gave all respondents. Fifty-seven participants completed written logs. Women's completed logs included 4 to 40 entries, with an average of 15. Men's logs numbered 3 to 20 entries and averaged 10. Three women and ten men failed to complete a log, citing lack of time, uncertainty regarding the task, or forgetfulness.[23]

At the start of each Phase 1 interview, I asked respondents to complete a short written activity while I reviewed their log and starred the entries I wanted to ask about in more depth.[24] I picked a subset of entries that varied in domain (e.g., food-related, schedule-related) and/or that stood out to me as either particularly interesting or confusing. Next, I asked detailed questions about each starred entry: what triggered the episode, what alternative options they considered, what role (if any) their spouse played, and how this example compared to typical events of this kind in their household. I asked respondents who had not completed the decision log in advance to recall a specific, recent decision in each of several routine categories (e.g., food, childcare, scheduling, social relationships). Next, I asked all participants a similar set of questions about irregular activities that were less likely to come up on a daily log: the last time they bought something for a child, dealt with a child's medical problem, made a home or car repair, took a vacation, established or modified a childcare arrangement, and selected a place to live.

My choice to focus on specific recent events was deliberate: I wanted respondents to avoid describing what "typically" happens, thereby minimizing the likelihood they'd report aspirational practices or emphasize exceptions to dominant patterns.[25] Detailed, process-oriented questions also helped me uncover cognitive activities respondents took for granted or carried out subconsciously. As the most salient component of the cognitive labor sequence, decisions were a useful starting point from which I could work backward. For instance, if a respondent reported the decision to make pasta for dinner, I asked a series of follow-up questions: What gave him this idea? Had he considered other options? Was he looking through the fridge when he made the decision? If not, how did he know what ingredients were on hand? This line of questioning helped reveal the cognitive labor embedded in processes respondents experienced as instinctive or primarily physical.

In a final portion of the Phase 1 interviews, I asked respondents a series of more abstract questions about how they made decisions. I also defined and gave examples of cognitive and physical labor and asked them to name both their ideal and actual division of both kinds of work. As I expected, the summary allocations they offered (e.g., I do 70 percent, my partner does 30 percent) did not always match the picture that had emerged from my more detailed questioning. Interestingly, these aggregate estimates were not consistently off in any particular direction: some respondents seemed to exaggerate the amount of work they contributed, while others downplayed their contributions. Phase 1 interviews averaged a little over an hour in length and concluded with a series of demographic questions.

I altered the interview protocol for Phases 2 and 3 to reflect my shifting understanding of what cognitive labor was and to make room for new research questions that had emerged from my earlier data. Though there was considerable overlap between the two interview guides, I made several key changes. First, I replaced the decision diary with a card-sort exercise conducted during the interview. In Phase 2, I handed respondents a set of 38 physical cards, and in Phase 3, I used a virtual whiteboard covered with 38 "post-its." The cards/post-its each listed a common household task, including 24 cognitive tasks (e.g., "decide what the family will have for dinner") and 14 physical tasks (e.g., "drive a child to/from an after-school activity"). These tasks were carefully selected to represent a diverse array of domains and cognitive labor subtypes, based on the typology I'd compiled following Phase 1.

I asked respondents to sort the tasks into five piles according to who typically completes the task for their household: the respondent, their partner, either/both (e.g., if they took turns, completed the task together, or otherwise shared the work), someone else (e.g., a child, grandparent, or housecleaner), or none of the above. During and after the sorting process, I asked respondents to elaborate on their labor arrangement, particularly for tasks placed in the "either/both" or "someone else" categories. For instance, if a respondent placed the "know whether we can afford a big purchase" card in the either/both pile, I asked whether both partners had access to paper or digital account statements, if and when they discussed financial matters, and whether one person was likely to have greater knowledge of their financial state on any given day.

The advantage of this approach was that it was faster than the decision diary debrief, which made space for me to include a new set of life-history questions regarding respondents' family of origin, educational and career trajectory, and relationship history.[26] These new questions proved especially helpful for understanding the pathways respondents took into a particular cognitive arrangement, as described in chapters 4–6. The disadvantage was that I quickly learned that respondents' definition of what constituted a "shared" task varied widely.[27] To assess Phase 2 and 3 respondents' labor division, I thus used a combination of the card-sort results and the interview transcripts. Though it would have been far simpler to rely on the card-sort alone, I found that this more painstaking process of compiling multiple sources of data was necessary to achieve an accurate picture of their labor allocation. Like Phase 1, Phase 2 and 3 interviews averaged a little over an hour each and concluded with demographic questions.

After each interview, I wrote up field notes, ranging from one paragraph to several pages in length. These field notes helped me process my impressions and solidified my memory of the interaction, which proved immensely helpful in the writing of this manuscript. When I reread my notes about the setting, the participant's appearance and mannerisms, and their interactions with their spouse, I was able to transport myself back to the interview even, in some cases, several years after the fact.

Data Analysis

After I conducted and transcribed the interviews,[28] the biggest analytical challenge I faced was finding a way to assess partners' relative cognitive workloads. Ultimately, I settled on assessing patterns of cognitive leadership across a series of topical domains. I inductively identified these domains after reviewing all Phase 1 transcripts, extracting all decisions mentioned, and sorting those decisions into nine categories: food, care for children, logistics/scheduling, cleaning/laundry, finances, social relationships, shopping/purchasing, home/car maintenance, and travel/leisure. These categories applied to most couples in the sample and encompassed the majority of decisions discussed.

Though several domains overlap with categories common in physical labor taxonomies, I focused on the *cognitive* component of each. For example, in the "cleaning" domain, I did not consider who vacuumed or scrubbed but rather who remembered when it was time to change the sheets, who initiated a cleaning session, who set standards on what constituted "clean enough," and who found and coordinated an external cleaning service. I applied this same taxonomy to the Phase 2 and 3 data, with one exception: because I was dealing with parents of slightly older children, I separated the childcare category into two domains. One "basic childcare" category focused on cognitive labor related to feeding, clothing, bathing, and supervising children. A second "management/engagement" category encompassed labor related to managing children's relationships with external institutions and individuals (e.g., schools, teachers, friends, tutors).

Once I established these categories, I looked holistically at a couple's dynamics in each: Who tended to initiate conversations? Who remembered the rationale for decisions in greater detail? Who ensured that a longer-term decision process kept moving forward? In most cases, I was able to identify a clear leader. Where I could not, it was usually because partners shared responsibility (e.g., one partner was the clear leader for car maintenance, but the other was the clear leader for home maintenance), in which case I classified the domain as shared. In rare cases, however, it was because I didn't have enough information to make a confident designation, in which case I classified the domain as "unknown." Finally, I also looked for crosscutting patterns related to kinds of cognitive work, such as anticipation and identification: Did one partner tend to bring up an issue, regardless of domain? Was one person the default "researcher" or ultimate decision maker?

I used these assessments to make a global designation of each couple as Woman-led, Man-led, or Balanced (for different-gender couples) and as Balanced or Imbalanced (for queer couples). The overall leader was the person who led at least two more domains than their partner. If the gap was zero or one, I classified the couple as Balanced.

Though I am confident this process enabled me to accurately identify the direction of any cognitive labor imbalance, it has at least two disadvantages. First, it gives equal weight to each domain, when in reality they have varying temporal, energetic, and emotional costs. I considered coming up with a weighting system but ultimately gave up when I recognized the variation across couples. For example, should the "home/car maintenance" category be weighted equally for car-free renters living in an urban center and for two-car homeowners living on a multi-acre property? Should "travel/leisure" be given the same weight for a couple with a robust social calendar and several international trips per year and another who self-describe as "homebodies"? Rather than apply my own subjective weights to the categories, I opted for a simple count.

A second downside is that using only a handful of categories (i.e., Man-led, Woman-led, etc.) masks variation in the *level* of inequality among couples. A couple in which the female partner leads nine domains and the male partner one domain is quite different from a couple in which she leads six and he leads four, though both would be classified as Woman-led in my system. While I considered adding additional categories (e.g., "slightly woman-led"), I ultimately decided that a simpler taxonomy would be more reader-friendly. Throughout the text I sometimes report on gap size, including in describing asymmetries between Woman- and Man-led couples or in describing a particular couple's story in depth.

I carried out the remainder of my analysis using the NVivo software. My approach most closely resembled the "flexible coding" strategy advocated by Deterding and Waters, though I took inspiration from several other sources as well.[29] I began with a round of open coding and memo-writing: I read each transcript carefully, highlighted recurring themes and passages I found particularly surprising or interesting, and synthesized the emerging insights in a series of memos, some about individual couples and others about cross-couple themes. Next, I applied index codes, based primarily on the questions in the interview guide, and assigned respondent attributes to each transcript. The process of applying these index codes built up my familiarity with the data set, in addition to proving helpful later on when I wanted to explore the way respondents—all of them, or a subset based on the coded attributes—spoke about a particular topic.

By this point in the process, I had developed many ideas about the data that I wanted to explore more systematically using analytic codes. For example,

I noticed that many respondents mentioned personality in their explanation for their cognitive labor allocation. I thus reviewed all the text already coded as "explanation" and developed analytic subcodes that represented the major themes within these data. "Personality," whether framed in negative or positive terms, was the most common such code. I repeated this process of generating and applying analytic codes multiple times for different research questions and emerging hypotheses. Throughout, I paid careful attention to apparently disconfirming evidence. Often, these data proved especially helpful in refining and/or placing boundaries around my emerging theories. For instance, the case of Anita and Glenn, detailed in chapter 3, initially seemed counter to my argument about the prevalence of personal essentialism. Ultimately, however, it helped me think about how the *absence* of such a narrative might help explain cases of marital disharmony in my data.

My Social Location

Try as she might, no interviewer can render herself a blank slate; factors like age, gender, race, and class—and, in a study like this one, marital and parental status—shape the assumptions others make about us and the assumptions we make about them. Another interviewer would undoubtedly have collected different data, even with the same set of questions. This is not a problem, per se, but it does merit careful reflection on how, and with what possible consequences, my own identity impacted the research.

When I began the study, I was a single, childless graduate student interviewing (mostly) married parents. Though in my mid-twenties, I was frequently assumed to be several years younger and, for this reason, presumably naive about issues related to marriage and childrearing. This may have made my apparent fascination with the minutiae of respondents' lives more legible: I could easily slot into the position of a novice eager to learn from my elders' expertise. This naivete was also helpful for projecting the nonjudgmental attitude with which I tried to conduct each interview, regardless of my own feelings about the labor allocation described. By the time I began Phase 3 interviews, roughly five years later, my inexperience was less taken-for-granted, and I got more questions from interviewees about my marital and parental status. At this point I was engaged but remained childless. This meant I was better able to build rapport around the joys and tribulations of being in a committed relationship but still understood to be less experienced than my respondents regarding both marriage and childrearing.

As briefly noted above, I suspect that my race (White) and class (as telegraphed by my status as a doctoral student at Harvard University) inhibited my ability to recruit a more racially and socioeconomically diverse sample. With the highly educated respondents who make up the bulk of my sample, meanwhile, my educational position seemed to open doors. Multiple respondents refused the small monetary incentive I offered for interview participation ($15 per person in Phase 1, and $25 in Phases 2 and 3), noting that they were instead motivated to help a graduate student. They had done research themselves, they said, or knew a close friend or sibling who'd conducted research and struggled to find participants.

I was particularly worried about how my gender (cisgender woman) would shape my interactions with the people I interviewed: Would women assume solidarity? Would men assume skepticism? On this dimension, I was simultaneously an in-group and an out-group member, depending on which portion of my sample I was speaking with. Indeed, I suspect that my gender—and individual respondents' assumptions about what that meant—did sometimes impact the way respondents communicated. Occasionally, male respondents said something similar to Matthew, describing his efforts to take on more cognitive labor: "I feel a duty to try to rectify this sort of unspoken disparity that [my wife and I] have in our decision-making process. I know it's laughable to say this to a woman." Matthew seemed to assume my gender implied something about my perspective—namely, that I would sympathize more with his wife than with him. On the flip side, female respondents occasionally made jokes about "how men are," presuming I would understand the humor and sympathize with their frustration. I tried to remain nonjudgmental and emotionally neutral, asking for clarification (Why is it laughable? What are men like?) rather than making assumptions. I also knew that the way respondents framed their accounts—sheepishly, humorously, proudly—was in itself important data regarding their perceptions of social norms and gender dynamics.[30]

Maintaining a dispassionate attitude was somewhat more difficult in the analysis and writing stages than in the interview context. My own commitment to egalitarianism and tendency toward Superhuman-like behaviors may have pointed me toward a particular initial interpretation of the data. I worked hard to challenge those views, including by exploring the high levels of conflict I observed among some Balanced and Man-led couples and taking seriously respondents' positive framing of Bumbler qualities. As my own different-gender relationship evolved in parallel with this research, I also developed a more visceral understanding of the ways in which couples of all kinds are buffeted by structural and social forces. Rather than placing blame on any individual's, couple's, or gender's shoulders, my hope is that this book makes clear how people acting in good faith can nevertheless recreate patterns they oppose, and the ways that we are all simultaneously complicit in and subject to a much broader system of constraints and opportunities.

NOTES

Introduction

1. All names, and some identifying details, have been changed to protect respondent confidentiality. I provide information about the race and occupations of focal participants, like Jackie, whose experiences I describe in depth. Demographic information, including race and social class markers for the full sample, is available in the appendix.

2. Yes, Jackie did say this, possibly mimicking the precision with which young children sometimes claim every last bit of their age.

3. Alternatively I might have asked them to report on the frequency with which they completed such tasks, or to guess at the percent of each task they typically completed, both of which are common ways of measuring housework.

4. An extensive body of research shows that women spend more time on housework and childcare than men, though the gap has narrowed over time, particularly in the 1960s through 1980s. See, e.g., Bianchi et al. 2000; Bianchi, Robinson, and Milkie 2006; Carlson and Petts 2022; Collins et al. 2021; Milkie et al. 2002. Hall and MacDermid (2009) estimate, based on a nationally representative sample of dual-earner different-gender couples, that about 9 percent of such couples are "parallel," in that men's and women's childcare, housework, and employment time are comparable.

5. I use "work" and "labor" interchangeably throughout the text. By contrast, Hochschild (2012) distinguishes "labor" as a component of paid employment from "work" as a more general, noncompensated activity. "Emotional labor," in her framework, is an activity performed by an employee; "emotion work" takes place in the private sphere. Given the widespread use in contemporary discourse of both "work" and "labor" in the context of domestic activities (e.g., housework, household labor), I have opted not to draw such a fine distinction between "cognitive work" and "cognitive labor."

6. Among women who completed decision diaries, the average number of entries was 15 (range: 4–40); among men, the average was 10 (range: 3–20).

7. I advertised the study to individuals who identified as LGBTQ+ and interviewed couples with a range of gender configurations, including same-gender female couples, same-gender male couples, and couples in which one or both partners identified as transgender and/or nonbinary. Throughout the text, I primarily use "queer couples" as shorthand for this group. See Velasco and Paxton 2022 for an insightful discussion of current trends regarding the use of constructive terms (such as "queer") and deconstructed identity markers (such as LGBTQIA+).

8. As I explain in the appendix, a minority of respondents could not secure their partner's participation in the study; for this reason, the individual count is not equal to two times the couple count.

9. Matthew was also somewhat unusual among men in Woman-led couples in the degree to which he recognized his wife's greater cognitive load and was attempting to take on more.

10. Not only are women better-educated than prior generations of women, they have also surpassed contemporary young men in college completion rates. See Diprete and Buchmann 2006; England, Levine, and Mishel 2020; and Van Bavel, Schwartz, and Esteve 2018.

11. The gender wage gap among full-time workers has diminished in recent decades (Blau and Kahn 2017; England, Levine, and Mishel 2020).

12. Women in recent decades make up a growing share of U.S. senators, representatives, and Fortune 500 CEOs, for instance (Pew Research Center 2023).

13. Hains 2012.

14. Slaughter 2012.

15. Sandberg 2013.

16. AAUW 2023; Kochhar 2023.

17. At their highest point (as of this writing), women made up 26 percent of the U.S. Senate; 28.5 percent of the House of Representatives; 10.6 percent of the Fortune 500 CEOs; and 30.4 percent of the Fortune 500 board members (Pew Research Center 2023).

18. Semega 2019.

19. Bianchi et al. 2012; Lachance-Grzela and Bouchard 2010.

20. While the overall trend in attitudes has been toward increased gender egalitarianism, some scholars argue that the predominant account of growing support for egalitarianism over-simplifies a more complex set of trends and that the pendulum may be swinging back in the other direction. Dernberger and Pepin (2020), for example, report that while young people are increasingly *open* to nontraditional gender arrangements, the majority still *prefer* something more traditional. Mize, Kaufman, and Petts (2021) document a shift toward more conventional attitudes regarding gender and the division of parenting labor during the Covid-19 pandemic.

21. England (2010) notes that change in the public sphere has been far greater than change in the private sphere; however, see Graf and Schwartz 2011 for a more optimistic counterpoint. Pepin and Cotter (2018) describe a parallel divergence in attitudes, with ideological support for egalitarianism in family life lagging support for egalitarianism in other realms.

22. Bianchi et al. 2000.

23. Married mothers' housework hours dropped from 33.9 in 1965 to 19.4 in 1995; married fathers' rose from 4.7 to 10.4 (Bianchi et al. 2000).

24. American Time Use Survey 2022 data indicated women spent roughly 1.5 times as many hours as men on "household activities," which includes travel (Bureau of Labor Statistics 2023).

25. England 2010.

26. For instance, Sullivan, Gershuny, and Robinson (2018) make the case for "lagged genera-tional change," arguing that the revolution is not stalled but rather slow.

27. See Hannan and Freeman 1984 for a discussion of "structural inertia" among organizations.

28. England, Levine, and Mishel 2020.

29. Ibid.; Goldin 2006.

30. Men did increase their housework time during this period. In fact, if we compare the percentage change, it looks like men's time was more dramatically altered than women's. However, because men were starting from such a low baseline (roughly five hours per week), the change is less significant in absolute terms (Bianchi et al. 2000).

31. Largely, but not entirely. One of the categories in Hochschild's study was "management of domestic life," defined as "remembering, planning, and scheduling domestic chores and events" (2012, 276).

32. Davis and Greenstein (2013), for instance, document a sharp increase from about 1990 forward in the number of articles published per year on related topics, up to more than one hundred per year in the early 2000s.

33. For an overview of these theories in sociology, see Coltrane 2000. In economics, Becker (1993) and related thinkers in the "new home economics" movement have been influential (Berk and Berk 1983).

34. The remote work era admittedly scrambles this logic somewhat, though emerging studies of the Covid-19 pandemic indicate that work-from-home status has asymmetric impacts on men's and women's time (André, Remery, and Yerkes 2023; Lyttelton, Zang, and Musick 2022, 2023).

35. Tichenor 2005. Some scholars have built on related findings to argue that men partnered with higher-earning women do less housework in order to counteract their "gender deviance" on the career front (Bittman et al. 2003; Brines 1994). However, more recent findings contradict that argument, showing that it is women's absolute rather than relative earnings that matter more for their housework time (Gupta 2007), or that it is high-earning women but not their male partners who attempt to perform gender through housework (Schneider 2011). What seems clear is that there is an interaction between gender and earnings, such that men's and women's earnings do not have parallel implications for their housework time.

36. West and Zimmerman 1987.

37. West and Zimmerman (1987, 126) describe gender as "an accomplishment, an achieved property of situated conduct." There is some overlap here with Butler's (2006) theory of gender performativity.

38. West and Zimmerman 1987, 136.

39. Berk (1985) memorably described the home as a "factory" that produces gender alongside other societal goods.

40. Lachance-Grzela and Bouchard 2010.

41. There have been exceptions, many of which I describe throughout the text. See Reich-Stiebert, Froehlich, and Voltmer 2023 for a review. They identify thirty-one studies, fifteen of which deal directly with "mental labor related to unpaid work and closely related topics" and the remainder of which discuss mental labor as "an additional outcome."

42. There may be elements of caricature in this depiction, though there's also evidence to suggest Americans, and Westerners more generally, place heavier emphasis on the individual than other cultures (Fischer 2008).

43. Cech 2021.

44. Many popular self-help books illustrate this sentiment: *You Are a Badass: How to Stop Doubting Your Greatness and Start Living an Awesome Life* by Jen Sincero; most books by Brené

Brown; *Untamed* by Glennon Doyle, which promises to help women "unleash our truest, wildest instincts."

45. Within psychology, this is known as the "person-situation debate." Contemporary psychologists acknowledge both context and personality as important drivers of behavior (Fleeson 2004; Mischel 2013).

46. Definitions of gendered selfhood vary. Risman (1999) characterizes gendered selfhood as an internalization of masculinity or femininity, such that maleness or femaleness becomes a property of the individual. Cech (2013) argues that gendered selfhood is about the type of person an individual understands themself to be, which in the aggregate tends to align with traditionally gendered traits and preferences. Martin (2004) suggests that the institution of gender is experienced as a self-concept, which is then displayed to others in the form of a personality.

47. Cech 2013, 2021; Charles and Grusky 2004.

48. Charles and Bradley 2009; Charles and Grusky 2004; England, Levine, and Mishel 2020.

49. Adult men and women do show significant gender differences in their vocational interests, as Su, Rounds, and Armstrong (2009) document in a meta-analysis. Of course, it does not necessarily follow that those differences are intrinsic rather than socialized.

50. Deloitte and Automotive News 2020; National Center for Education Statistics 2023.

51. Meta-analyses typically show some gender differences in both temperament (conceptualized as an early indicator of personality) and personality. Girls score higher on measures of attention and agreeableness, for example (Else-Quest et al. 2006; Hyde 2014). However, there is considerable debate about the *significance* of those differences. Hyde (2014) notes that average gender differences are typically small to moderate, though at the tails of the distribution, gender differences are much larger. This, Hyde writes, leads to "a common problem in which people infer, from marked gender differences in extreme scores, that differences between girls and boys are categorical . . . when in fact average gender differences are moderate, representing substantial overlap between the male and female distributions" (383). A further issue is that temperament scores are influenced by experience and cannot be assumed innate.

52. Whitney was the birthing mother for their eldest, while Vanessa was carrying their second child.

53. Numerous scholars have critiqued earlier assumptions that gender was irrelevant for same-gender couples or that an "egalitarian ethic" necessarily translated into egalitarian practices. See, e.g., Brewster 2017; Goldberg 2013; Reczek 2020.

54. Katz-Wise, Priess, and Hyde 2010; Yavorsky, Kamp Dush, and Schoppe-Sullivan 2015.

55. Davis and Greenstein 2009.

56. My East Coast recruitment sites may have led to an oversampling of moderate and liberal parents. Middle- and upper-middle-class individuals with more conservative views would likely be more ambivalent about, or even hostile toward, the gender-egalitarian ideals that predominated among this sample (Davis and Greenstein 2009).

57. In Massachusetts, the median household income is $96,505 (in 2022 dollars) and in New Jersey, it is $97,126 (U.S. Census Bureau 2022a, 2022b).

58. Exactly what those differences might be, I wasn't sure. On the one hand, educational attainment is positively correlated with egalitarian gender ideology (Scarborough, Sin, and Risman 2019) and negatively correlated with women's housework time (Bianchi et al. 2000; Evertsson et al. 2009). On the other, some research demonstrates how classed employment

conditions (e.g., overwork, partners working alternate shifts) can scramble the typical patterns (Deutsch and Saxon 1998; Gerstel and Clawson 2014; Hochschild and Machung 2012; Usdansky 2011). Recent evidence also shows that the "super-rich" (i.e., the top 1 percent) are significantly more likely than other couples to practice a traditional male breadwinner and female home-maker arrangement (Yavorsky et al. 2023). Further complicating matters, prior research in this area has focused almost exclusively on the division of physical rather than cognitive labor.

59. For example, Dow (2016a, 2019) shows how middle-class Black mothers face a unique combination of expectations and structural constraints that influence their parenting strategies and behaviors as well as the approach they take to combining paid work and family responsibili-ties. Barnes, writing about highly educated Black women who left the workforce to care for their children, describes them as practicing a form of "strategic motherhood" that is different in form but a continuation in spirit of Black women's long-standing role in "ensur[ing] familial and communal survival" (2016, 6). While not specifically focused on gender, Warikoo's (2020) in-terviews demonstrate differences between White U.S.-born and Asian immigrant parents'—primarily mothers'—approaches to promoting their children's emotional health.

60. Scholars, chiefly those writing in the Black feminist tradition, have rightly critiqued those who write about White, middle-class women's experiences as if they were generalizable to all women. See, for example, Collins 2022; Dow 2016a; Glenn 1992.

61. Time diaries may be completed by participants in real time or constructed by an inter-viewer shortly after the fact. For example, the American Time Use Survey (ATUS) is administered by an interviewer who asks the respondent to recreate the previous day in detail (Bureau of Labor Statistics 2021).

62. My primary inspiration was Berk 1985; however, card-sort exercises have been used in diverse ways by many other researchers (Neufeld et al. 2004). For example, in Doucet's (1996) Household Portrait method, partners work together to allocate cards into categories based on their shared understanding of who does what. Outside academia, Rodsky's (2019) Fair Play method centers on a deck of task cards that couples sort through and assign to each partner.

63. See Scharrer et al. 2021 for an overview of depictions of TV dads, which trend toward the negative. Lareau, in the memorably titled article "My Wife Can Tell Me Who I Know: Methodological and Conceptual Problems in Studying Fathers," bluntly describes fathers as "not useful sources of information for the routines of family life" (2000, 407).

Chapter 1. Doing, Feeling—and Thinking

1. For a flavor of these debates in historical terms, see Boydston 1994; Folbre 1991; Siegel 1994; and Silbaugh 1996. More recently, the "Unpaid Work in the GDP by 2030" (Gale 2022) campaign picked up on these earlier threads.

2. Marx 1976. Of course, the Industrial Revolution was not confined to the United States; however, I focus in this section on its effects there.

3. Folbre 1991.

4. Marx 1976.

5. The idea that men and women operate in different "worlds" is a much older idea; Kerber (1988), for example, traces it as far back as Tocqueville. However, the nineteenth century is widely considered its heyday (Folbre 1991).

6. This conception of the domestic sphere is also known as "the cult of domesticity" or "the cult of true womanhood" (Welter 1966). The so-called true woman was expected to be pure, pious, domestic, and submissive.

7. In her 1841 book *A Treatise on Domestic Economy*, Beecher summarizes this sentiment: "In matters pertaining to the education of their children . . . and in all questions relating to morals or manners, [women] have a superior influence" (33).

8. "Historical accounts," writes Silbaugh, "show that the separate spheres of labor are not only distinct, but stratified" (1996, 21). Later, she adds that while women's "emotional role was praised, their material labor was obscured" (24). Psychologists term a contemporary version of this phenomenon "benevolent sexism," which characterizes women as "pure creatures who ought to be protected, supported, and adored. . . . This idealization of women simultaneously implies that they are weak and best suited for conventional gender roles; being put on a pedestal is confining, yet the man who places a woman there is likely to interpret this as cherishing, rather than restricting, her" (Glick and Fiske 2001, 109).

9. Crenshaw writes that "because the experiential base upon which many feminist observations [including those regarding the separate spheres ideology] are grounded is white, theoretical statements drawn from them are overgeneralized at best, and often wrong" (1997, 67), insofar as they do not account for the intersection of race and gender.

10. Landry 2002; Silbaugh 1996. Black women's *reproductive* labor has also been exploited for centuries (Roberts 1998).

11. Siegel 1994.

12. This history also helps explain contemporary racial differences in conceptions of "ideal" feminine behavior, particularly whether a woman should work for pay. Black women have been more likely than White women to work for pay for most of the post–Civil War years (Boustan and Collins 2013; Dow 2015).

13. Kneeland 1929, 35.

14. Ibid.

15. Folbre 1991.

16. Siegel 1994.

17. Dreilinger 2021; Richards 2000; Stage and Vincenti 1997.

18. Dreilinger 2021. In the preface to her 1928 book *The Home-Maker and Her Job*, pioneering home economist Gilbreth writes, "This book applies to the home the methods of eliminating waste that have been successful in industry" (vii). A few years earlier, Frederick (1923), a self-described "household efficiency engineer," published *Household Engineering: Scientific Management in the Home*, which promised to teach women "the application of the principles of efficiency engineering and scientific management to the everyday tasks of housekeeping."

19. This functionalist perspective is exemplified by the work of Talcott Parsons. See, e.g., Parsons and Bales 1960.

20. Ferree, Khan, and Morimoto 2007, 440.

21. This passage may give the false impression that this disciplinary evolution was easy and is now complete. As Ferree and colleagues' 2007 history of women in sociology makes clear, the integration of women was a long and fraught—and still ongoing—process.

22. Coltrane 2000.

23. Ibid. For example, British sociologist Oakley, author of the pathbreaking 1975 book *The Sociology of Housework*, asked respondents about "cleaning, household shopping, cooking,

washing up, washing, ironing, mending, buying/making clothes, and buying/making house durables" (210).

24. Locke 1982. Espeland and Stevens (2008, 417) write more broadly about "the authority of numbers," which they argue is vested in several qualities, including "our sense of their accuracy or validity as representations of some part of the world" and "their long and evolving association with rationality and objectivity."

25. See Espeland and Stevens 1998 for a sociological discussion of commensuration.

26. Economic historian Goldin writes that creators of economic measures like GDP and GNP agonized over whether to include unpaid family labor but ultimately opted against the idea because "no reliable basis is available for estimating their value" (2021, 48).

27. Kneeland 1929, 36.

28. Ibid. In their attempt to study "household management," arguably the closest thing to cognitive labor that appears in major surveys, Winkler and Ireland (2009) ran into this problem, which they attribute in part to the lack of space for recording "secondary" activities.

29. Daniels 1987, 407.

30. Papanek 1979.

31. Ruddick 1995; Walzer 1996.

32. Rosenthal 1985.

33. Mederer 1993.

34. See, for instance, Chesley and Flood 2016; Cooke and Hook 2018; and Yavorsky, Kamp Dush, and Schoppe-Sullivan 2015. However, in just the past few years, there have been promising signs of change. As I describe in more depth in the conclusion, several scholarly teams are engaged in the work of developing quantitative measures of cognitive labor and related constructs. Examples include Weeks 2024, Petts and Carlson 2023, and Haupt and Gelbgiser 2023.

35. Robinson and Godbey 2010.

36. In her prescient 1987 article, for example, Daniels describes "invisible labor" as any effort that is "arduous, skilled, and recognized as useful" but does not match the "folk conception" of work as public and financially remunerated (403). The examples she gives include such diverse activities as emotional labor in families, political activism, community service, and care for the ill or disabled.

37. Hochschild 1979, 2012.

38. Unlike Hochschild, I use the terms "cognitive labor" and "cognitive work" interchangeably.

39. For example, see Cretaz 2020; Hartley 2017; Wong 2018.

40. Beck 2018.

41. I conceive of emotional and cognitive labor as conceptually distinct but significantly overlapping in practice. Other scholars have put forth somewhat different definitions of how these two constructs relate. For example, Dean, Churchill, and Ruppanner (2022) describe the combination of cognitive and emotional labor as "the mental load," while Fielding-Singh and Cooper (2023) argue that cognitive and emotional labor are "mutually constitutive" (453), albeit distinct processes. Finally, Wayne et al. (2023) describe the "invisible family load" as a combination of managerial, cognitive, and emotional responsibilities.

42. Daminger 2019. Though others have come up with slightly different taxonomies, there is often overlap among them. For example, Robertson and colleagues named six forms of mental labor: "(a) planning and strategizing, (b) monitoring and anticipating needs, (c) metaparenting,

(d) knowing (learning and remembering), (e) managerial thinking (including delegating and instructing), and (f) self-regulation" (2019, 184).

43. Psychologists call this the Zeigarnik Effect, after the Russian psychologist who found that subjects remembered incomplete tasks better than completed ones (Savitsky, Medvec, and Gilovich 1997).

44. Duffy 2007; Glenn 1992; Hochschild 1979; Jang, Allen, and Regina 2021.

45. Here I'm paraphrasing the *Oxford English Dictionary*'s (2023) definition of work as "action or activity involving physical or mental effort and undertaken in order to achieve a result, esp. as a means of making one's living or earning money."

46. Robinson and Godbey 2010.

47. Ibid.

48. See Sullivan 2013 for a thoughtful discussion of the need for distinct theories to explain childcare and housework time-use patterns.

49. The scholars Milkie, Nomaguchi, and Schieman (2019) and Nomaguchi, Milkie, and Bianchi (2005) show that a perceived "time deficit" with children is a stressor with deleterious effects on parents' health and well-being. This may be partly a function of modern parenting ideology, which tells us that children are precious, sacred beings whose development should be carefully cultivated, ideally by a family member who finds such care emotionally fulfilling (Hays 1996; Ishizuka 2019; Lareau 2011; Zelizer 1994).

50. To be sure, this is a complex issue. Many aspects of childcare are indeed tedious. When parents say they wish they could spend more time with their children, they may not be referring specifically to more diaper changes and midnight feedings. My point is simply that it's more complex and nuanced than the calculus typically applied to housework, which holds that more time spent on chores is worse.

51. Though physical tasks also come with both burdens and benefits, they are not the same as those associated with cognitive tasks, a finding that helps explain why efforts to assess cognitive work using tools designed to study physical labor are unlikely to succeed.

52. Astute early readers pointed out that the work of keeping a house maintained is also abstract and never-ending. Here, though, I'm trying to distinguish between the work of anticipating or monitoring (e.g., keeping track of a child's wardrobe) and that of identifying options for meeting an already-anticipated need (e.g., to fix the roof).

53. There is a long sociological tradition of inferring marital power dynamics on the basis of decision making, with the spouse who gets the last word usually understood to be more powerful (Blood and Wolfe 1960; Komter 1989).

54. Hardill et al. (1997) describe this kind of big-picture versus day-to-day decision making as "orchestration" and "implementation" power, respectively, arguing that the latter decisions are "time-consuming but less important" (316).

55. Hochschild and Machung 2012. For more on Hochschild's ideas about appreciation and gratitude vis-à-vis household labor, see Hochschild 2003.

56. Much more commonly, as we'll see in the next chapter, one partner identifies options, and then the couple decides together. Cases where partners separated the work of identification and decision making were largely confined to lower-stakes issues such as where to order takeout or which movie to watch.

57. Kneeland 1929, 36.

58. Offer 2014, 916. Offer calculated mental labor time based on respondents' answers to the question "What was on your mind?" when paged at random intervals throughout the day. She constructed three measures of mental labor (cross-domain, family-specific, and job-specific) based on their responses. See pp. 924–25 for details.

59. However, Offer (2014) does find that family-related cognitive labor has a negative impact on mothers' emotional well-being but not on fathers', and she reports that mothers spend a slightly larger proportion of their waking hours (26.14 percent) on mental labor of all types than fathers do (21.46 percent).

60. Winkler and Ireland 2009.

61. Ibid., 302.

62. Emma 2018.

63. Hartley 2017.

64. For example, one reason Grant's 2021 op-ed, "There's a Name for the Blah You're Feeling: It's Called Languishing," was so popular was that it did exactly what the title suggests: gave a term to a vague cluster of "symptoms" that did not fall under any existing (or at least, well-known) framework.

65. Kristen logged a number of additional items, but for brevity's sake I only included a fraction in my earlier description of her day.

66. Winkler and Ireland (2009) point out that without the ability to report on "secondary activities," household management is likely to be underreported. More recently Folbre (2023) has argued that we need to go "beyond the clock" in order to fully capture the work involved in caring for children and shows how far tallies of "active care" underestimate parents' care efforts.

67. In this case, participants typically marked the start as the time when an issue first arose and the end as the time it was fully resolved. E.g., a "what to have for dinner" decision might begin with a conversation at 4:30 p.m. and end at 8:00 p.m. when one partner picked up Thai takeout. Presumably, however, other things happened during this 3.5-hour block.

68. Mani et al. 2013; Mullainathan and Shafir 2013; Vohs et al. 2008.

69. For example, Julie Morgenstern titled her 2005 productivity guide *Never Check Email in the Morning*; more recently, Cal Newport (2016) has advocated for knowledge workers to carve out time for "deep work" free of any digital distractions.

70. Mark, Gonzalez, and Harris 2005.

71. Ahn and colleagues (2017) identify "mnemonic work" (i.e., helping one's partner remember tasks) as a form of labor and show that it is largely a female-typed activity among different-gender couples. See Harrington and Reese-Melancon 2022 for similar findings.

72. Scholars refer to these as "core" or "routine" tasks and distinguish them from "occasional" or "discretionary" tasks like finances and household maintenance (Bianchi et al. 2000; Coltrane 2000).

Chapter 2. The Gendered Division of Cognitive Labor

1. Time-use research indicates that contemporary men are spending more time on childcare than their predecessors; however, men's childcare time is disproportionately allocated toward the arguably more enjoyable work of playing, teaching, and going on outings together (Monna and Gauthier 2008; Negraia, Augustine, and Prickett 2018).

2. A large body of research on physical housework consistently shows women spending more time than men on such activities (Lachance-Grzela and Bouchard 2010; Tai and Treas 2013). Childcare is also consistently gendered: women spend more time caring for children and are especially likely to take on routine care tasks like feeding and bathing (Bianchi et al. 2012; Craig 2006; Craig and Mullan 2011; Monna and Gauthier 2008).

3. I describe my methodology in considerably more detail in the appendix but offer a short, nontechnical description here.

4. Small 2017. There's also evidence that men and women, but perhaps especially men, have a tendency to misrepresent their housework contributions when asked to make general assessments about time spent or proportion of labor completed (Kamo 2000; Lee and Waite 2005).

5. The Food Frequency Questionnaire (FFQ) is a more sophisticated version of the example I provide here. Its limitations are well-documented (Shim, Oh, and Kim 2014).

6. In addition to asking about the events logged on decision diaries, I asked Phase 1 interviewees about the last time they dealt with irregular events such as a child's illness, a move, or something broken in the home. The process of scheduling interviews was also a helpful window into dynamics in the logistics and scheduling domain: Did each partner schedule their own interview, or did one partner schedule for both? Who communicated last-minute changes to time or place?

7. In Phase 1 of data collection, with parents of children five years old and younger, I examined only nine domains, including one for cognitive childcare. In later phases, I split the childcare category into two—basic childcare and managing children's engagement—to reflect the additional responsibilities described by parents of school-aged children.

8. I also classified a smaller number of domains as "shared," if partners seemed roughly equally responsible.

9. To qualify as Woman-led, there had to be a gap of two or more domains between partners, to allow for a margin of error and potential differences in the scope of each domain. If Carla had led four domains and Robert three, for instance, I would have classified them as "Balanced."

10. The full range was 4–10 domains led by the woman partner.

11. This is consistent with time-use research showing that women typically spend more time alone with their child(ren) (Craig and Mullan 2011; Raley, Bianchi, and Wang 2012).

12. Forty-one percent and 42 percent of couples were man-led in these domains, respectively.

13. Financial tasks such as managing a monthly budget and paying bills were less clearly gendered. See Cooper 2014 for a discussion of how social class intersects with gender when it comes to families' financial management.

14. This is consistent with Tai and Treas (2013), who report that the majority of married couples describe their decision making as joint.

15. Lareau (2000), for example, noted the limitations of fathers as accurate sources of information about children's lives in an article memorably titled, "My Wife Can Tell Me Who I Know."

16. Recent research shows a similar gendered pattern among parents choosing their child's elementary school (Brown 2022).

17. Blood and Wolfe 1960; Komter 1989; Kranichfeld 1987; Miller and Carlson 2016.

18. For more on the role of mutuality in couples' decision making, see Wong and Daminger 2024.

19. Bianchi et al. 2000; Coltrane 2000.

20. In this section, I report primarily on the different-gender couples I interviewed in the second phase of data collection because I did not collect sufficient information to assess physical labor allocation in the first round.

21. Sonya's comments echo earlier research on women as "managers" and men as "helpers" (Coltrane 2000).

22. This "offsetter" narrative could be thought of as a version of Hochschild and Machung's (2012) "upstairs-downstairs" family myth. For those earlier interviewees, however, the "myth" was the equation of two sets of tasks that were far from equivalent in their labor costs. Here, the issue is less about the commensurability of the two dimensions than about the accuracy of the assertion that the male partner did most of the physical labor.

23. At no point in the interview did I offer my own assessment of a couple's (in)equality. However, numerous respondents made comments like Denise's, after completing the card-sort exercise: "You know, laying [the cards] out like this, it's like, 'oh my god, he does all the boy stuff, and I do all the girl stuff!'"

24. Bertrand, Kamenica, and Pan 2015; Fry et al. 2023.

25. If we separate higher earners from those who work longer hours but do not earn more, the same patterns hold. Ninety-one percent of couples with higher-earning men were Woman-led, but 64 percent of couples with higher-earning women were *also* Woman-led. Ninety-eight percent of couples with longer-working men were Woman-led, but 58 percent of couples with longer-working women were *also* Woman-led.

26. This finding parallels research on the relationship between employment and physical housework, which finds that women's higher earnings are less likely than men's to translate into lower physical housework burdens (Lyonette and Crompton 2015; Schneider 2011; Tichenor 2005).

Chapter 3. "It's Not a Gender Thing, It's a Me Thing"

1. For reviews, see Lachance-Grzela and Bouchard 2010 and Perry-Jenkins and Gerstel 2020.

2. Cotter, Hermsen, and Vanneman 2011; Scarborough, Sin, and Risman 2019. However, note that some recent research presents a more complicated story regarding attitudinal change and argues for distinguishing among beliefs about the marketplace, the family, and mothers' employment, or between gender egalitarianism and gender flexibility (Dernberger and Pepin 2020; Pepin and Cotter 2018).

3. This group partially overlapped with the couples described in the previous chapter, who argued that they had already reached this offsetting equilibrium; others held offsetting up as their ideal but did not believe they'd yet reached it.

4. In hoping for something that "feels equitable," Ray intuited a finding from prior research: *feelings* of fairness and equity are imperfectly related to a couple's *actual* labor allocation (Sanchez and Kane 1996; Wilkie, Ferree, and Ratcliff 1998).

5. Pugh 2013, 47.

6. Festinger 1957.

7. Another option is simply getting distracted and forgetting about the conflict (Festinger 1957; McGrath 2017).

8. Beagan et al. 2008; Van Hooff 2011; Nyman, Reinikainen, and Eriksson 2018.

9. Hochschild and Machung 2012.

10. Ibid., 44–45.

11. This finding contrasts with other research suggesting that both men and women, but especially the former, tend to exaggerate their household contributions (Kamo 2000; Lee and Waite 2005). My participants, of all genders, sometimes matched my own assessment, sometimes described their allocation as more equal, and sometimes perceived it as less equal. This variation may be partly attributable to the study design (in-depth interview versus anonymous survey; both partners included versus only one). The magnitude and direction of the gap between my assessment and a respondent's also seemed to correspond with the broader narrative the respondent offered throughout the interview; their feelings about the fairness or appropriateness of their allocation; and their relationship satisfaction levels.

12. I focus here on the account I heard most often from Woman-led couples, and the one that appeared most consequential in terms of reducing spousal conflict and maintaining cognitive labor inequality. Other accounts referenced skill differentials, habit, and upbringing.

13. My use of "account" comes from Scott and Lyman (1968, 48), who define the account as a statement "made to explain untoward behavior and bridge the gap between actions and expectations." See also Damaske 2011, 2013.

14. This finding parallels arguments about "racism without racists" or "colorblind racism," narrative frames that justify the avoidance of discussions about race and racism while paradoxically facilitating the persistence of racial inequality (Bonilla-Silva 2021).

15. Elsewhere I describe this phenomenon as "de-gendering," defined as recasting gender inequality as personal inequality by distinguishing a coincidentally gendered outcome from supposedly gender-neutral intentions and processes (Daminger 2020). Personal essentialism, which I explain in the next subsection, is one category of de-gendering.

16. Bonilla-Silva 2021; Forman and Lewis 2015; Hagerman 2018.

17. Charles and Bradley 2009; Charles and Grusky 2004; Ridgeway 2011.

18. Folbre 1991; Kerber 1988; Siegel 1994.

19. Glick and Fiske (2001) make a similar point in their discussion of "benevolent sexism."

20. Cotter, Hermsen, and Vanneman 2011; Knight and Brinton 2017; Scarborough, Sin, and Risman 2019.

21. For a scholarly example of this perspective, see Hakim 2001.

22. Gray 2012.

23. Ibid., 5.

24. Ibid., 4.

25. Ibid.

26. This finding is in keeping with other research, which shows a positive association between egalitarian attitudes and educational attainment (Davis and Greenstein 2009).

27. Pathological language like this is reminiscent of earlier discussions of female "hysteria" (Chodoff 1974; Micale 1989).

28. Scharrer et al. (2021) discuss trends over time in the depiction of television fathers, noting the persistence of "disparagement humor" in which fathers are frequently the butt of the joke.

29. Full lyrics are available here: https://www.classical-music.com/features/works/theres -a-hole-in-my-bucket-lyrics/.

30. Austrew 2023; Ehrstein 2022; McLuhan et al. 2014.

31. Hartley 2017; Lockman 2019.

32. Recent research by philosophers McClelland and Sliwa (2022) puts forth an intriguing hypothesis regarding mental "affordances," which supports Colleen's suspicion that Ted didn't "see" the air pump. McClelland and Sliwa argue that there may be gender differences in whether and how strongly people see objects as "affording" housework-related action. In the terms of their argument, Ted might see the pump as merely an object, whereas Colleen might see it as an object affording the action of "putting away."

33. My data do not allow me to determine the order of events. It is possible, for instance, that Anita once believed Glenn was "naturally" indisposed to notice problems like a broken table, but as their marriage deteriorated she changed her interpretation. Alternately, it is possible that her interpretation of his behavior as deliberate contributed to the decline of their relationship. Without longitudinal data, I can only conclude that the absence of personal essentialist rhetoric among Woman-led couples was *associated* with relatively high levels of rancor. However, prior research provides some evidence that marital distress can "initiate searching for and finding unfairness in one's relationship" (Grote and Clark 2001, 288).

34. Bridget noted that she picked 70 percent as her ideal in part because the "cessation of control" required to turn over cognitive labor to her husband scared her. In chapter 4, I unpack her fears in more detail.

35. For more detail on the relationship between choice and circumstance, see Daminger 2020.

36. Damaske 2021; Rao 2020.

37. Beagan et al. 2008.

Chapter 4. Gendered Investment, Gendered Deployment

1. Randall's language echoes that of an interviewee quoted in Hjálmsdóttir and Bjarnadóttir (2021, 277), who says she has "turned into a foreman here at home" during the Covid-19 lockdown.

2. My data allow me to examine the origins of these patterns within the context of the couple's relationship and transition to parenthood; however, I do not have sufficient data to explore pre-relational processes in great detail. Other scholars' work shows that girls and boys are placed on different trajectories from a very early age, which likely provides the backdrop for the gendered processes in adulthood that I document here. See, e.g., Kane 2012; Martin 1998; Stacey 2021.

3. Research shows considerable individual variation in spatial navigation skills, with some evidence suggesting these differences are patterned by sex (Wolbers and Hegarty 2010). The causes of such differences are debated, however, with some scholars pointing to sex hormones and others noting the role of factors such as prior experience wayfinding and anxiety related to navigation (Lawton and Kallai 2002). It seems likely, as Burte and Montello (2017, 3) argue, that differences are the result of "some combination of innate or learned spatial abilities and/or acquired strategies for learning and estimating spatial properties."

4. Research on "transactive memory systems" shows that people in close interdependent relationships tend to divide and conquer when it comes to remembering information, based on their perceptions of each other's expertise, and that gender stereotypes shape those perceptions

(Hollingshead and Fraidin 2003). For skills such as financial literacy, being assigned the leadership role in managing family finances leads one partner to develop skills while the other's skills atrophy, eventually producing a gap in the competencies of the two partners that may have been small or nonexistent to start (Ward and Lynch 2019).

5. Leah and Mateo's experience points to the importance of structural factors, including access to paid parental leave, that intersect with individuals' ability to invest in family-related skills, knowledge, and relationships. Paternity leave is positively associated with father involvement in childcare and other forms of household labor, and longer and/or solo paternity leaves have larger effects (Bünning 2015; Petts and Knoester 2018). I return to the importance of structural factors later in the chapter.

6. Calarco and colleagues (2021) report that different-gender couples dealing with new responsibilities generated by the Covid-19 pandemic typically allocated more childcare to mothers "by default rather than through active negotiation."

7. Ample evidence indicates that digital parenting networks tend to be dominated by women, and some scholars argue that this helps perpetuate gender inequality in parenting labor (Brady and Guerin 2010; Lupton, Pedersen, and Thomas 2016).

8. Doucet (2000, 2006, 2009) has also pointed out the challenges fathers face integrating into female-dominated parenting networks and argues that these challenges help preserve the link between women and primary responsibility for childcare.

9. Research shows that women are held more accountable, particularly for children's outcomes, than men. These judgments start even before the child is born, when mothers' behaviors during pregnancy are monitored and expectant mothers begin anticipating future parenting demands (Bass 2015; Hernandez and Calarco 2021; Waggoner 2017).

10. Scholars have argued that a deterrent to men's greater investment in building parenting-related skills and relationships is women's "gatekeeping" behavior (Allen and Hawkins 1999; Puhlman and Pasley 2013). Allen and Hawkins (1999, 200) define maternal gatekeeping as "a collection of beliefs and behaviors that ultimately inhibit a collaborative effort between men and women in family work by limiting men's opportunities for learning and growing through caring for home and children." Later scholars have argued for an expanded definition that includes positive behaviors that help facilitate father involvement (Lee and Schoppe-Sullivan 2023; Puhlman and Pasley 2013).

11. It is difficult to determine the accuracy of beliefs like Jennifer's, given the hypothetical nature of her fears, but recent experimental research confirms that gender shapes perceptions of responsibility for housework and childcare tasks (Doan and Quadlin 2018) and judgments regarding home cleanliness (Thébaud, Kornrich, and Ruppanner 2019).

12. Again, it's likely that some of those gaps predated the relationship, given what we know about gendered socialization patterns (Carter 2014; Cunningham 2001; Martin 1998; Stacey 2021). However, my data focus primarily on what happened from the start of the relationship and particularly during the early days of parenthood.

13. Though I did not ask about this directly, women are also considerably more likely than their husbands to have prior experience with childcare, such as through a teenage babysitting job (Besen-Cassino 2018).

14. Definitions of "executive function" and of its specific subcomponents vary widely across studies (Baggetta and Alexander 2016). Based on their review of extant research on executive function, Baggetta and Alexander (2016, 24) recommend defining executive function as "a set

of cognitive processes that: 1) guides action and behaviors essential to aspects of learning and everyday human performance tasks; 2) contributes to the monitoring or regulation of such tasks; and 3) pertains not only to the cognitive domain, but also socioemotional and behavioral domains of human performance."

15. The most commonly cited components of executive function are inhibitory control (i.e., one's ability to deliberately manage automatic thoughts or responses); working memory; shifting (also called "cognitive flexibility"); planning; and attention (Baggetta and Alexander 2016). Decision making is also included in some definitions, e.g., Grissom and Reyes 2019.

16. A meta-analysis shows that while individual components (i.e., working memory, inhibition, and cognitive flexibility) can be improved via training, there is limited evidence that those gains will translate into improvements in other components not explicitly trained (Kassai et al. 2019). The authors conclude that the best training programs will target multiple components simultaneously.

17. Grissom and Reyes 2019.

18. Ibid.

19. Alex took on a few more physical labor tasks but, consistent with recent research on gender and unemployment, his wife still completed the majority of such work (Damaske 2020, 2021; Rao 2020, 2021).

20. Findings from Damaske 2020, 2021 suggest that Alex's ability to take his time returning to work, while in the meantime leaning into his hobbies and engaging in extensive reflection about his career goals, was likely a product of the privileges afforded middle-class men. Damaske finds that women and working-class men are more likely to have diverted and urgent job searches, respectively.

21. Many of those support staff are likely to be women. For example, roughly 85 percent of nurses and 94 percent of secretaries/administrative assistants identify as female (Beckhusen 2022; Day and Christnacht 2019).

22. Emens 2015, 2019.

23. An analogous theory is the "strength model" of self-control, which argues that exercising willpower in one situation depletes one's capacity to exercise restraint subsequently (Vohs et al. 2008; Wang et al. 2010). However, the accuracy of this model may depend on individuals' theories of self-control: those who *believe* self-control is a limited resource are more likely to show diminished self-control over time (Job, Dweck, and Walton 2010).

24. My findings here parallel those of Tichenor (2005), who found that women who outearn their husbands do not necessarily do commensurately less housework. Women whose higher income translates into less housework are typically partnered with men who perceive the woman's job as more important.

25. Again, this echoes Tichenor's (2005) finding that it is the *perception* of relative career importance, more so than the economics, that impacted whether higher-earning women in her study did a lower share of the housework.

26. While breadwinning responsibility is historically associated with husbands and fathers (Coltrane 1996; Gerson 1993; Riggs 1997; Townsend 2002), *management* of financial affairs is a bit more complicated. Cooper (2014, 152), for instance, highlights the intersection between financial management and social class, noting that "when there is extra money in the household to be managed or invested, it is the men who control it, whereas when money is tight, women are in charge of the everyday management."

Chapter 5. Nontraditional Paths

1. These same cultural imperatives appear to underpin the widespread experience of "maternal guilt" described in prior research (Collins 2021; Constantinou, Varela, and Buckby 2021; Fielding-Singh and Cooper 2023; Sutherland 2010).

2. Collectively, I refer to Man-led and Balanced different-gender couples as "nontraditional" when describing patterns not specific to either group.

3. To my knowledge, no prior study has examined different-gender couples with a nontraditional cognitive labor allocation; instead, couples have been selected on the basis of their division of household chores (e.g., cooking meals, cleaning) and childcare (Deutsch 2000; Ehrensaft 1987; Risman and Johnson-Sumerford 1998; Schwartz 1994). Several of these studies hint that apparently nontraditional couples might be classified differently if cognitive labor were included. Deutsch (2000) reports, for example, that household management skews more heavily female among her sample; Ehrensaft (1987) finds that women in egalitarian relationships do more "worrying" and household scheduling; and Zimmerman and coauthors (2002) describe couples who understand themselves as egalitarian but put much more of the "family organization" work on the female partner.

4. This is a relatively uncommon household structure: Pew Research Center estimates that 7 percent of American fathers are at-home parents, compared to 26 percent of mothers (Fry 2023). Further, only a minority of the 7 percent of men say they are home in order to care for their family; many are instead home because they are ill or disabled, unable to find work, or in school.

5. Exceptions to this pattern were concentrated among couples with an at-home father, such as Meg and Bram.

6. In this quote, Antoni is referring to Siobhan's postgraduate training in child development.

7. Carrie's experiences are consistent with prior research on the presumed incompatibility between the "ideal mother" and "ideal worker" roles (Blair-Loy 2003, 2010; Thébaud and Taylor 2021).

8. Issues related to children's diet, health, and weight can be particularly fraught for mothers, who are typically positioned as "responsible" for such matters (Brenton 2017; DeVault 1991; Elliott and Bowen 2018; Fielding-Singh and Cooper 2023).

9. The "doing gender" theory makes clear that while it is possible to do gender in nonnormative ways, individuals who do so risk being "held to account" for their actions (West and Zimmerman 1987). "Virtually any activity," West and Zimmerman elaborate, "can be assessed as to its womanly or manly nature" (136).

10. For more on male caregivers' experiences, and particularly their challenges related to social integration in gendered parenting communities, see Doucet 2000, 2006, 2009; Lee and Lee 2018; and Rochlen, McKelley, and Whittaker 2010.

11. Allen and Hawkins 1999; Puhlman and Pasley 2013.

12. I classified six different-gender couples as Man-led and eight as Balanced. Together these groups constitute approximately 20 percent of my different-gender sample.

13. This is consistent with Rosenthal's (1985) report that "kinkeeping"—i.e., the work of maintaining extended family relationships—is typically woman-led.

14. I was initially skeptical in large part because Woman-led couples frequently implied that a task was shared but, when probed, revealed that partners had distinct roles.

15. Carlson 2022.

16. Seventy-nine percent of nontraditional men and 86 percent of nontraditional women had at least a four-year college degree, compared to 81 percent and 83 percent of men and women in the full different-gender sample.

17. Nontraditional couples did have a higher average household income than their Woman-led peers ($192,500 vs. $150,000). Data on the relationship between social class and gender egalitarian behaviors is complicated. Education is positively correlated with time spent on housework for men, but negatively for women (Bianchi et al. 2000; Sullivan 2010). Some scholars find that greater privilege is associated with lower equality, whether because lower-income couples are more likely to work alternate shifts or because higher-income couples can more easily afford to live on one partner's income (Deutsch and Saxon 1998; Presser 1994; Usdansky 2011; Yavorsky et al. 2023).

18. In one Balanced couple, the female partner's hours and earnings were lower. This couple was unusual along several dimensions, however, including the fact that this was the only couple in which I was not able to interview the female partner; the only working-class couple to share cognitive labor equally; and the only couple in which physical labor was woman-led but cognitive labor was shared or man-led.

19. See Van Bavel, Schwartz, and Esteve 2018 for a review of recent research countering or complicating the gender display theory, which would predict that women's greater economic resources would translate into a *greater* housework load.

20. These figures are calculated with data from different-gender couples only.

21. Coltrane 2000; Lachance-Grzela and Bouchard 2010.

22. This finding parallels Deutsch's (2000): in a study of egalitarian couples—defined on the basis of their physical labor practices—Deutsch reports that equality is more often the unintended consequence of external constraints than the result of premeditated intention.

23. Carrie's general disdain for the institution of marriage, based on her strong negative feelings about her parents' relationship, was shared by several other nontraditional women. This accords with Deutsch's (2000) argument that women in egalitarian relationships tend to have more "emotional" power than their counterparts in traditional unions, because they are married to men with a stronger investment in the marital relationship and in having children. Of course, it could also simply be that these women's early experiences shaped their preferences in similar ways.

24. Ronald's deference to Carrie's career is notable in light of long-standing findings that women are more likely to make career sacrifices to support a man's career than vice versa (Bielby and Bielby 1992; Brandén 2014), though recent research documents sources of variation (Wong 2017, 2023).

25. Unknowingly, Ronald stumbled on a curious finding unearthed by other researchers, who note that perceptions of fairness, even more than actual labor allocation, drive relationship satisfaction (Lennon and Rosenfield 1994; Wilkie, Ferree, and Ratcliff 1998).

26. Carrie grew up in a working-class family and Ronald in a middle-class household; this may be one factor influencing their different approaches to structure (Streib 2015).

27. Both Kurt and Meredith and Richard and Shannon fell into this second group of more adaptive than intentional couples.

28. In this way, Meredith strongly echoes many of the young women in Gerson's (2011) interview study who preferred self-reliance to a gender-traditional marriage.

29. Kurt and Meredith were committed evangelical Christians, a belief system associated with more traditional notions of gender roles (Moon, Tobin, and Sumerau 2019). The spouses described their ideal division of cognitive labor as 50/50 (Meredith) or an offsetting 70/30 male skew for physical labor and 70/30 female skew for cognitive labor (Kurt). Nevertheless, I suspect that their religious background may have contributed to some of the frustrations described below.

30. Oláh and Gähler 2014.

Chapter 6. "Which of You Is 'the Woman'?"

1. My own assessment was that while Olga acts as chief cognitive laborer for the household, the couple roughly shares physical labor—though Andrea takes on a greater share of what scholars call the "core" or "routine" physical tasks related to cleaning and childcare (Coltrane 2000; Lachance-Grzela and Bouchard 2010).

2. I use the term "queer" rather than "same-gender" because not all of my respondents were in same-gender relationships. Some participants identified as nonbinary; some couples identified as queer despite being different-gender, usually because one partner was transgender. I also refer to "same-gender female" and "same-gender male" couples, except in cases where the participants themselves applied a different label, because not all members of same-gender couples identified as either lesbian or gay; some, for instance, described themselves as bisexual.

3. As a result, throughout this chapter I frequently describe Balanced and Imbalanced queer couples together, though I draw attention to notable group differences where relevant. The fact that equality/inequality was not a stark dividing line among the queer couples lends credence to some scholars' argument that we cannot assume that (in)equality *means* the same thing in all relational contexts, nor that inequality is inherently negative (Goldberg 2013; Moore 2008; Reczek 2020).

4. Dustin and Paul were one of four "offsetter" couples, meaning that one partner handled most of the physical labor and the other most of the cognitive. This pattern was more common among same- than different-gender couples but was not the dominant pattern among either group.

5. This is consistent with earlier research on the division of physical labor among same-gender male and female couples, which generally shows that such couples tend to be more equal than different-gender couples, though not necessarily 50/50 (Biblarz and Savci 2010; Brewster 2017).

6. This would be consistent with Moore's (2008) argument, based on a sample of Black, lesbian stepfamilies, that managing household labor could be a source of relationship power rather than solely a burden.

7. Calarco and colleagues' (2021) finding that different-gender couples rely heavily on mothers' domestic labor "by default" rather than via deliberation would seem to support Patrick's hypothesis.

8. This does not mean that gender is irrelevant for their—or any other—same-gender relationship, as scholars using the gender-as-relational (GAR) approach argue (Thomeer, Umberson, and Reczek 2020; Umberson, Thomeer, and Lodge 2015).

9. See Pfeffer 2010, 2017 for an in-depth study of household labor practices among couples comprised of a cisgender woman and transgender man.

10. This is consistent with Goldberg and colleagues' (2012) findings based on a sample of same- and different-gender adoptive parent couples. The authors report that feminine and

masculine tasks were less segregated among same-gender couples (i.e., less likely to be concentrated in one partner's purview).

11. This is consistent with some scholars' argument that butch/femme couples may subvert rather than reproduce heteropatriarchal dynamics (Lev 2008).

12. My data do not enable me to compare the total amount of cognitive labor completed by different-gender, same-gender female, and same-gender male couples. In the absence of a metric like time, I focused on detecting differences *between* partners rather than across couples. However, the qualitative evidence I have points to more similarities than differences in the cognitive labor patterns of same-gender male and female couples. For instance, very few queer respondents, regardless of gender, indicated that the cognitive tasks included in the card-sort activity did not happen in their household. Nearly all exceptions were concentrated among couples with very young children who were not yet in school or day care, and thus weren't yet going on playdates or field trips or attending summer camps. It is possible that the way queer men and women performed cognitive tasks was qualitatively different by gender, but I did not detect any such systematic variation.

13. One exception in my data was a woman who'd had a child with her now ex-husband before re-partnering with a woman.

14. Gager 1998; Thompson 1991.

15. Scholars have documented an "egalitarian ethic," or tendency to strongly value relationship equality, among queer couples (Downing and Goldberg 2011) but have also noted that this ethic belies considerable diversity among queer couples. Further, self-reports of equality are sometimes exaggerated (Carrington 2002). As Goldberg (2013, 90) writes, couples "may be concerned not only with being seen as accommodating to heteronormativity but also with failing to live up to the prevailing norms of the LGB community (i.e., violating homonormativity)." Of course, different-gender couples can also be unreliable narrators and they, too, save face via family myths (Hochschild and Machung 2012; Kamo 2000).

16. This is consistent with other research on the division of housework among same-gender couples. For example, in a review of literature on lesbian couples, Brewster (2017, 61–62) argues that a major distinction between lesbian couples with an unequal (specifically, a heteronormative) division of housework and their different-gender peers is "a high level of cognizance about the process" and "continuous evaluation, negotiation, and communication about their needs."

17. This was true in a more limited sense among Woman-led couples, in that men commonly invested in a small subset of male-typed domestic tasks.

18. Goldberg 2013; Moore 2008.

19. To some extent, Cody and James offer a version of a point I've previously argued: namely, that while couples often perceive their labor allocation as a function of external constraints, at least some of those constraints were generated by the couple's earlier choices, rather than forced on them from the outside (Daminger 2020).

Conclusion

1. Brekhus 2020; Fischer 2008; Giddens 1986. Future research should explore cross-national variation in both cognitive labor patterns and the narratives that sustain them. Collins's (2019, 2020, 2021) work, for instance, demonstrates how individualist thinking is considerably more prominent among American than European mothers.

2. As originally formulated, the doing gender theory hints at the role of attitudes, perceptions, and other cognitive elements of our gender performance. However, West and Zimmerman's (1987) emphasis on interaction has obscured questions about the internal experience of gender (Meadow 2018; Messerschmidt 2009). This focus makes sense in light of their key insight that doing gender is about being held to account by others. Behavior is visible to others in a way that cognition is not. And yet behavior and cognition are inextricably linked; we cannot fully understand behavior without paying attention to the cognition that precedes it.

3. Scholars have noted that in recent years women's options appear to have expanded further than men's, such that men's and boys' gender is policed more heavily (Kane 2012; Meadow 2018; Pascoe 2007).

4. For example, we expect many women to enter the workforce but also to feel conflicted about leaving their children behind (Christopher 2012; Gerson and Damaske 2020; Hays 1996). We expect many men to scrub toilets but to do so in response to a wife's request rather than at their own initiative (Coltrane 1996; Doucet 2001).

5. The question of whether such success is cause or consequence of these couples' nontraditional patterns remains unresolved. I suspect it varies across couples: for the couples I describe as "adaptive" in chapter 5, it may be closer to cause, and for those I describe as "intentional," it seems more likely effect.

6. Craig and Brown 2016; England, Levine, and Mishel 2020; Iversen and Rosenbluth 2010; Offer and Schneider 2011.

7. Kincaid 2021.

8. Petts and Carlson 2023. See also the work of Ciciolla and Luthar (2019), who show how perceptions of responsibility for household management are negatively correlated with mothers' well-being and relationship satisfaction.

9. Weeks 2024.

10. For example, Weeks (2024) developed a twenty-four-item scale in which respondents are asked to report who in their family "typically handles" various cognitive household tasks. In another recent study, Petts and Carlson (2023, 193) include only two items but offer specific examples for each: "household management/organizing (e.g., planning, assigning tasks, keeping track of household needs, scheduling repairs, etc.)" and "organizing/planning for child (e.g., scheduling doctor appointments, planning play dates, organizing activities)."

11. Christopher 2020. Preliminary findings from De Laat and Doucet (2024) show a relatively weak correlation between the way fathers report on their allocation of abstract responsibilities in surveys versus qualitative interviews. By contrast, they find a stronger correlation between survey and interview reports on the allocation of concrete tasks.

12. Jerolmack and Khan 2014; Krumpal 2013.

13. Bianchi, Robinson, and Milkie 2006; Robinson and Godbey 2010.

14. Allen 2016; Dow 2019; Edwards 2018; Herd and Moynihan 2019; León-Pérez, Richards, and Non 2021; Vesely, Letiecq, and Goodman 2019.

15. Collins 2022; Dow 2016a, 2019; Stack 1983.

16. Parts of this history are described in chapter 1. See Federici 1995; Folbre 1991; Kneeland 1929; Siegel 1994; and Silbaugh 1996.

17. E.g., Emma 2018; Hartley 2017.

18. Caron 2021; Grose 2021.

19. Volpe 2023.

20. For an exception, see Ziesel 2021. Organizations like Fathering Together are also providing an important counterpoint to the largely woman-centered content.

21. Ferree, Khan, and Morimoto 2007; Mirin 2021.

22. Unfortunately, this has too often meant simply pushing such labor from one group of women to another, less privileged set (Dill 2016; Ehrenreich and Hochschild 2004; Parreñas 2015; Rollins 1985).

23. Collins's (2019, 2020) interviews with American mothers suggest they have strongly internalized this self-blame, understanding themselves, rather than the broader policy context, as responsible for their struggles managing work and family responsibilities.

24. Orloff 1993.

25. Cooper 2014; Ramey and Ramey 2010.

26. See Cha 2013 and Goldin 2021 for more on how the hours requirements and on-call expectations of many white-collar jobs can interfere with gender equity in household labor.

27. Lareau 2011; Monna and Gauthier 2008; Nomaguchi and Milkie 2020; Sullivan 2010.

28. Milkie and Warner (2014) describe the largely maternal work of ensuring children retain their parents' position in the class hierarchy as "status safeguarding." See also Cooper 2014 and Ramey and Ramey 2010.

29. For more on this topic, see Collins 2019 and Orloff 1993. Their work is particularly compelling because it is comparative, documenting cross-national variation in women's experiences that they tie directly to variations in social policy regimes, among other factors.

30. Collins 2019; Gerson 1985; Reid 2015; Stone 2007.

31. The recommendations in this paragraph overlap somewhat with those offered by Emens (2015, 2019). For example, Emens (2015, 1466) recommends that government agencies "evaluate their forms and procedures . . . to see if any of their burdens create unnecessary and unjustified time demands on citizens" and identifies the Paperwork Reduction Act as an important but limited measure.

32. Edwards 2018; Herd and Moynihan 2019.

33. Lamont and Small 2008; Swidler 1986.

34. Dweck 2007. More recent research has challenged Dweck's earlier findings, placing scope conditions around when, where, and for whom "growth mindset" interventions are most effective (Burnette et al. 2023; Yeager and Dweck 2020).

35. Cha 2013; Cha and Weeden 2014; Goldin 2021.

36. Acker 1990; Blair-Loy 2003; Reid 2015.

37. Schneider, Harknett, and their collaborators have established an impressive body of work documenting the class and gender implications of practices like just-in-time scheduling, which are common for shift workers. See, for example, Harknett and Schneider 2022; Harknett, Schneider, and Luhr 2020; and Luhr, Schneider, and Harknett 2022.

38. Kelly and Moen (2020) argue compellingly against the idea of "flexibility as accommodation," which they argue leads to the mistaken assumption that only some subgroups (largely women with caregiving demands) require flexibility. For more on the "flexibility stigma," see Cech and Blair-Loy 2014; Chung 2022; Coltrane et al. 2013; and Williams 2001.

39. Buzard, Gee, and Stoddard 2023.

40. If you prefer to follow a more formal system, I recommend Rodsky's (2019) *Fair Play*. The book and associated card deck are the tools I most often suggest to couples who ask me for practical advice about reallocating their cognitive as well as physical labor.

41. The recommendations in this paragraph overlap somewhat with the process Oster (2021) suggests in *The Family Firm*, though Oster is considerably less focused on the allocation of labor between partners.

Methodological Appendix

1. Specifically, I read Budig and England 2001; Correll, Benard, and Paik 2007; and Hochschild and Machung 2012.

2. Mani et al. 2013; Mullainathan and Shafir 2013.

3. Daniels 1987; Hochschild 1979; Hochschild and Machung 2012; Offer 2014; Rosenthal 1985. See Reich-Stiebert et al. 2023 for a systematic review.

4. Blood and Wolfe 1960; Gillespie 1971; Komter 1989.

5. Jerolmack and Khan 2014; Kamo 2000.

6. Gerson and Damaske 2020; Lamont and Swidler 2014; Pugh 2013.

7. Robinson and Godbey 2010. Regardless of the precise method used, self-report consumption data is often misreported; however, shorter and more specific periods of recall (e.g., a list of all foods eaten in the previous twenty-four hours) tend to be somewhat more accurate than general questionnaires about the frequency with which one eats particular foods (Park et al. 2018). The latest advancements in the field of dietary assessment center on moving away from self-report altogether by relying on technology such as smartphones, which produce photographic records of consumption that can be assessed using artificial intelligence, and wearables, which track metrics such as number of bites taken (Archundia Herrera and Chan 2018; Rollo et al. 2016).

8. Tversky and Kahneman 1973.

9. Darrah, Freeman, and English-Lueck 2007; Yavorsky, Kamp Dush, and Schoppe-Sullivan 2015.

10. Cotter, Hermsen, and Vanneman 2011; Knight and Brinton 2017; Scarborough, Sin, and Risman 2019; Usdansky 2011. Note, however, that there is some disagreement among scholars about the relationship between class and egalitarian behavior, as opposed to ideology. See Usdansky 2011 for more detail.

11. Hays 1996; Lareau 2011.

12. Though I did interview three queer couples in Phase 1, I analyzed them with the Phase 3 data.

13. Thomeer, Umberson, and Reczek 2020.

14. Ehrstein 2022.

15. NJ Department of State 2016.

16. The one exception was also the sole couple in which I only interviewed the male partner.

17. This was not unexpected, as roughly 15 percent of households headed by a same-gender couple include a child under eighteen, compared to approximately 38 percent of the much larger population of households headed by a different-gender couple (Taylor 2020).

18. Brantley 2023; Dow 2016b, 2019; Hughes et al. 2006.

19. Christopher 2013; Dow 2015, 2016a.

20. Ahn, Haines, and Mason 2017; Harrington and Reese-Melancon 2022; Hollingshead and Fraidin 2003.

21. See Cerchiaro 2023 for a thoughtful discussion of the kinds of data produced by individual versus joint couple interviews, both of which can be valuable for distinct research questions and goals.

22. Jenner and Myers 2019; Oates et al. 2022; Thunberg and Arnell 2022.

23. This adds up to 70 participants, rather than 64, because it includes the members of three queer couples who completed the logs but are counted elsewhere as part of the Phase 3 data.

24. I asked them to make a list of all the categories of housework and childcare that were involved in running their family. Initially, I planned to code and analyze these lists; however, I ultimately did not find they added especially helpful information and have not included these data in my analyses.

25. Small 2017.

26. Gerson and Damaske 2020.

27. Christopher (2020) makes a similar observation.

28. Transcription efforts were divided between myself and an external firm hired to assist.

29. Deterding and Waters 2021. Also influential in my thinking were Emerson, Fretz, and Shaw 2011; Gerson and Damaske 2020; and Weiss 1994.

30. Pugh (2013) argues that in-depth interviews provide at least four kinds of information: the honorable, the schematic, the visceral, and meta-feelings. By focusing on things like respondents' tone, their use of humor, and their expressions of guilt or shame, I was able to tap into these multiple levels of meaning.

BIBLIOGRAPHY

AAUW. 2023. "Native Women and the Pay Gap." https://www.aauw.org/resources/article/native-women-and-the-pay-gap/.

Acker, Joan. 1990. "Hierarchies, Jobs, Bodies: A Theory of Gendered Organizations." *Gender & Society* 4(2):139–58.

Ahn, Janet N., Elizabeth L. Haines, and Malia F. Mason. 2017. "Gender Stereotypes and the Coordination of Mnemonic Work within Heterosexual Couples: Romantic Partners Manage Their Daily To-Dos." *Sex Roles* 77(7–8):1–18. https://doi.org/10.1007/s11199-017-0743-1.

Allen, Quaylan. 2016. "'Tell Your Own Story': Manhood, Masculinity and Racial Socialization among Black Fathers and Their Sons." *Ethnic and Racial Studies* 39(10):1831–48.

Allen, Sarah M., and Alan J. Hawkins. 1999. "Maternal Gatekeeping: Mothers' Beliefs and Behaviors That Inhibit Greater Father Involvement in Family Work." *Journal of Marriage and Family* 61(1):199–212.

André, Stéfanie, Chantal Remery, and Mara A. Yerkes. 2023. "Extending Theoretical Explanations for Gendered Divisions of Care during the COVID-19 Pandemic." *Journal of Marriage and Family* 1–18. https://doi.org/10.1111/jomf.12950.

Archundia Herrera, M. Carolina, and Catherine B. Chan. 2018. "Narrative Review of New Methods for Assessing Food and Energy Intake." *Nutrients* 10(8):1064. https://doi.org/10.3390/nu10081064.

Austrew, Ashley. 2023. "Weaponized Incompetence: What It Is and How to Know If It's Happening in Your Relationship." Care.com. https://www.care.com/c/what-is-weaponized-incompetence/.

Baggetta, Peter, and Patricia A. Alexander. 2016. "Conceptualization and Operationalization of Executive Function." *Mind, Brain, and Education* 10(1):10–33. https://doi.org/10.1111/mbe.12100.

Barnes, Riché J. Daniel. 2016. *Raising the Race: Black Career Women Redefine Marriage, Motherhood, and Community.* New Brunswick, NJ: Rutgers University Press.

Bass, Brooke C. 2015. "Preparing for Parenthood? Gender, Aspirations, and the Reproduction of Labor Market Inequality." *Gender & Society* 29(3):362–85. https://doi.org/10.1177/0891243214546936.

Beagan, Brenda, Gwen E. Chapman, Andrea D'Sylva, and B. Raewyn Bassett. 2008. "'It's Just Easier for Me to Do It': Rationalizing the Family Division of Foodwork." *Sociology* 42(4):653–71. https://doi.org/10.1177/0038038508091621.

Beck, Julie. 2018. "The Concept Creep of 'Emotional Labor.'" *The Atlantic.* https://www
.theatlantic.com/family/archive/2018/11/arlie-hochschild-housework-isnt-emotional
-labor/576637/.

Becker, Gary. 1993. *A Treatise on the Family.* Cambridge, MA: Harvard University Press.

Beckhusen, Julia. 2022. "Administrative Professionals Day Recognizes 2% of U.S. Workforce,
Mostly Women Who Earn Less than Average Worker." *Census.Gov.* https://www.census.gov
/library/stories/2022/04/recognizing-nations-administrative-professionals.html.

Beecher, Catharine E. 1841. *A Treatise on Domestic Economy for the Use of Young Ladies at Home
and at School.* Boston: Marsh, Capen, Lyon & Webb.

Berk, Richard A., and Sarah F. Berk. 1983. "Supply-Side Sociology of the Family: The Challenge
of the New Home Economics." *Annual Review of Sociology* 9:375–95.

Berk, Sarah F. 1985. *The Gender Factory: The Apportionment of Work in American Households.* New
York: Plenum Press.

Bertrand, Marianne, Emir Kamenica, and Jessica Pan. 2015. "Gender Identity and Relative Income within Households." *Quarterly Journal of Economics* 130(2):571–614. https://doi.org
/10.1093/qje/qjv001.

Besen-Cassino, Yasemin. 2018. *The Cost of Being a Girl: Working Teens and the Origins of the
Gender Wage Gap.* Philadelphia: Temple University Press.

Bianchi, Suzanne M., Melissa A. Milkie, Liana C. Sayer, and John P. Robinson. 2000. "Is Anyone
Doing the Housework? Trends in the Gender Division of Household Labor." *Social Forces*
79(1):191–228.

Bianchi, Suzanne M., John P. Robinson, and Melissa A. Milkie. 2006. *Changing Rhythms of
American Family Life.* New York: Russell Sage Foundation.

Bianchi, Suzanne M., Liana C. Sayer, Melissa A. Milkie, and John P. Robinson. 2012. "Housework: Who Did, Does or Will Do It, and How Much Does It Matter?" *Social Forces* 91(1):55–63.
https://doi.org/10.1093/sf/sos120.

Biblarz, Timothy J., and Evren Savci. 2010. "Lesbian, Gay, Bisexual, and Transgender Families."
Journal of Marriage and Family 72(3):480–97. https://doi.org/10.1111/j.1741-3737.2010
.00714.x.

Bielby, William, and Denise Bielby. 1992. "I Will Follow Him: Family Ties, Gender-Role Beliefs, and Reluctance to Relocate for a Better Job." *American Journal of Sociology* 97(5):
1241–67.

Bittman, Michael, Paula England, Nancy Folbre, Liana C. Sayer, and George Matheson. 2003.
"When Does Gender Trump Money? Bargaining and Time in Household Work." *American
Journal of Sociology* 109(1):186–214.

Blair-Loy, Mary. 2003. *Competing Devotions: Career and Family among Women Executives.* Cambridge, MA: Harvard University Press.

———. 2010. "Moral Dimensions of the Work-Family Nexus." *Handbook of the Sociology of
Morality,* ed. S. Hitlin and S. Vaisey, 439–53. New York: Springer.

Blau, Francine D., and Lawrence M. Kahn. 2017. "The Gender Wage Gap: Extent, Trends, and
Explanations." *Journal of Economic Literature* 55(3):789–865. https://doi.org/10.1257/jel
.20160995.

Blood, Robert O., and Donald M. Wolfe. 1960. *Husbands and Wives: The Dynamics of Family
Living.* New York: Free Press.

Bonilla-Silva, Eduardo. 2021. *Racism without Racists: Color-Blind Racism and the Persistence of Racial Inequality in America*. 6th ed. Lanham, MD: Rowman & Littlefield.

Boustan, Leah Platt, and William J. Collins. 2013. "The Origins and Persistence of Black-White Differences in Women's Labor Force Participation." NBER Working Paper No. 19040.

Boydston, Jeanne. 1994. *Home and Work: Housework, Wages, and the Ideology of Labor in the Early Republic*. New York: Oxford University Press.

Brady, Ellen, and Suzanne Guerin. 2010. "'Not the Romantic, All Happy, Coochy Coo Experience': A Qualitative Analysis of Interactions on an Irish Parenting Web Site." *Family Relations* 59(1):14–27. https://doi.org/10.1111/j.1741-3729.2009.00582.x.

Brandén, Maria. 2014. "Gender, Gender Ideology, and Couples' Migration Decisions." *Journal of Family Issues* 35(7):950–71. https://doi.org/10.1177/0192513X14522244.

Brantley, Mia. 2023. "Burdens of the What-if: Vicarious Anti-Black Racism and Stress for Black Mothers." *Journal of Marriage and Family* 85(4):941–61. https://doi.org/10.1111/jomf.12914.

Brekhus, Wayne H. 2020. *The Sociology of Identity: Authenticity, Multidimensionality, and Mobility*. Cambridge: Polity Press.

Brenton, Joslyn. 2017. "The Limits of Intensive Feeding: Maternal Foodwork at the Intersections of Race, Class, and Gender." *Sociology of Health & Illness* 39(6):863–77. https://doi.org/10.1111/1467-9566.12547.

Brewster, Melanie E. 2017. "Lesbian Women and Household Labor Division: A Systematic Review of Scholarly Research from 2000 to 2015." *Journal of Lesbian Studies* 21(1):47–69. https://doi.org/10.1080/10894160.2016.1142350.

Brines, Julie. 1994. "Economic Dependency, Gender, and the Division of Labor at Home." *American Journal of Sociology* 100(3):652–88.

Brown, Bailey A. 2022. "Intensive Mothering and the Unequal School-Search Burden." *Sociology of Education* 95(1):3–22. https://doi.org/10.1177/00380407211048453.

Budig, Michelle J., and Paula England. 2001. "The Wage Penalty for Motherhood." *American Sociological Review* 66(2):204–25.

Bünning, Mareike. 2015. "What Happens after the 'Daddy Months'? Fathers' Involvement in Paid Work, Childcare, and Housework after Taking Parental Leave in Germany." *European Sociological Review* 31(6):738–48. https://doi.org/10.1093/esr/jcv072.

Bureau of Labor Statistics. 2021. "Data Sources: Handbook of Methods: U.S. Bureau of Labor Statistics." https://www.bls.gov/opub/hom/atus/data.htm.

———. 2023. "Table 1. Time Spent in Primary Activities and Percent of the Civilian Population Engaging in Each Activity, Averages per Day by Sex, 2022 Annual Averages—2022 A01 Results." https://www.bls.gov/news.release/atus.t01.htm.

Burnette, Jeni L., Joseph Billingsley, George C. Banks, Laura E. Knouse, Crystal L. Hoyt, Jeffrey M. Pollack, and Stefanie Simon. 2023. "A Systematic Review and Meta-Analysis of Growth Mindset Interventions: For Whom, How, and Why Might Such Interventions Work?" *Psychological Bulletin* 149(3–4):174–205. https://doi.org/10.1037/bul0000368.

Burte, Heather, and Daniel R. Montello. 2017. "How Sense-of-Direction and Learning Intentionality Relate to Spatial Knowledge Acquisition in the Environment." *Cognitive Research: Principles and Implications* 2(1):18. https://doi.org/10.1186/s41235-017-0057-4.

Butler, Judith. 2006. *Gender Trouble: Feminism and the Subversion of Identity*. New York: Routledge.

Buzard, Kristy, Laura K. Gee, and Olga Stoddard. 2023. "Who You Gonna Call? Gender Inequality in External Demands for Parental Involvement." *SSRN Elsevier.* https://doi.org /10.2139/ssrn.4456100.

Calarco, Jessica M., Emily Meanwell, Elizabeth M. Anderson, and Amelia S. Knopf. 2021. "By Default: How Mothers in Different-Sex Dual-Earner Couples Account for Inequalities in Pandemic Parenting." *Socius* 7. https://doi.org/10.1177/23780231211038783.

Carlson, Daniel L. 2022. "Reconceptualizing the Gendered Division of Housework: Number of Shared Tasks and Partners' Relationship Quality." *Sex Roles* 86(9–10):528–43. https://doi .org/10.1007/s11199-022-01282-5.

Carlson, Daniel L., and Richard J. Petts. 2022. "US Parents' Domestic Labor during the First Year of the COVID-19 Pandemic." *Population Research and Policy Review* 41(6):2393–2418. https://doi.org/10.1007/s11113-022-09735-1.

Caron, Christina. 2021. "How Same-Sex Parents Share the Mental Load." *New York Times,* August 25. https://www.nytimes.com/2021/08/25/parenting/same-sex-relationships .html.

Carrington, Christopher. 2002. *No Place like Home: Relationships and Family Life among Lesbians and Gay Men.* Chicago: University of Chicago Press.

Carter, Michael. 2014. "Gender Socialization and Identity Theory." *Social Sciences* 3(2):242–63. https://doi.org/10.3390/socsci3020242.

Cech, Erin A. 2013. "The Self-Expressive Edge of Occupational Sex Segregation." *American Journal of Sociology* 119(3):747–89.

———. 2021. *The Trouble with Passion: How Searching for Fulfillment at Work Fosters Inequality.* Berkeley: University of California Press.

Cech, Erin A., and Mary Blair-Loy. 2014. "Consequences of Flexibility Stigma among Academic Scientists and Engineers." *Work and Occupations* 41(1):86–110. https://doi.org/10.1177 /0730888413515497.

Cerchiaro, Francesco. 2023. "Advancing Research in Couple Studies: Why, When, and How to Combine Individual and Couple Interview." *Quality & Quantity* 57:1465–82.

Cha, Youngjoo. 2013. "Overwork and the Persistence of Gender Segregation in Occupations." *Gender & Society* 27(2):158–84. https://doi.org/10.1177/0891243212470510.

Cha, Youngjoo, and Kim A. Weeden. 2014. "Overwork and the Slow Convergence in the Gender Gap in Wages." *American Sociological Review* 79(3):457–84. https://doi.org/10.1177 /0003122414528936.

Charles, Maria, and Karen Bradley. 2009. "Indulging Our Gendered Selves? Sex Segregation by Field of Study in 44 Countries." *American Journal of Sociology* 114(4):924–76.

Charles, Maria, and David B. Grusky. 2004. *Occupational Ghettos: The Worldwide Segregation of Women and Men.* Palo Alto: Stanford University Press.

Chesley, Noelle, and Sarah Flood. 2016. "Signs of Change? At-Home and Breadwinner Parents' Housework and Child-Care Time." *Journal of Marriage and Family* 79(2):511–34. https://doi .org/10.1111/jomf.12376.

Chodoff, Paul. 1974. "The Diagnosis of Hysteria: An Overview." *American Journal of Psychiatry* 131(10):1073–78.

Christopher, Emily. 2020. "Capturing Conflicting Accounts of Domestic Labour: The Household Portrait as a Methodology." *Sociological Research Online* 26(3):451–68. https://doi.org /10.1177/1360780420951804.

Christopher, Karen. 2012. "Extensive Mothering." *Gender & Society* 26(1):73–96. https://doi.org /10.1177/0891243211427700.

———. 2013. "African Americans' and Latinas' Mothering Scripts: An Intersectional Analysis." *Notions of Family: Intersectional Perspectives*, ed. M. H. Kohlman, D. B. Krieg, and B. J. Dickerson, 187–208. Bingley: Emerald Group Publishing Limited.

Chung, Heejung. 2022. *The Flexibility Paradox: Why Flexible Working Leads to (Self)-Exploitation.* Bristol: Policy Press.

Ciciolla, Lucia, and Suniya S. Luthar. 2019. "Invisible Household Labor and Ramifications for Adjustment: Mothers as Captains of Households." *Sex Roles* 81(7):467–86. https://doi.org /10.1007/s11199-018-1001-x.

Collins, Caitlyn. 2019. *Making Motherhood Work: How Women Manage Careers and Caregiving.* Princeton: Princeton University Press.

———. 2020. "Who to Blame and How to Solve It: Mothers' Perceptions of Work-Family Conflict across Western Policy Regimes." *Journal of Marriage and Family* 82(3):849–74. https://doi.org/10.1111/jomf.12643.

———. 2021. "Is Maternal Guilt a Cross-National Experience?" *Qualitative Sociology* 44(1):1–29. https://doi.org/10.1007/s11133-020-09451-2.

Collins, Caitlyn, Liana C. Landivar, Leah Ruppanner, and William J. Scarborough. 2021. "COVID-19 and the Gender Gap in Work Hours." *Gender, Work & Organization* 28(S1):101–12. https://doi.org/https://doi.org/10.1111/gwao.12506.

Collins, Patricia H. 2022. *Black Feminist Thought, 30th Anniversary Edition: Knowledge, Consciousness, and the Politics of Empowerment.* New York: Routledge.

Coltrane, Scott. 1996. *Family Man: Fatherhood, Housework, and Gender Equality.* New York: Oxford University Press.

———. 2000. "Research on Household Labor: Modeling and Measuring the Social Embeddedness of Routine Family Work." *Journal of Marriage and Family* 62(4):1208–33.

Coltrane, Scott, Elizabeth C. Miller, Tracy DeHaan, and Lauren Stewart. 2013. "Fathers and the Flexibility Stigma." *Journal of Social Issues* 69(2):279–302. https://doi.org/10.1111/josi .12015.

Constantinou, Georgia, Sharon Varela, and Beryl Buckby. 2021. "Reviewing the Experiences of Maternal Guilt: The 'Motherhood Myth' Influence." *Health Care for Women International* 42(4–6):852–76. https://doi.org/10.1080/07399332.2020.1835917.

Cooke, Lynn P., and Jennifer L. Hook. 2018. "Productivity or Gender? The Impact of Domestic Tasks across the Wage Distribution." *Journal of Marriage and Family* 80(3):721–36. https:// doi.org/10.1111/jomf.12467.

Cooper, Marianne. 2014. *Cut Adrift: Families in Insecure Times.* Berkeley: University of California Press.

Correll, Shelley J., Stephen Benard, and In Paik. 2007. "Getting a Job: Is There a Motherhood Penalty?" *American Journal of Sociology* 112(5):1297–1339. https://doi.org/10.1086/511799.

Cotter, David, Joan M. Hermsen, and Reeve Vanneman. 2011. "The End of the Gender Revolution? Gender Role Attitudes from 1977 to 2008." *American Journal of Sociology* 117(1):259–89. https://doi.org/10.1086/658853.

Craig, Lyn. 2006. "Does Father Care Mean Fathers Share? A Comparison of How Mothers and Fathers in Intact Families Spend Time with Children." *Gender & Society* 20(2):259–81. https://doi.org/10.1177/0891243205285212.

Craig, Lyn, and Judith E. Brown. 2016. "Feeling Rushed: Gendered Time Quality, Work Hours, Nonstandard Work Schedules, and Spousal Crossover." *Journal of Marriage and Family* 79(1):225–42. https://doi.org/10.1111/jomf.12320.

Craig, Lyn, and Killian Mullan. 2011. "How Mothers and Fathers Share Childcare: A Cross-National Time-Use Comparison." *American Sociological Review* 76(6):834–61. https://doi .org/10.1177/0003122411427673.

Crenshaw, Kimberle. 1997. "Demarginalizing the Intersection of Race and Sex: A Black Feminist Critique of Antidiscrimination Doctrine, Feminist Theory, and Antiracist Politics." In *Feminist Legal Theories*, ed. K. Maschke. New York: Routledge.

Cretaz, Britni de la. 2020. "How to Get Your Partner to Take on More Emotional Labor." *New York Times*, May 8. https://www.nytimes.com/article/emotional-labor.html.

Cunningham, Mick. 2001. "The Influence of Parental Attitudes and Behaviors on Children's Attitudes toward Gender and Household Labor in Early Adulthood." *Journal of Marriage and Family* 63(1):111–22. https://doi.org/10.1111/j.1741-3737.2001.00111.x.

Damaske, Sarah. 2011. *For the Family? How Class and Gender Shape Women's Work*. New York: Oxford University Press.

———. 2013. "Work, Family, and Accounts of Mothers' Lives Using Discourse to Navigate Intensive Mothering Ideals." *Sociology Compass* 7(6):436–44. https://doi.org/10.1111/soc4 .12043.

———. 2020. "Job Loss and Attempts to Return to Work: Complicating Inequalities across Gender and Class." *Gender & Society* 34(1):7–30. https://doi.org/10.1177/08912432198 69381.

———. 2021. *The Tolls of Uncertainty: How Privilege and the Guilt Gap Shape Unemployment in America*. Princeton: Princeton University Press.

Daminger, Allison. 2019. "The Cognitive Dimension of Household Labor." *American Sociological Review* 84(4):609–33. https://doi.org/10.1177/0003122419859007.

———. 2020. "De-Gendered Processes, Gendered Outcomes: How Egalitarian Couples Make Sense of Non-Egalitarian Household Practices." *American Sociological Review* 85(5):806–29. https://doi.org/10.1177/0003122420950208.

Daniels, Arlene K. 1987. "Invisible Work." *Social Problems* 34(5):403–15.

Darrah, Charles N., James M. Freeman, and J. A. English-Lueck. 2007. *Busier than Ever!: Why American Families Can't Slow Down*. Palo Alto: Stanford University Press.

Davis, Shannon N., and Theodore N. Greenstein. 2009. "Gender Ideology: Components, Predictors, and Consequences." *Annual Review of Sociology* 35(1):87–105. https://doi.org/10 .1146/annurev-soc-070308-115920.

———. 2013. "Why Study Housework? Cleaning as a Window into Power in Couples." *Journal of Family Theory & Review* 5(2):63–71. https://doi.org/10.1111/jftr.12004.

Day, Jennifer C., and Cheridan Christnacht. 2019. "Women Hold 76% of All Health Care Jobs, Gaining in Higher-Paying Occupations." *Census.Gov*. https://www.census.gov/library /stories/2019/08/your-health-care-in-womens-hands.html.

De Laat, Kim, and Andrea Doucet. 2024. "How Do We Measure Father Involvement? Methodological and Epistemological Issues in a Canadian Mixed-Methods Study on Household Tasks and Responsibilities." Conference Presentation. Work Family Researchers Network Biennial Conference. Montreal, Canada.

Dean, Liz, Brendan Churchill, and Leah Ruppanner. 2022. "The Mental Load: Building a Deeper Theoretical Understanding of How Cognitive and Emotional Labor Overload Women and Mothers." *Community, Work & Family* 25(1):13–29. https://doi.org/10.1080/13668803.2021.2002813.

Deloitte and Automotive News. 2020. *Women at the Wheel: Key Findings from the 2020 Diversity, Equity, and Inclusion in Automotive Study.* https://www2.deloitte.com/content/dam/Deloitte/us/Documents/manufacturing/us-women-at-the-wheel-2020-executive-summary-final.pdf.

Dernberger, Brittany, and Joanna Pepin. 2020. "Gender Flexibility, but Not Equality: Young Adults' Division of Labor Preferences." *Sociological Science* 7:36–56. https://doi.org/10.15195/v7.a2.

Deterding, Nicole M., and Mary C. Waters. 2021. "Flexible Coding of In-Depth Interviews." *Sociological Methods & Research* 50(2):708–39. https://doi.org/10.1177/0049124118799377.

Deutsch, Francine M. 2000. *Halving It All: How Equally Shared Parenting Works.* Rev. ed. Cambridge, MA: Harvard University Press.

Deutsch, Francine M., and Susan E. Saxon. 1998. "Traditional Ideologies, Nontraditional Lives." *Sex Roles* 38(5/6):331–62.

DeVault, Marjorie L. 1991. *Feeding the Family: The Social Organization of Caring as Gendered Work.* Chicago: University of Chicago Press.

Dill, Bonnie T. 2016. *Across the Boundaries of Race & Class: An Exploration of Work & Family among Black Female Domestic Servants.* New York: Garland.

Diprete, Thomas A., and Claudia Buchmann. 2006. "Gender-Specific Trends in the Value of Education and the Emerging Gender Gap in College Completion." *Demography* 43(1):1–24. https://doi.org/10.1353/dem.2006.0003.

Doan, Long, and Natasha Quadlin. 2018. "Partner Characteristics and Perceptions of Responsibility for Housework and Child Care." *Journal of Marriage and Family* 81(1):145–63. https://doi.org/10.1111/jomf.12526.

Doucet, Andrea. 1996. "Encouraging Voices: Towards More Creative Methods for Collecting Data on Gender and Household Labour." In *Gender Relations in Public and Private: New Research Perspectives,* ed. L. Morris and E. Stina Lyon, 156–75. New York: St. Martin's Press.

———. 2000. "'There's a Huge Gulf between Me as a Male Carer and Women': Gender, Domestic Responsibility, and the Community as an Institutional Arena." *Community, Work & Family* 3(2):163–84. https://doi.org/10.1080/713658907.

———. 2001. "'You See the Need Perhaps More Clearly than I Have': Exploring Gendered Processes of Domestic Responsibility." *Journal of Family Issues* 22(3):328–57.

———. 2006. "'Estrogen-Filled Worlds': Fathers as Primary Caregivers and Embodiment." *Sociological Review* 54(4):696–716. https://doi.org/10.1111/j.1467-954X.2006.00667.x.

———. 2009. "Dad and Baby in the First Year: Gendered Responsibilities and Embodiment." *ANNALS of the American Academy of Political and Social Science* 624(1):78–98. https://doi.org/10.1177/0002716209334069.

Dow, Dawn M. 2015. "Negotiating 'The Welfare Queen' and 'The Strong Black Woman.'" *Sociological Perspectives* 58(1):36–55. https://doi.org/10.1177/0731121414556546.

———. 2016a. "Integrated Motherhood: Beyond Hegemonic Ideologies of Motherhood." *Journal of Marriage and Family* 78(1):180–96. https://doi.org/10.1111/jomf.12264.

———. 2016b. "The Deadly Challenges of Raising African American Boys: Navigating the Controlling Image of the 'Thug.'" *Gender & Society* 30(2):161–88. https://doi.org/10.1177/089 1243216629928.

———. 2019. *Mothering while Black: Boundaries and Burdens of Middle-Class Parenthood.* Berkeley: University of California Press.

Downing, Jordan B., and Abbie E. Goldberg. 2011. "Lesbian Mothers' Constructions of the Division of Paid and Unpaid Labor." *Feminism & Psychology* 21(1):100–120. https://doi.org/10 .1177/0959353510375869.

Dreilinger, Danielle. 2021. *The Secret History of Home Economics: How Trailblazing Women Harnessed the Power of Home and Changed the Way We Live.* New York: W. W. Norton.

Duffy, Mignon. 2007. "Doing the Dirty Work: Gender, Race, and Reproductive Labor in Historical Perspective." *Gender & Society* 21(3):313–36. https://doi.org/10.1177/0891243207300764.

Dweck, Carol S. 2007. *Mindset: The New Psychology of Success.* New York: Penguin Random House.

Edwards, Linsey Nicole. 2018. "Time and Efficacy: Neighborhoods, Temporal Constraints, and the Persistence of Poverty." PhD diss., Princeton University.

Ehrenreich, Barbara, and Arlie Russell Hochschild, eds. 2004. *Global Woman: Nannies, Maids, and Sex Workers in the New Economy.* New York: Henry Holt and Company.

Ehrensaft, Diane. 1987. *Parenting Together: Men and Women Sharing the Care of Their Children.* New York: Free Press.

Ehrstein, Yvonne. 2022. "'Facilitating Wife' and 'Feckless Manchild': Working Mothers' Talk about Divisions of Care on Mumsnet." *Feminism & Psychology* 32(3):394–412. https://doi .org/10.1177/09593535221094260.

Elliott, Sinikka, and Sarah Bowen. 2018. "Defending Motherhood: Morality, Responsibility, and Double Binds in Feeding Children." *Journal of Marriage and Family* 80(2):499–520. https:// doi.org/10.1111/jomf.12465.

Else-Quest, Nicole M., Janet S. Hyde, H. Hill Goldsmith, and Carol A. Van Hulle. 2006. "Gender Differences in Temperament: A Meta-Analysis." *Psychological Bulletin* 132(1):33–72. https:// doi.org/10.1037/0033-2909.132.1.33.

Emens, Elizabeth F. 2015. "Admin." *Georgetown Law Journal* 103(6):1409–81.

———. 2019. *Life Admin: How I Learned to Do Less, Do Better, and Live More.* Boston: Houghton Mifflin Harcourt.

Emerson, Robert M., Rachel I. Fretz, and Linda L. Shaw. 2011. *Writing Ethnographic Fieldnotes.* 2nd ed. Chicago: University of Chicago Press.

Emma. 2018. *The Mental Load: A Feminist Comic.* New York: Seven Stories Press.

England, Paula. 2010. "The Gender Revolution." *Gender & Society* 24(2):149–66. https://doi.org /10.1177/0891243210361475.

England, Paula, Andrew Levine, and Emma Mishel. 2020. "Progress toward Gender Equality in the United States Has Slowed or Stalled." *Proceedings of the National Academy of Sciences* 117(13):6990–97. https://doi.org/10.1073/pnas.1918891117.

Espeland, Wendy N., and Mitchell L. Stevens. 1998. "Commensuration as a Social Process." *Annual Review of Sociology* 24:313–43.

———. 2008. "A Sociology of Quantification." *European Journal of Sociology/Archives Européennes de Sociologie* 49(3):401–36.

Evertsson, Marie, Paula England, Irma Mooi-Reci, Joan Hermsen, Jeanne De Bruijn, and David Cotter. 2009. "Is Gender Inequality Greater at Lower or Higher Educational Levels? Common Patterns in the Netherlands, Sweden, and the United States." *Social Politics: International Studies in Gender, State & Society* 16(2):210–41.

Federici, Silvia. 1995. "Wages against Housework." In *The Politics of Housework*, ed. E. Malos, 187–94. Cheltenham: New Clarion Press.

Ferree, Myra M., Shamus R. Khan, and Shauna A. Morimoto. 2007. "Assessing the Feminist Revolution: The Presence and Absence of Gender in Theory and Practice." In *Sociology in America: A History*, ed. C. Calhoun. Chicago: University of Chicago Press.

Festinger, Leon. 1957. *A Theory of Cognitive Dissonance*. Palo Alto: Stanford University Press.

Fielding-Singh, Priya, and Marianne Cooper. 2023. "The Emotional Management of Motherhood: Foodwork, Maternal Guilt, and Emotion Work." *Journal of Marriage and Family* 85(2):436–57. https://doi.org/10.1111/jomf.12878.

Fischer, Claude S. 2008. "Paradoxes of American Individualism." *Sociological Forum* 23(2):363–72. https://doi.org/10.1111/j.1573-7861.2008.00066.x.

Fleeson, William. 2004. "Moving Personality beyond the Person-Situation Debate." *Current Directions in Psychological Science* 13(2):41–87.

Folbre, Nancy. 1991. "The Unproductive Housewife: Her Evolution in Nineteenth-Century Economic Thought." *Signs: Journal of Women in Culture and Society* 16(3):463–84. https://doi.org/10.1086/494679.

———. 2023. "Beyond the Clock: Rethinking the Meaning of Unpaid Childcare in the U.S." *Time & Society* 32(4):367–84.

Forman, Tyrone A., and Amanda E. Lewis. 2015. "Beyond Prejudice? Young Whites' Racial Attitudes in Post–Civil Rights America, 1976 to 2000." *American Behavioral Scientist* 59(11):1394–1428.

Frederick, Christine. 1923. *Household Engineering: Scientific Management in the Home*. Chicago: American School of Home Economics.

Fry, Richard. 2023. "Almost 1 in 5 Stay-at-Home Parents in the U.S. Are Dads." *Pew Research Center*. https://www.pewresearch.org/short-reads/2023/08/03/almost-1-in-5-stay-at-home-parents-in-the-us-are-dads/.

Fry, Richard, Carolina Aragao, Kiley Hurst, and Kim Parker. 2023. "In a Growing Share of U.S. Marriages, Husbands and Wives Earn About the Same." *Pew Research Center*. https://www.pewresearch.org/social-trends/2023/04/13/in-a-growing-share-of-u-s-marriages-husbands-and-wives-earn-about-the-same/.

Gager, Constance T. 1998. "The Role of Valued Outcomes, Justifications, and Comparison Referents in Perceptions of Fairness among Dual-Earner Couples." *Journal of Family Issues* 19(5):622–48.

Gale, Rebecca. 2022. "Should Unpaid Labor Like Childcare Be Part of the GDP? One Group Is Trying to Make It Happen." *Fortune*. https://fortune.com/2022/04/28/eve-rodsky-unpaid-labor-part-of-gdp-by-2030/.

Gerson, Kathleen. 1985. *Hard Choices: How Women Decide about Work, Career and Motherhood*. Berkeley: University of California Press.

———. 1993. *No Man's Land: Men's Changing Commitments to Family and Work*. New York: Basic Books.

———. 2011. *The Unfinished Revolution: Coming of Age in a New Era of Gender, Work, and Family.* Oxford: Oxford University Press.

Gerson, Kathleen, and Sarah Damaske. 2020. *The Science and Art of Interviewing.* New York: Oxford University Press.

Gerstel, Naomi, and Dan Clawson. 2014. *Unequal Time: Gender, Class, and Family in Employment Schedules.* New York: Russell Sage Foundation.

Giddens, Anthony. 1986. *The Constitution of Society: Outline of the Theory of Structuration.* Reprint. Berkeley: University of California Press.

Gilbreth, Lillian. 1928. *The Home-Maker and Her Job.* New York: D. Appleton and Company.

Gillespie, Dair L. 1971. "Who Has the Power? The Marital Struggle." *Journal of Marriage and Family* 33(3):445–58.

Glenn, Evelyn N. 1992. "From Servitude to Service Work: Historical Continuities in the Racial Division of Paid Reproductive Labor." *Signs* 18(1):1–43.

Glick, Peter, and Susan T. Fiske. 2001. "An Ambivalent Alliance: Hostile and Benevolent Sexism as Complementary Justifications for Gender Inequality." *American Psychologist* 56(2):109–18. https://doi.org/10.1037/0003-066X.56.2.109.

Goldberg, Abbie E. 2013. "'Doing' and 'Undoing' Gender: The Meaning and Division of Housework in Same-Sex Couples." *Journal of Family Theory & Review* 5(2):85–104. https://doi.org/10.1111/jftr.12009.

Goldberg, Abbie E., JuliAnna Z. Smith, and Maureen Perry-Jenkins. 2012. "The Division of Labor in Lesbian, Gay, and Heterosexual New Adoptive Parents." *Journal of Marriage and Family* 74(4):812–28. https://doi.org/10.1111/j.1741-3737.2012.00992.x.

Goldin, Claudia. 2006. "The Quiet Revolution That Transformed Women's Employment, Education, and Family." *American Economic Review* 96(2):1–21. https://doi.org/10.1257/000282806777212350.

———. 2021. *Career and Family: Women's Century-Long Journey toward Equity.* Princeton: Princeton University Press.

Graf, Nikki L., and Christine R. Schwartz. 2011. "The Uneven Pace of Change in Heterosexual Romantic Relationships." *Gender & Society* 25(1):101–7. https://doi.org/10.1177/0891243210390356.

Grant, Adam. 2021. "There's a Name for the Blah You're Feeling: It's Called Languishing." *New York Times*, April 19. https://www.nytimes.com/2021/04/19/well/mind/covid-mental-health-languishing.html.

Gray, John. 2012. *Men Are from Mars, Women Are from Venus: The Classic Guide to Understanding the Opposite Sex.* New York: Harper.

Grissom, Nicola M., and Teresa M. Reyes. 2019. "Let's Call the Whole Thing Off: Evaluating Gender and Sex Differences in Executive Function." *Neuropsychopharmacology* 44(1):86–96. https://doi.org/10.1038/s41386-018-0179-5.

Grose, Jessica. 2021. "Why Women Do the Household Worrying." *New York Times*, April 21. https://www.nytimes.com/2021/04/21/parenting/women-gender-gap-domestic-work.html.

Grote, Nancy K., and Margaret S. Clark. 2001. "Perceiving Unfairness in the Family: Cause or Consequence of Marital Distress?" *Journal of Personality and Social Psychology* 80(2):281–93. https://doi.org/10.1037//0022-3514.80.2.281.

Gupta, Sanjiv. 2007. "Autonomy, Dependence, or Display? The Relationship between Married Women's Earnings and Housework." *Journal of Marriage and Family* 69(2):399–417.

Hagerman, Margaret A. 2018. *White Kids: Growing Up with Privilege in a Racially Divided America.* New York: New York University Press.

Hains, Rebecca. 2012. *Growing Up with Girl Power: Girlhood on Screen and in Everyday Life.* New York: Peter Lang.

Hakim, Catherine. 2001. *Work-Lifestyle Choices in the 21st Century: Preference Theory.* Oxford: Oxford University Press.

Hall, Scott S., and Shelley M. MacDermid. 2009. "A Typology of Dual Earner Marriages Based on Work and Family Arrangements." *Journal of Family and Economic Issues* 30(3):215–25. https://doi.org/10.1007/s10834-009-9156-9.

Hannan, Michael T., and John Freeman. 1984. "Structural Inertia and Organizational Change." *American Sociological Review* 49(2):149–64. https://doi.org/10.2307/2095567.

Hardill, Irene, Anne E. Green, Anna C. Dudleston, and David W. Owen. 1997. "Who Decides What? Decision Making in Dual-Career Households." *Work, Employment and Society* 11(2):313–26. https://doi.org/10.1177/0950017097112006.

Harknett, Kristen, and Daniel Schneider. 2022. "Mandates Narrow Gender Gaps in Paid Sick Leave Coverage for Low-Wage Workers in the US." *Health Affairs* 41(11):1575–82. https://doi.org/10.1377/hlthaff.2022.00727.

Harknett, Kristen, Daniel Schneider, and Sigrid Luhr. 2020. "Who Cares If Parents Have Unpredictable Work Schedules?: Just-in-Time Work Schedules and Child Care Arrangements." *Social Problems* 69(1):164–83. https://doi.org/10.1093/socpro/spaa020.

Harrington, Erin E., and Celinda Reese-Melancon. 2022. "Who Is Responsible for Remembering? Everyday Prospective Memory Demands in Parenthood." *Sex Roles* 86(3):189–207. https://doi.org/10.1007/s11199-021-01264-z.

Hartley, Gemma. 2017. "Women Aren't Nags—We're Just Fed Up." *Harper's Bazaar.* https://www.harpersbazaar.com/culture/features/a12063822/emotional-labor-gender-equality/.

Haupt, Andreas, and Dafna Gelbgiser. 2023. "The Gendered Division of Cognitive Household Labor, Mental Load, and Family-Work Conflict in European Countries." *European Societies.* https://doi.org/10.1080/14616696.2023.2271963.

Hays, Sharon. 1996. *The Cultural Contradictions of Motherhood.* New Haven: Yale University Press.

Herd, Pamela, and Donald P. Moynihan. 2019. *Administrative Burden: Policymaking by Other Means.* New York: Russell Sage Foundation.

Hernandez, Elaine M., and Jessica M. Calarco. 2021. "Health Decisions amidst Controversy: Prenatal Alcohol Consumption and the Unequal Experience of Influence and Control in Networks." *Social Science & Medicine* 286:114319. https://doi.org/10.1016/j.socscimed.2021.114319.

Hjálmsdóttir, Andrea, and Valgerður S. Bjarnadóttir. 2021. "'I Have Turned into a Foreman Here at Home': Families and Work–Life Balance in Times of COVID-19 in a Gender Equality Paradise." *Gender, Work & Organization* 28(1):268–83. https://doi.org/10.1111/gwao.12552.

Hochschild, Arlie. 1979. "Emotion Work, Feeling Rules, and Social Structure." *American Journal of Sociology* 85(3):551–75.

———. 2003. *The Commercialization of Intimate Life: Notes from Home and Work.* Berkeley: University of California Press.

————. 2012. *The Managed Heart: Commercialization of Human Feeling*. 3rd ed. Berkeley: University of California Press.

Hochschild, Arlie, and Anne Machung. 2012. *The Second Shift: Working Families and the Revolution at Home*. Rev. ed. New York: Penguin Books.

Hollingshead, Andrea B., and Samuel N. Fraidin. 2003. "Gender Stereotypes and Assumptions about Expertise in Transactive Memory." *Journal of Experimental Social Psychology* 39(4):355–63. https://doi.org/10.1016/S0022-1031(02)00549-8.

Hughes, Diane, James Rodriguez, Emilie P. Smith, Deborah J. Johnson, Howard C. Stevenson, and Paul Spicer. 2006. "Parents' Ethnic-Racial Socialization Practices: A Review of Research and Directions for Future Study." *Developmental Psychology* 42(5):747–70. https://doi.org/10.1037/0012-1649.42.5.747.

Hyde, Janet S. 2014. "Gender Similarities and Differences." *Annual Review of Psychology* 65(1): 373–98. https://doi.org/10.1146/annurev-psych-010213-115057.

Ishizuka, Patrick. 2019. "Social Class, Gender, and Contemporary Parenting Standards in the United States: Evidence from a National Survey Experiment." *Social Forces* 98(1):31–58. https://doi.org/10.1093/sf/soy107.

Iversen, Torben, and Frances M. Rosenbluth. 2010. *Women, Work, and Politics: The Political Economy of Gender Inequality*. New Haven: Yale University Press.

Jang, Seulki, Tammy D. Allen, and Joseph Regina. 2021. "Office Housework, Burnout, and Promotion: Does Gender Matter?" *Journal of Business and Psychology* 36(5):793–805. https://doi.org/10.1007/s10869-020-09703-6.

Jenner, Brandy M., and Kit C. Myers. 2019. "Intimacy, Rapport, and Exceptional Disclosure: A Comparison of In-Person and Mediated Interview Contexts." *International Journal of Social Research Methodology* 22(2):165–77. https://doi.org/10.1080/13645579.2018.1512694.

Jerolmack, Colin, and Shamus Khan. 2014. "Talk Is Cheap." *Sociological Methods & Research* 43(2):178–209. https://doi.org/10.1177/0049124114523396.

Job, Veronika, Carol S. Dweck, and Gregory M. Walton. 2010. "Ego Depletion—Is It All in Your Head?: Implicit Theories about Willpower Affect Self-Regulation." *Psychological Science* 21(11):1686–93. https://doi.org/10.1177/0956797610384745.

Kamo, Yoshinori. 2000. "'He Said, She Said': Assessing Discrepancies in Husbands' and Wives' Reports on the Division of Household Labor." *Social Science Research* 29(4):459–76. https://doi.org/10.1006/ssre.2000.0674.

Kane, Emily W. 2012. *The Gender Trap: Parents and the Pitfalls of Raising Boys and Girls*. New York: New York University Press.

Kassai, Reka, Judit Futo, Zsolt Demetrovics, and Zsofia K. Takacs. 2019. "A Meta-Analysis of the Experimental Evidence on the Near- and Far-Transfer Effects among Children's Executive Function Skills." *Psychological Bulletin* 145(2):165. https://doi.org/10.1037/bul0000180.

Katz-Wise, Sabra L., Heather A. Priess, and Janet S. Hyde. 2010. "Gender-Role Attitudes and Behavior across the Transition to Parenthood." *Developmental Psychology* 46(1):18–28. https://doi.org/10.1037/a0017820.

Kelly, Erin L., and Phyllis Moen. 2020. *Overload*. Princeton: Princeton University Press.

Kerber, Linda K. 1988. "Separate Spheres, Female Worlds, Woman's Place: The Rhetoric of Women's History." *Journal of American History* 75(1):9–39. https://doi.org/10.2307/1889653.

Kincaid, Reilly. 2021. "Maternal Decision-Making and Family-to-Work Spillover: Does Gender Ideology Matter?" *Sociological Focus* 54(3):223–38. https://doi.org/10.1080/00380237.2021 .1923597.

Kneeland, Hildegarde. 1929. "Woman's Economic Contribution in the Home." *ANNALS of the American Academy of Political and Social Science* 143(1):33–40. https://doi.org/10.1177 /000271622914300105.

Knight, Carly R., and Mary C. Brinton. 2017. "One Egalitarianism or Several? Two Decades of Gender-Role Attitude Change in Europe." *American Journal of Sociology* 122(5):1485–1532.

Kochhar, Rakesh. 2023. "The Enduring Grip of the Gender Pay Gap." *Pew Research Center.* https:// www.pewresearch.org/social-trends/2023/03/01/the-enduring-grip-of-the-gender-pay-gap/.

Komter, Aafke. 1989. "Hidden Power in Marriage." *Gender & Society* 3(2):187–216.

Kranichfeld, Marion L. 1987. "Rethinking Family Power." *Journal of Family Issues* 8(1): 42–56.

Krumpal, Ivar. 2013. "Determinants of Social Desirability Bias in Sensitive Surveys: A Literature Review." *Quality & Quantity* 47:2025–47.

Lachance-Grzela, Mylène, and Geneviève Bouchard. 2010. "Why Do Women Do the Lion's Share of Housework? A Decade of Research." *Sex Roles* 63(11–12):767–80. https://doi.org /10.1007/s11199-010-9797-z.

Lamont, Michèle, and Mario L. Small. 2008. "How Culture Matters: Enriching Our Understanding of Poverty." In *The Colors of Poverty: Why Racial and Ethnic Disparities Persist*, 76–102. New York: Russell Sage Foundation.

Lamont, Michèle, and Ann Swidler. 2014. "Methodological Pluralism and the Possibilities and Limits of Interviewing." *Qualitative Sociology* 37(2):153–71. https://doi.org/10.1007/s11133 -014-9274-z.

Landry, Bart. 2002. *Black Working Wives: Pioneers of the American Family Revolution.* Berkeley: University of California Press.

Lareau, Annette. 2000. "My Wife Can Tell Me Who I Know: Methodological and Conceptual Problems in Studying Fathers." *Qualitative Sociology* 23(4):407–33.

———. 2011. *Unequal Childhoods: Class, Race, and Family Life.* 2nd ed. Berkeley: University of California Press.

Lawton, Carol A., and Janos Kallai. 2002. "Gender Differences in Wayfinding Strategies and Anxiety about Wayfinding: A Cross-Cultural Comparison." *Sex Roles* 47:389–401.

Lee, Jin-kyung, and Sarah J. Schoppe-Sullivan. 2023. "Paternal Identity, Maternal Gate Opening, and Fathers' Longitudinal Positive Engagement." *Journal of Family Psychology* 37(2):243–55. https://doi.org/10.1037/fam0001028.

Lee, Joyce Y., and Shawna J. Lee. 2018. "Caring Is Masculine: Stay-at-Home Fathers and Masculine Identity." *Psychology of Men & Masculinity* 19(1):47–58. https://doi.org/10.1037 /men0000079.

Lee, Yun-Suk, and Linda J. Waite. 2005. "Husbands' and Wives' Time Spent on Housework: A Comparison of Measures." *Journal of Marriage and Family* 67(2):328–36.

Lennon, Mary C., and Sarah Rosenfield. 1994. "Relative Fairness and the Division of Housework: The Importance of Options." *American Journal of Sociology* 100(2):506–31.

León-Pérez, Gabriela, Caroline Richards, and Amy L. Non. 2021. "Precarious Work and Parenting Stress among Mexican Immigrant Women in the United States." *Journal of Marriage and Family* 83(3):881–97. https://doi.org/10.1111/jomf.12761.

Lev, Arlene I. 2008. "More than Surface Tension: Femmes in Families." *Journal of Lesbian Studies* 12(2–3):127–44. https://doi.org/10.1080/10894160802161299.

Locke, Edwin A. 1982. "The Ideas of Frederick W. Taylor: An Evaluation." *Academy of Management Review* 7(1):14–24.

Lockman, Darcy. 2019. *All the Rage: Mothers, Fathers, and the Myth of Equal Partnership*. New York: Harper.

Luhr, Sigrid, Daniel Schneider, and Kristen Harknett. 2022. "Parenting without Predictability: Precarious Schedules, Parental Strain, and Work-Life Conflict." *Russell Sage Foundation Journal of the Social Sciences* 8(5):24–44.

Lupton, Deborah, Sarah Pedersen, and Gareth M. Thomas. 2016. "Parenting and Digital Media: From the Early Web to Contemporary Digital Society." *Sociology Compass* 10(8):730–43. https://doi.org/10.1111/soc4.12398.

Lyonette, Clare, and Rosemary Crompton. 2015. "Sharing the Load? Partners' Relative Earnings and the Division of Domestic Labour." *Work, Employment and Society* 29(1):23–40. https://doi.org/10.1177/0950017014523661.

Lyttelton, Thomas, Emma Zang, and Kelly Musick. 2022. "Telecommuting and Gender Inequalities in Parents' Paid and Unpaid Work before and during the COVID-19 Pandemic." *Journal of Marriage and Family* 84(1):230–49. https://doi.org/10.1111/jomf.12810.

———. 2023. "Parents' Work Arrangements and Gendered Time Use during the COVID-19 Pandemic." *Journal of Marriage and Family* 85(2):657–73. https://doi.org/10.1111/jomf.12897.

Mani, Anandi, Sendhil Mullainathan, Eldar Shafir, and Jiaying Zhao. 2013. "Poverty Impedes Cognitive Function." *Science* 341(6149):976–80.

Mark, Gloria, Victor M. Gonzalez, and Justin Harris. 2005. "No Task Left Behind?: Examining the Nature of Fragmented Work." In *Proceedings of the SIGCHI Conference on Human Factors in Computing Systems*, 321–30. New York: ACM.

Martin, Karin A. 1998. "Becoming a Gendered Body: Practices of Preschools." *American Sociological Review* 63(4):494–511.

Martin, Patricia Y. 2004. "Gender as Social Institution." *Social Forces* 82(4):1249–73. https://doi.org/10.1353/sof.2004.0081.

Marx, Karl. 1976. *Capital: A Critique of Political Economy, Vol. 1*. New York: Penguin Classics.

McClelland, Tom, and Paulina Sliwa. 2022. "Gendered Affordance Perception and Unequal Domestic Labour." *Philosophy and Phenomenological Research* 107(2):501–24. https://doi.org/10.1111/phpr.12929.

McGrath, April. 2017. "Dealing with Dissonance: A Review of Cognitive Dissonance Reduction." *Social and Personality Psychology Compass* 11(12):e12362. https://doi.org/10.1111/spc3.12362.

McLuhan, Arthur, Dorothy Pawluch, William Shaffir, and Jack Haas. 2014. "The Cloak of Incompetence: A Neglected Concept in the Sociology of Everyday Life." *American Sociologist* 45(4):361–87. https://doi.org/10.1007/s12108-014-9240-y.

Meadow, Tey. 2018. *Trans Kids: Being Gendered in the Twenty-First Century*. Berkeley: University of California Press.

Mederer, Helen J. 1993. "Division of Labor in Two-Earner Homes: Task Accomplishment versus Household Management as Critical Variables in Perceptions about Family Work." *Journal of Marriage and Family* 55(1):133–45.

Messerschmidt, James W. 2009. "'Doing Gender': The Impact and Future of a Salient Sociological Concept." *Gender & Society* 23(1):85–88. https://doi.org/10.1177/08912432 08326253.

Micale, Mark S. 1989. "Hysteria and Its Historiography: A Review of Past and Present Writings." *History of Science* 27(3):223–61. https://doi.org/10.1177/007327538902700301.

Milkie, Melissa A., Suzanne M. Bianchi, Marybeth J. Mattingly, and John P. Robinson. 2002. "Gendered Division of Childrearing: Ideals, Realities, and the Relationship to Parental Well-Being." *Sex Roles* 47(1–2):21–38.

Milkie, Melissa A., Kei Nomaguchi, and Scott Schieman. 2019. "Time Deficits with Children: The Link to Parents' Mental and Physical Health." *Society and Mental Health* 9(3):277–95. https://doi.org/10.1177/2156869318767488.

Milkie, Melissa A., and Catharine H. Warner. 2014. "Status Safeguarding: Mothers' Work to Secure Children's Place in the Social Hierarchy." In *Intensive Mothering: The Cultural Contradictions of Modern Motherhood*, ed. L. R. Ennis, 66–85. Bradford, Ontario: Demeter Press.

Miller, Amanda J., and Daniel L. Carlson. 2016. "Great Expectations? Working- and Middle-Class Cohabitors' Expected and Actual Divisions of Housework." *Journal of Marriage and Family* 78(2):346–63. https://doi.org/10.1111/jomf.12276.

Mirin, Arthur A. 2021. "Gender Disparity in the Funding of Diseases by the U.S. National Institutes of Health." *Journal of Women's Health* 30(7):956–63. https://doi.org/10.1089/jwh.2020.8682.

Mischel, Walter. 2013. *Personality and Assessment*. New York: Psychology Press.

Mize, Trenton D., Gayle Kaufman, and Richard J. Petts. 2021. "Visualizing Shifts in Gendered Parenting Attitudes during COVID-19." *Socius* 7. https://doi.org/10.1177/23780231211 013128.

Monna, Berenice, and Anne H. Gauthier. 2008. "A Review of the Literature on the Social and Economic Determinants of Parental Time." *Journal of Family and Economic Issues* 29(4): 634–53. https://doi.org/10.1007/s10834-008-9121-z.

Moon, Dawne, Theresa W. Tobin, and J. E. Sumerau. 2019. "Alpha, Omega, and the Letters in Between: LGBTQI Conservative Christians Undoing Gender." *Gender & Society* 33(4): 583–606. https://doi.org/10.1177/0891243219846592.

Moore, Mignon R. 2008. "Gendered Power Relations among Women: A Study of Household Decision Making in Black, Lesbian Stepfamilies." *American Sociological Review* 73(2): 335–56.

Morgenstern, Julie. 2005. *Never Check E-Mail in the Morning: And Other Unexpected Strategies for Making Your Work Life Work*. Reprint. New York: Touchstone.

Mullainathan, Sendhil, and Eldar Shafir. 2013. *Scarcity: Why Having Too Little Means So Much*. New York: Times Books.

National Center for Education Statistics. 2023. "Characteristics of Public School Teachers." *Condition of Education*. U.S. Department of Education, Institute of Education Sciences. https://nces.ed.gov/programs/coe/indicator/clr.

Negraia, Daniela V., Jennifer M. Augustine, and Kate C. Prickett. 2018. "Gender Disparities in Parenting Time across Activities, Child Ages, and Educational Groups." *Journal of Family Issues* 39(11):3006–28. https://doi.org/10.1177/0192513X18770232.

Neufeld, Anne, Margaret J. Harrison, Gwen R. Rempel, Sylvie Larocque, Sharon Dublin, Miriam Stewart, and Karen Hughes. 2004. "Practical Issues in Using a Card Sort in a Study of Nonsupport and Family Caregiving." *Qualitative Health Research* 14(10):1418–28. https://doi.org/10.1177/1049732304271228.

Newport, Cal. 2016. *Deep Work: Rules for Focused Success in a Distracted World.* New York: Grand Central Publishing.

NJ Department of State. 2016. "General Election Results, Gloucester County." https://www.state.nj.us/state/elections/assets/pdf/election-results/2016/2016-gen-elect-presidential-results-gloucester.pdf.

Nomaguchi, Kei, and Melissa A. Milkie. 2020. "Parenthood and Well-Being: A Decade in Review." *Journal of Marriage and Family* 82(1):198–223. https://doi.org/10.1111/jomf.12646.

Nomaguchi, Kei M., Melissa A. Milkie, and Suzanne M. Bianchi. 2005. "Time Strains and Psychological Well-Being: Do Dual-Earner Mothers and Fathers Differ?" *Journal of Family Issues* 26(6):756–92. https://doi.org/10.1177/0192513X05277524.

Nyman, Charlott, Lasse Reinikainen, and Kristina Eriksson. 2018. "The Tension between Gender Equality and Doing Gender: Swedish Couples' Talk about the Division of Housework." *Women's Studies International Forum* 68:36–46. https://doi.org/10.1016/j.wsif.2018.01.010.

Oakley, Ann. 1975. *Sociology of Housework.* 2nd ed. New York: Pantheon Books.

Oates, Maggie, Kyle Crichton, Lorrie Cranor, Storm Budwig, Erica J. L. Weston, Brigette M. Bernagozzi, and Julie Pagaduan. 2022. "Audio, Video, Chat, Email, or Survey: How Much Does Online Interview Mode Matter?" *PLOS ONE* 17(2):e0263876. https://doi.org/10.1371/journal.pone.0263876.

Offer, Shira. 2014. "The Costs of Thinking about Work and Family: Mental Labor, Work-Family Spillover, and Gender Inequality among Parents in Dual-Earner Families." *Sociological Forum* 29(4):916–36. https://doi.org/10.1111/socf.12126.

Offer, Shira, and Barbara Schneider. 2011. "Revisiting the Gender Gap in Time-Use Patterns: Multitasking and Well-Being among Mothers and Fathers in Dual-Earner Families." *American Sociological Review* 76(6):809–33. https://doi.org/10.1177/0003122411425170.

Oláh, Livia S., and Michael Gähler. 2014. "Gender Equality Perceptions, Division of Paid and Unpaid Work, and Partnership Dissolution in Sweden." *Social Forces* 93(2):571–94. https://doi.org/10.1093/sf/sou066.

Orloff, Ann. 1993. "Gender and the Social Rights of Citizenship: The Comparative Analysis of Gender Relations and Welfare States." *American Sociological Review* 58(3):303–28.

Oster, Emily. 2021. *The Family Firm: A Data-Driven Guide to Better Decision Making in the Early School Years.* New York: Penguin Press.

Oxford English Dictionary. 2023. "Work." https://www.oed.com/dictionary/work_n?tab=meaning_and_use#13818326.

Papanek, Hanna. 1979. "Family Status Production: The 'Work' and 'Non-Work' of Women." *Signs* 4(4):775–81.

Park, Yikyung, Kevin W. Dodd, Victor Kipnis, Frances E. Thompson, Nancy Potischman, Dale A. Schoeller, David J. Baer, Douglas Midthune, Richard P. Troiano, Heather Bowles, and Amy F. Subar. 2018. "Comparison of Self-Reported Dietary Intakes from the Automated Self-Administered 24-h Recall, 4-d Food Records, and Food-Frequency Questionnaires against Recovery Biomarkers." *American Journal of Clinical Nutrition* 107:80–93.

Parreñas, Rhacel. 2015. *Servants of Globalization: Migration and Domestic Work*. 2nd ed. Stanford: Stanford University Press.

Parsons, Talcott, and Robert Bales. 1960. *Family: Socialization and Interaction Process*. New York: Free Press.

Pascoe, C. J. 2007. *Dude, You're a Fag: Masculinity and Sexuality in High School*. Berkeley: University of California Press.

Pepin, Joanna, and David Cotter. 2018. "Separating Spheres? Diverging Trends in Youth's Gender Attitudes about Work and Family." *Journal of Marriage & Family* 80(1):7–24.

Perry-Jenkins, Maureen, and Naomi Gerstel. 2020. "Work and Family in the Second Decade of the 21st Century." *Journal of Marriage and Family* 82(1):420–53. https://doi.org/10.1111/jomf.12636.

Petts, Richard J., and Daniel L. Carlson. 2023. "Managing a Household during a Pandemic: Cognitive Labor and Parents' Psychological Well-Being." *Society and Mental Health* 13(3):187–207. https://doi.org/10.1177/21568693231169521.

Petts, Richard J., and Chris Knoester. 2018. "Paternity Leave-Taking and Father Engagement." *Journal of Marriage and Family* 80(5):1144–62. https://doi.org/10.1111/jomf.12494.

Pew Research Center. 2023. "The Data on Women Leaders." https://www.pewresearch.org/social-trends/fact-sheet/the-data-on-women-leaders/.

Pfeffer, Carla A. 2010. "'Women's Work'? Women Partners of Transgender Men Doing Housework and Emotion Work." *Journal of Marriage and Family* 72(1):165–83. https://doi.org/10.1111/j.1741-3737.2009.00690.x.

———. 2017. *Queering Families: The Postmodern Partnerships of Cisgender Women and Transgender Men*. New York: Oxford University Press.

Presser, Harriet B. 1994. "Employment Schedules among Dual-Earner Spouses and the Division of Household Labor by Gender." *American Sociological Review* 59(3):348. https://doi.org/10.2307/2095938.

Pugh, Allison J. 2013. "What Good Are Interviews for Thinking about Culture? Demystifying Interpretive Analysis." *American Journal of Cultural Sociology* 1(1):42–68. https://doi.org/10.1057/ajcs.2012.4.

Puhlman, Daniel J., and Kay Pasley. 2013. "Rethinking Maternal Gatekeeping." *Journal of Family Theory & Review* 5(3):176–93. https://doi.org/10.1111/jftr.12016.

Raley, Sara, Suzanne M. Bianchi, and Wendy Wang. 2012. "When Do Fathers Care? Mothers' Economic Contribution and Fathers' Involvement in Child Care." *American Journal of Sociology* 117(5):1422–59. https://doi.org/10.1086/663354.

Ramey, Garey, and Valerie A. Ramey. 2010. "The Rug Rat Race." *Brookings Papers on Economic Activity* 2010(1):129–76. https://doi.org/10.1353/eca.2010.0003.

Rao, Aliya H. 2020. *Crunch Time: How Married Couples Confront Unemployment*. Berkeley: University of California Press.

———. 2021. "The Ideal Job-Seeker Norm: Unemployment and Marital Privileges in the Professional Middle-Class." *Journal of Marriage and Family* 83(4):1038–57. https://doi.org/10.1111/jomf.12748.

Reczek, Corinne. 2020. "Sexual- and Gender-Minority Families: A 2010 to 2020 Decade in Review." *Journal of Marriage and Family* 82(1):300–325. https://doi.org/10.1111/jomf.12607.

Reich-Stiebert, Natalia, Laura Froehlich, and Jan-Bennet Voltmer. 2023. "Gendered Mental Labor: A Systematic Literature Review on the Cognitive Dimension of Unpaid Work within the Household and Childcare." *Sex Roles* 88:475–94.

Reid, Erin. 2015. "Embracing, Passing, Revealing, and the Ideal Worker Image: How People Navigate Expected and Experienced Professional Identities." *Organization Science* 26(4): 997–1017. https://doi.org/10.1287/orsc.2015.0975.

Richards, M. Virginia. 2000. "The Postmodern Perspective on Home Economics History." *Journal of Family and Consumer Sciences* 92(1):81–84.

Ridgeway, Cecilia L. 2011. *Framed by Gender: How Gender Inequality Persists in the Modern World.* New York: Oxford University Press.

Riggs, Janet M. 1997. "Mandates for Mothers and Fathers: Perceptions of Breadwinners and Care Givers." *Sex Roles* 37(7/8):565–80.

Risman, Barbara J. 1999. *Gender Vertigo: American Families in Transition.* New Haven: Yale University Press.

Risman, Barbara J., and Danette Johnson-Sumerford. 1998. "Doing It Fairly: A Study of Postgender Marriages." *Journal of Marriage and Family* 60(1):23–40.

Roberts, Dorothy. 1998. *Killing the Black Body: Race, Reproduction, and the Meaning of Liberty.* New York: Vintage Books.

Robertson, Lindsey G., Tamara L. Anderson, M. Elizabeth L. Hall, and Christina L. Kim. 2019. "Mothers and Mental Labor: A Phenomenological Focus Group Study of Family-Related Thinking Work." *Psychology of Women Quarterly* 43(2):184–200. https://doi.org/10.1177/0361684319825581.

Robinson, John, and Geoffrey Godbey. 2010. *Time for Life: The Surprising Ways Americans Use Their Time.* University Park: Pennsylvania State University Press.

Rochlen, Aaron B., Ryan A. McKelley, and Tiffany A. Whittaker. 2010. "Stay-at-Home Fathers' Reasons for Entering the Role and Stigma Experiences: A Preliminary Report." *Psychology of Men & Masculinity* 11(4):279–85. https://doi.org/10.1037/a0017774.

Rodsky, Eve. 2019. *Fair Play: A Game-Changing Solution for When You Have Too Much to Do (and More Life to Live).* New York: G. P. Putnam's Sons.

Rollins, Judith. 1985. *Between Women: Domestics and Their Employers.* Philadelphia: Temple University Press.

Rollo, Megan E., Rebecca L. Williams, Tracy Burrows, Sharon I. Kirkpatrick, Tamara Bucher, and Clare E. Collins. 2016. "What Are They Really Eating? A Review on New Approaches to Dietary Intake Assessment and Validation." *Current Nutrition Reports* 5(4):307–14. https://doi.org/10.1007/s13668-016-0182-6.

Rosenthal, Carolyn J. 1985. "Kinkeeping in the Familial Division of Labor." *Journal of Marriage and Family* 47(4):965–74.

Ruddick, Sara. 1995. *Maternal Thinking: Toward a Politics of Peace.* Boston: Beacon Press.

Sanchez, Laura, and Emily W. Kane. 1996. "Women's and Men's Constructions of Perceptions of Housework Fairness." *Journal of Family Issues* 17(3):358–87.

Sandberg, Sheryl. 2013. *Lean In: Women, Work, and the Will to Lead.* New York: Alfred A. Knopf.

Savitsky, Kenneth, Victoria H. Medvec, and Thomas Gilovich. 1997. "Remembering and Regretting: The Zeigarnik Effect and the Cognitive Availability of Regrettable Actions and Inactions." *Personality and Social Psychology Bulletin* 23(3):248–57. https://doi.org/10.1177/0146167297233004.

Scarborough, William J., Ray Sin, and Barbara Risman. 2019. "Attitudes and the Stalled Gender Revolution: Egalitarianism, Traditionalism, and Ambivalence from 1977 through 2016." *Gender & Society* 33(2):173–200. https://doi.org/10.1177/0891243218809604.

Scharrer, Erica, Stephen Warren, Eean Grimshaw, Gichuhi Kamau, Sarah Cho, Menno Reijven, and Congcong Zhang. 2021. "Disparaged Dads? A Content Analysis of Depictions of Fathers in U.S. Sitcoms over Time." *Psychology of Popular Media* 10(2):275–87. https://doi.org/10 .1037/ppm0000289.

Schneider, Daniel. 2011. "Market Earnings and Household Work: New Tests of Gender Performance Theory." *Journal of Marriage and Family* 73(4):845–60. https://doi.org/10.1111 /j.1741-3737.2011.00851.x.

Schwartz, Pepper. 1994. *Peer Marriage: How Love between Equals Really Works*. New York: Free Press.

Scott, Marvin B., and Stanford M. Lyman. 1968. "Accounts." *American Sociological Review* 33(1): 46–62.

Semega, Jessica. 2019. "Pay Is Up. Poverty Is Down. How Women Are Making Strides." *Census .Gov*. https://www.census.gov/library/stories/2019/09/payday-poverty-and-women.html.

Shim, Jee-Seon, Kyungwon Oh, and Hyeon Chang Kim. 2014. "Dietary Assessment Methods in Epidemiologic Studies." *Epidemiology and Health* 36:e2014009. https://doi.org/10.4178 /epih/e2014009.

Siegel, Reva B. 1994. "Home as Work: The First Woman's Rights Claims Concerning Wives' Household Labor, 1850–1880." *Yale Law Journal* 103(5):1073–1217.

Silbaugh, Katharine. 1996. "Turning Labor into Love: Housework and the Law." *Northwestern University Law Review* 91(1):1–86.

Slaughter, Anne-Marie. 2012. "Why Women Still Can't Have It All." *The Atlantic*. https://www .theatlantic.com/magazine/archive/2012/07/why-women-still-cant-have-it-all/309020/.

Small, Mario L. 2017. *Someone to Talk To*. New York: Oxford University Press.

Stacey, Lawrence. 2021. "The Family as Gender and Sexuality Factory: A Review of the Literature and Future Directions." *Sociology Compass* 15(4):e12864.

Stack, Carol B. 1983. *All Our Kin: Strategies for Survival in a Black Community*. New York: Basic Books.

Stage, Sarah, and Virginia B. Vincenti, eds. 1997. *Rethinking Home Economics: Women and the History of a Profession*. Ithaca: Cornell University Press.

Stone, Pamela. 2007. *Opting Out? Why Women Really Quit Careers and Head Home*. Berkeley: University of California Press.

Streib, Jessi. 2015. *The Power of the Past: Understanding Cross-Class Marriages*. New York: Oxford University Press.

Su, Rong, James Rounds, and Patrick I. Armstrong. 2009. "Men and Things, Women and People: A Meta-Analysis of Sex Differences in Interests." *Psychological Bulletin* 135(6):859–84. https:// doi.org/10.1037/a0017364.

Sullivan, Oriel. 2010. "Changing Differences by Educational Attainment in Fathers' Domestic Labour and Child Care." *Sociology* 44(4):716–33. https://doi.org/10.1177/0038038510 369351.

———. 2013. "What Do We Learn about Gender by Analyzing Housework Separately from Child Care? Some Considerations from Time-Use Evidence." *Journal of Family Theory & Review* 5(2):72–84. https://doi.org/10.1111/jftr.12007.

Sullivan, Oriel, Jonathan Gershuny, and John P. Robinson. 2018. "Stalled or Uneven Gender Revolution? A Long-Term Processual Framework for Understanding Why Change Is Slow." *Journal of Family Theory & Review* 10(1):263–79. https://doi.org/10.1111/jftr.12248.

Sutherland, Jean-Anne. 2010. "Mothering, Guilt and Shame." *Sociology Compass* 4(5):310–21. https://doi.org/10.1111/j.1751-9020.2010.00283.x.

Swidler, Ann. 1986. "Culture in Action: Symbols and Strategies." *American Sociological Review* 51(2):273–86.

Tai, Tsui-o, and Judith Treas. 2013. "Housework Task Hierarchies in 32 Countries." *European Sociological Review* 29(4):780–91. https://doi.org/10.1093/esr/jcs057.

Taylor, Danielle. 2020. "Same-Sex Couples Are More Likely to Adopt or Foster Children." *Census.Gov*. https://www.census.gov/library/stories/2020/09/fifteen-percent-of-same-sex-couples-have-children-in-their-household.html.

Thébaud, Sarah, Sabino Kornrich, and Leah Ruppanner. 2019. "Good Housekeeping, Great Expectations: Gender and Housework Norms." *Sociological Methods & Research* 50(3):1186–1214. https://doi.org/10.1177/0049124119852395.

Thébaud, Sarah, and Catherine J. Taylor. 2021. "The Specter of Motherhood: Culture and the Production of Gendered Career Aspirations in Science and Engineering." *Gender & Society* 35(3):395–421. https://doi.org/10.1177/08912432211006037.

Thomeer, Mieke B., Debra Umberson, and Corinne Reczek. 2020. "The Gender-as-Relational Approach for Theorizing about Romantic Relationships of Sexual and Gender Minority Mid- to Later-Life Adults." *Journal of Family Theory & Review* 12(2):220–37. https://doi.org/10.1111/jftr.12368.

Thompson, Linda. 1991. "Family Work: Women's Sense of Fairness." *Journal of Family Issues* 12(2):181–96.

Thunberg, Sara, and Linda Arnell. 2022. "Pioneering the Use of Technologies in Qualitative Research—A Research Review of the Use of Digital Interviews." *International Journal of Social Research Methodology* 25(6):757–68. https://doi.org/10.1080/13645579.2021.1935565.

Tichenor, Veronica J. 2005. *Earning More and Getting Less: Why Successful Wives Can't Buy Equality*. New Brunswick, NJ: Rutgers University Press.

Townsend, Nicholas. 2002. *The Package Deal: Marriage, Work and Fatherhood in Men's Lives*. Philadelphia: Temple University Press.

Tversky, Amos, and Daniel Kahneman. 1973. "Availability: A Heuristic for Judging Frequency and Probability." *Cognitive Psychology* 5(2):207–32. https://doi.org/10.1016/0010-0285(73)90033-9.

Umberson, Debra, Mieke B. Thomeer, and Amy C. Lodge. 2015. "Intimacy and Emotion Work in Lesbian, Gay, and Heterosexual Relationships." *Journal of Marriage and Family* 77(2):542–56. https://doi.org/10.1111/jomf.12178.

U.S. Census Bureau. 2022a. "U.S. Census Bureau QuickFacts: Massachusetts." Retrieved January 5, 2024 (https://www.census.gov/quickfacts/fact/table/MA/INC110222).

———. 2022b. "U.S. Census Bureau QuickFacts: New Jersey." https://www.census.gov/quickfacts/fact/table/NJ/SBO001217.

Usdansky, Margaret L. 2011. "The Gender-Equality Paradox: Class and Incongruity between Work-Family Attitudes and Behaviors." *Journal of Family Theory & Review* 3(3):163–78. https://doi.org/10.1111/j.1756-2589.2011.00094.x.

Van Bavel, Jan, Christine R. Schwartz, and Albert Esteve. 2018. "The Reversal of the Gender Gap in Education and Its Consequences for Family Life." *Annual Review of Sociology* 44(1):341–60. https://doi.org/10.1146/annurev-soc-073117-041215.

Van Hooff, Jenny H. 2011. "Rationalising Inequality: Heterosexual Couples' Explanations and Justifications for the Division of Housework along Traditionally Gendered Lines." *Journal of Gender Studies* 20(1):19–30. https://doi.org/10.1080/09589236.2011.542016.

Velasco, Kristopher, and Pamela Paxton. 2022. "Deconstructed and Constructive Logics: Explaining Inclusive Language Change in Queer Nonprofits, 1998–2016." *American Journal of Sociology* 127(4):1267–1310. https://doi.org/10.1086/718279.

Vesely, Colleen K., Bethany L. Letiecq, and Rachael D. Goodman. 2019. "Parenting across Two Worlds: Low-Income Latina Immigrants' Adaptation to Motherhood in the United States." *Journal of Family Issues* 40(6):711–38. https://doi.org/10.1177/0192513X18821398.

Vohs, Kathleen D., Roy F. Baumeister, Brandon J. Schmeichel, Jean M. Twenge, Noelle M. Nelson, and Dianne M. Tice. 2008. "Making Choices Impairs Subsequent Self-Control: A Limited-Resource Account of Decision Making, Self-Regulation, and Active Initiative." *Journal of Personality and Social Psychology* 94(5):883–98. https://doi.org/10.1037/0022-3514.94.5.883.

Volpe, Allie. 2023. "Social Media Can't Be Your Couples' Therapist." *Vox.* https://www.vox.com/even-better/23963847/social-media-relationship-advice-toxic-gaslighting-red-flags-emotional-load.

Waggoner, Miranda R. 2017. *The Zero Trimester: Pre-Pregnancy Care and the Politics of Reproductive Risk.* Oakland: University of California Press.

Walzer, Susan. 1996. "Thinking about the Baby: Gender and Divisions of Infant Care." *Social Problems* 43(2):219–34.

Wang, Jing, Nathan Novemsky, Ravi Dhar, and Roy F. Baumeister. 2010. "Trade-Offs and Depletion in Choice." *Journal of Marketing Research* 47(5):910–19. https://doi.org/10.1509/jmkr.47.5.910.

Ward, Adrian F., and John G. Lynch. 2019. "On a Need-to-Know Basis: How the Distribution of Responsibility between Couples Shapes Financial Literacy and Financial Outcomes." *Journal of Consumer Research* 45(5):1013–36. https://doi.org/10.1093/jcr/ucy037.

Warikoo, Natasha. 2020. "Addressing Emotional Health while Protecting Status: Asian American and White Parents in Suburban America." *American Journal of Sociology* 126(3):545–76. https://doi.org/10.1086/712820.

Wayne, Julie H., Maura J. Mills, Yi-Ren Wang, Russell A. Matthews, and Marilyn V. Whitman. 2023. "Who's Remembering to Buy the Eggs? The Meaning, Measurement, and Implications of Invisible Family Load." *Journal of Business and Psychology* 38(6):1159–84. https://doi.org/10.1007/s10869-023-09887-7.

Weeks, Ana C. 2024. "The Political Consequences of the Mental Load." Working paper. https://scholar.harvard.edu/sites/scholar.harvard.edu/files/anacweeks/files/weeks_ml_170124.pdf.

Weiss, Robert S. 1994. *Learning from Strangers: The Art and Method of Qualitative Interview Studies.* New York: Free Press.

Welter, Barbara. 1966. "The Cult of True Womanhood: 1820–1860." *American Quarterly* 18(2):151–74.

West, Candace, and Don H. Zimmerman. 1987. "Doing Gender." *Gender & Society* 1(2):125–51.

Wilkie, Jane R., Myra M. Ferree, and Kathryn S. Ratcliff. 1998. "Gender and Fairness: Marital Satisfaction in Two-Earner Couples." *Journal of Marriage and Family* 60(3):577–94.

Williams, Joan. 2001. *Unbending Gender: Why Family and Work Conflict and What to Do about It*. New York: Oxford University Press.

Winkler, Anne E., and Thomas R. Ireland. 2009. "Time Spent in Household Management: Evidence and Implications." *Journal of Family and Economic Issues* 30(3):293–304. https://doi.org/10.1007/s10834-009-9160-0.

Wolbers, Thomas, and Mary Hegarty. 2010. "What Determines Our Navigational Abilities?" *Trends in Cognitive Sciences* 14(3):138–46. https://doi.org/10.1016/j.tics.2010.01.001.

Wong, Jaclyn S. 2017. "Competing Desires: How Young Adult Couples Negotiate Moving for Career Opportunities." *Gender & Society* 31(2):171–96. https://doi.org/10.1177/08912432 17695520.

———. 2023. *Equal Partners?: How Dual-Professional Couples Make Career, Relationship, and Family Decisions*. Berkeley: University of California Press.

Wong, Jaclyn S., and Allison Daminger. 2024. "The Myth of Mutuality: Decision-Making, Marital Power, and the Persistence of Gender Inequality." *Gender & Society* 38(2):157–86. https://doi.org/10.1177/08912432241230555.

Wong, Kristin. 2018. "There's a Stress Gap between Men and Women. Here's Why It's Important." *New York Times*, November 14. https://www.nytimes.com/2018/11/14/smarter-living/stress-gap-women-men.html.

Yavorsky, Jill E., Claire M. Kamp Dush, and Sarah J. Schoppe-Sullivan. 2015. "The Production of Inequality: The Gender Division of Labor across the Transition to Parenthood." *Journal of Marriage and Family* 77(3):662–79. https://doi.org/10.1111/jomf.12189.

Yavorsky, Jill E., Lisa A. Keister, Yue Qian, and Sarah Thébaud. 2023. "Separate Spheres: The Gender Division of Labor in the Financial Elite." *Social Forces* 102(2):609–32.

Yeager, David S., and Carol S. Dweck. 2020. "What Can Be Learned from Growth Mindset Controversies?" *American Psychologist* 75(9):1269–84. https://doi.org/10.1037/amp0000 794.

Zelizer, Viviana A. 1994. *Pricing the Priceless Child*. Princeton: Princeton University Press.

Ziesel, Joshua. 2021. "I Wanted to Be a Better Husband. So I Planned My Kid's Birthday Party." *Washington Post*. https://www.washingtonpost.com/outlook/2021/06/18/dad-pandemic -mental-labor/.

Zimmerman, Toni S., Shelley A. Haddock, Scott Ziemba, and Aimee Rust. 2002. "Family Organizational Labor." *Journal of Feminist Family Therapy* 13(2–3):65–90. https://doi.org/10 .1300/J086v13n02_05.

INDEX

abstractness of cognitive tasks, 31, 34–35, 38–39, 47

"account," 186n13

action-oriented chores. *See* physical labor

adaptive couples, 115, 194n5

administrative tasks, 93, 146

"affordances," 187n32

agency, sense of, 111–12, 115, 118–20, 134, 138, 143, 149

age range, 164

Alan (participant), 19–21, 51, 53, 92

Alex (participant), 51, 64, 89, 92–93, 189nn19 and 20

Amanda (participant), 88

Amber (participant), 69

American Time Use Survey (ATUS), 176n24, 179n61

Amy (participant), 67–68, 76

analytic coding, 170–71

Andrea (participant), 117–20, 125, 132, 192n1

Anita (participant), 75, 171, 187n33

Annette (participant), 106–8

Anthony (participant), 124

anticipation work, 27–28; in Balanced couples, 106–7; benefits and burdens of, 31, 32, 36, 43, 49–50; in decision diaries, 2–3, 46; example of, 2–3; invisibility of, 37, 47, 49–50; measurement of, 141; by men, 51, 55; as women's specialty, 47–50, 71–72

Antoni (participant), 102–4, 190n6

anxiety, 72, 139

appreciation for household labor, 35, 66

April (participant), 71

archetypes, 10, 70–72; in Balanced couples, 114; as barrier, 72–78, 83, 138, 146–47, 149; as liabilities, 71–72; in Man-led couples, 100; in queer couples, 12, 119, 125, 128, 130; as valued qualities, 72, 173. *See also* Bumbler archetype; Superhuman archetype

"the authority of numbers" (Espeland & Stevens), 181n24

awareness of inequality, 142–45

"background job" (Bridget), 50

Balanced couples, 105–8; conflict in, 107–8, 114–15, 172; definition of, 4, 101, 105, 169, 190n2; examples of, 105–8; *versus* Imbalanced couples, 118, 121–22; *versus* Man-led couples, 108–15; paid work in, 109, 112; percentage of, 10, 16, 190n12; personal essentialism in, 115, 139; physical labor in, 107; queer couples, 5, 16, 118, 121–22; satisfaction levels, 16, 101, 107–8, 113–15; Sharers, 106–8, 121, 150; Splitters, 105–6, 122, 150; unintentional pathway in, 112–15; *versus* Woman-led couples, 108–15

Beecher, Catherine E., 180n7

benefits of cognitive labor, 31–35, 46, 121, 137

benevolent sexism, 180n8, 186n19

biases, in data collection, 141, 158

Billy (participant), 122

bisexual participants, 192n2. *See also* queer couples

Black feminist tradition, 142, 179n60

blame, 54–55, 81, 88–89, 96, 104, 188n9, 190n8, 195n23

Kendra (participant), 85, 127

Kenneth (participant), 67, 76

Kevin (participant), 67–68, 76

Kim (participant), 49, 74

Kincaid, Reilly, 140

"kinkeeping" (Rosenthal), 25–26, 190n13

Kneeland, Hildegarde, 23, 25, 26, 35–36

Kristen (participant), 19–21, 28, 29, 37–38, 51–53, 183n65

Kristy (participant), 120–21, 125, 126, 132

Kurt (participant), 105, 109, 112–15, 191n27, 192n29

labor, *versus* work, 29–30, 175n5, 181n38, 182n45

labor allocation: adjustments to (*see* reallocation efforts); arguments about (*see* conflict about labor allocation); awareness of, 142–45; cognitive *versus* physical, 55–57, 64 (*see also* cognitive labor; physical labor); couple types, 10, 16, 160–61, 169–70 (see also *specific type*); desire for equality, 15, 57, 63–66, 69, 123–24, 141, 149–52, 172; employment and (*see* paid work); gendered, 7–10 (*see also* gender division of cognitive labor); institutional role in, 144–47; negotiating changes to (*see* reallocation efforts); offsetting patterns, 56–57, 64, 66, 138, 185n22, 192n4; organizational role in, 147–49; parenthood (*see* childcare; parenting); reimagination of, 143–45; satisfaction with (*see* satisfaction levels); taxonomy of, 45–46, 140–41, 166–71

labor specialties: men's, 47, 50–52, 64, 137–38; women's, 46–50, 64, 71–72. See also *specific task*

"lagged generational change," 176n26

Lareau, Annette, 179n63, 184n15

laundry, 24, 45–46; in queer couples, 120, 122, 131; as women's specialty, 46–47

Leah (participant), 48, 83–84, 89, 188n5

Lean In (Sandberg), 5

leisure category, 45–46, 170

lesbian couples. *See* queer couples

Leslie (participant), 122, 124

Levi (participant), 67

LGBTQ+ couples. *See* queer couples

life-history questions, 168

Linda (participant), 122

Lindsay (participant), 123, 129–30

Lisa (participant), 47, 92, 96

list-making: men's skill deployment, 92–93, 102; in queer couples, 121; as women's specialty, 47, 56, 62, 74–75, 77, 80

Liz (participant), 48, 85

logistics, 45–46; example of, 184n6; men's involvement in, 103, 105; in queer couples, 122, 123; as women's specialty, 45–46

logs. *See* decision diaries

Lori (participant), 120–21, 125, 132

Luis (participant), 72, 73

"magic wand" offer, 63–66, 119, 128

maintenance, 24, 45–46, 170; as men's specialty, 47, 50–51, 80, 89, 105; in queer couples, 122, 129

"management of domestic life" (Hochschild), 177n31

management theory, 23

Mandy (participant), 64, 72, 92–93

Man-led couples, 99–105; *versus* Balanced couples, 108–15; conflict in, 172; definition of, 4, 100, 169, 190n2; examples of, 99–105; identification of, 43–46; intentional pathway in, 102–3, 109–12; paid work in, 101–2, 109, 112; percentage of, 10, 16, 190n12; personal essentialism in, 100, 111–12, 115, 139; satisfaction levels, 16, 109, 115; social forces affecting, 100, 103–5, 111, 139, 149; *versus* Woman-led couples, 100–105, 108–15, 142

market economy, 22

Marx, Karl, 21

Mateo (participant), 48, 83–84, 89, 188n5

maternal gatekeeping, 88, 105, 188n10

maternal guilt, 190n1, 195n23

maternity leave, 61, 84, 89, 102, 118, 188n5